Dear

A be

and out of - enjoy!

Much love

L + ?

xx   ?x

THE
LANGUAGE-LOVER'S
LEXIPEDIA

To Sonny and Jude, who inspired me.

To Rachel, who believed in me.

To my parents, who've always had my back.

THE
LANGUAGE-LOVER'S
LEXIPEDIA

AN A–Z OF
LINGUISTIC CURIOSITIES

JOSHUA BLACKBURN

BLOOMSBURY
LONDON • OXFORD • NEW YORK • NEW DELHI • SYDNEY

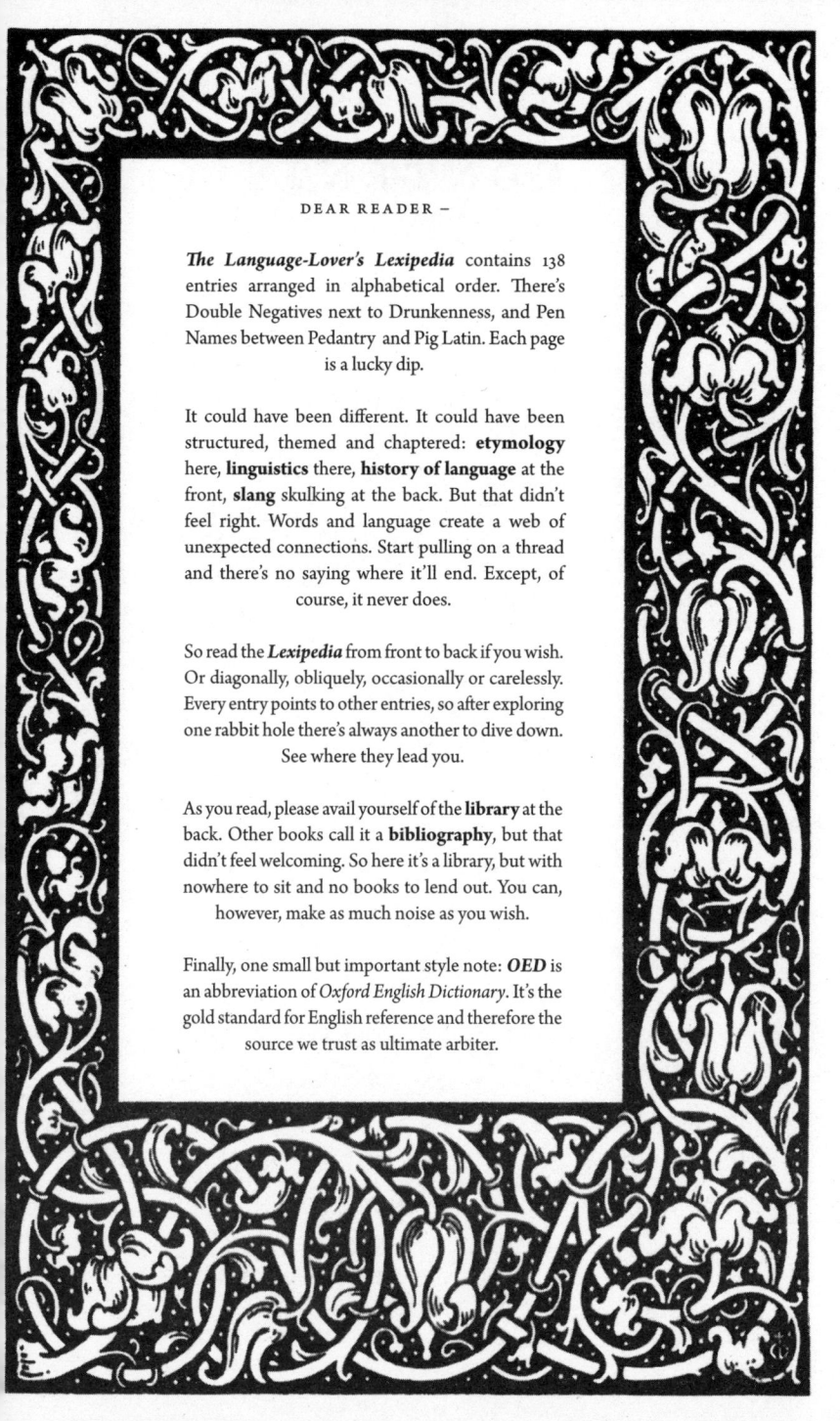

DEAR READER –

The Language-Lover's Lexipedia contains 138 entries arranged in alphabetical order. There's Double Negatives next to Drunkenness, and Pen Names between Pedantry and Pig Latin. Each page is a lucky dip.

It could have been different. It could have been structured, themed and chaptered: **etymology** here, **linguistics** there, **history of language** at the front, **slang** skulking at the back. But that didn't feel right. Words and language create a web of unexpected connections. Start pulling on a thread and there's no saying where it'll end. Except, of course, it never does.

So read the *Lexipedia* from front to back if you wish. Or diagonally, obliquely, occasionally or carelessly. Every entry points to other entries, so after exploring one rabbit hole there's always another to dive down. See where they lead you.

As you read, please avail yourself of the **library** at the back. Other books call it a **bibliography**, but that didn't feel welcoming. So here it's a library, but with nowhere to sit and no books to lend out. You can, however, make as much noise as you wish.

Finally, one small but important style note: **OED** is an abbreviation of *Oxford English Dictionary*. It's the gold standard for English reference and therefore the source we trust as ultimate arbiter.

CONTENTS

INTRODUCTION

¶ In 2020 I invented a game. It was during Covid lockdown, and I was coming face to face with my kids' English homework. Stuck in an endless loop of comprehensions and grammar tests, time seemed to slow down. My boys were bored. I was bored. It was boring.

¶ This frustrated me. The English language is anything but boring. Language itself is the single greatest invention in history; greater than the wheel, gunpowder and sliced bread put together. And English is endlessly fascinating; its origins, its mechanics, its riddles, its quirks, its beauty, its use, its... *everything*. So why is the English we teach our kids so joyless?

¶ As an antidote to this dull homework, I invented games to encourage my boys to be more curious about language. They had silly names, like Word Splat, Word War and the intriguing Tyrannosaurus Lex (more fun to say than to play), but they were just lockdown nonsense. Except one. League of the Lexicon was a quiz game about words and language. As I started playing it with friends, writing more and more questions, it became something of an obsession. Even when the pandemic was over, I kept working on it. It had become more grown up and challenging, but retained its delight in the wonders of language.

¶ Two years later, I launched League of the Lexicon on the crowdfunding website Kickstarter. I hoped for the best, but hardly expected it. In three frantic weeks it became the most successful word game in the platform's history. Then Waterstones made it their Game of the Month and Mensa America made it one of their Recommended Games. Even more extraordinary, luminaries like Susie Dent, Stephen Fry and David Crystal said lovely things about it, and it was appearing in *The Wall Street Journal*, *Wired* magazine and the BBC.

¶ At first, I had imposter syndrome. I'm not even an English graduate, and couldn't explain a fronted adverbial if my dangling modifiers depended on it. But my game wasn't made for English professors, and with apologies to those who care about such things, I've survived just fine not knowing what a fronted adverbial is*. League of the Lexicon was a game for language lovers, pure and simple.

---

*I've since looked them up. They're adverbs that go at the front of sentences, as in: 'Yesterday, I found out what a fronted adverbial was.'

¶ As the game's Question-Writer-in-Chief, I have been immersed in language for the last five years. I've become a collector of archaic words, an aficionado of slang and an accumulator of linguistic morsels. But it's the questions I enjoy most – those 'Hmmm... I never thought about that'-type questions that occur to me mid-conversation or while staring at an ad on the London Underground. Questions like:

Where does punctuation come from? How are Chinese dictionaries ordered? What was the last letter to enter the alphabet? Why do tongue-twisters twist tongues? Why are words with a K funny? (And why are words with a T not?) Why do we have silent letters? How do you invent a language? Why are pedants pedantic? How are IKEA product names chosen? Why is the plural of mongoose not 'mongeese'? How many words did Shakespeare actually coin? Why is envy green and cowardice yellow? Who was John Doe? What's the last word in the dictionary? And given all these questions, where did the question mark come from?

¶ Such are the things that occupy me. They are what I call my 'rabbit holes', because I dive down them, never knowing what I'll find, only to emerge days later, with more books, more questions and more to wonder about.

¶ These rabbit holes were the genesis of the *Lexipedia*. When I started this book, the working title was *The Infinite Encyclopaedia of Linguistic Curiosity*. My editors were against it. They pointed out that it wasn't infinite, and what's more, it was a mouthful. Both fair comments. But although I abandoned the title, it described what I was trying to write. Because language is infinite. Because I wanted the rigour of an encyclopaedia. And because everything was driven by a spirit of restless curiosity.

¶ I set out to write 100 entries. By the time I reached 138 my editors insisted I stop. Little did they know that in my trusty notebook there are over 300 more rabbit holes ready to get lost in. This is the joy of language, and it's pure catnip for curious minds.

London
2025

Be curious.

A.

ABRACADABRA

¶ The first known mention of the magical word *abracadabra* is in *De Medicina Praecepta Saluberrima*, a collection of medical treatments written in didactic poetry by Roman physician Quintus Serenus Sammonicus in the second century. 'Abracadabra' is used in Sammonicus's prescription for 'semitertian fever' (malaria), which required the word be written repeatedly on a piece of papyrus, with a letter removed each time; as the word is reduced, so too the disease. The papyrus would then be rolled into a cone, strung with cat gut and worn as an amulet.

¶ The origins of the word are unknown. Despite accounts linking it to Aramaic demons, Gnostic charms and Jewish mysticism, the *OED* concludes of all theories that 'supporting evidence is lacking'. Such mystery feels appropriate for an ancient incantation that was clearly doing the rounds of medieval Europe. Elisha ben Gad of Ancona included it in his collection of Kabbala-inspired spells and remedies, *The Tree of Knowledge* (1535), and it was still being used during the Great Plague of London in 1665. In *A Journal of the Plague Year*, Daniel Defoe describes the 'hellish charms and trumpery' hanging around people's necks, specifically mentioning *abracadabra*.

¶ English occultist and twaddle-peddler Aleister Crowley called *abrahadabra* (his spelling) 'The Word of Double Power in the Voice of the Master', and encyclopaedias of magic and witchcraft continue to revere it; but by the eighteenth century it had become a derisive word similar to 'hocus pocus' or 'nonsense', and was left to conjurors and stage magicians to use as a flourish during performances.

```
A B R A C A D A B R A
A B R A C A D A B R
A B R A C A D A B
A B R A C A D A
A B R A C A D
A B R A C A
A B R A C
A B R A
A B R
A B
A
```

OTHER MAGIC WORDS

ABLANATHANALBA SISOPETRON
A Greek-Cypriot magical curse.

ABRAXAS
A Gnostic incantation found on amulets.

AKRAKANARBA
An Ancient Greek incantation similar to abracadabra.

ANANIZAPTA
A medieval charm against epilepsy and intoxication.

ABEK WABEK FABEK
An incantation which, when repeated three times, can stop a nosebleed.

ALAN
A magic word used in spells to safeguard pigs.

ADVERTISING SLOGANS IN LATIN

¶ **Slogan** comes from the Scottish Gaelic **sluagh-ghairm**, meaning 'war cry', which evolved to **slorgorne**. Clan Cameron, for instance, mustered under the call, 'Sons of the Hounds, Come Here and Get Flesh!', while the slorgorne of Clan Robertson was 'Fierce when Roused!'.

¶ But while Highland clans gave English the word, today's slogans, on which brands and politicians depend, owe more to the mottos of classical and post-classical Latin. Had the Romans not got there first, **Fortune favours the brave** ('fortuna favet fortibus') would have made a fine strapline for Adidas, and Chanel would have been quite happy with **Beauty conquers** ('pulchritudo vincit').

¶ Given these similiarites, and drawing inspiration from the words of Cicero, Lucretius and Petronius, classical scholar Katie Walker translated some celebrated straplines for the *Lexipedia*. While the language and the lines are separated by some 2,000 years, their linguistic essence remains the same. But then, as Walker said, 'Rhetoric is the mother of the advertising slogan'. So, **sumpsistine lac**?

CLASSICAL MOTTO OR AD SLOGAN?

Below are five Latin mottos and five brand slogans. Can you identify which is which?

Say thank you.	*Beauty is confidence.*
Now or never.	*Be ready.*
Live forward.	*See and believe.*
Live while you can.	*Faster, higher, stronger.*
Today, not tomorrow.	*Strong is beautiful.*

(Answers on page 214.)

AGE MODO!
Just do it! (Nike)

OPTIMUM QUODQUE VIRO IMPETRANDUM.
The best a man can get. (Gillette)

RER' ALITER.
Think different. (Apple)

ID AMATURIO.
I'm lovin' it. (McDonalds)

CUM OPERAE PRETIUM SIS.
Because I'm worth it. (L'Oréal)

NULLA PRO INFECTO SUNT.
Impossible is nothing. (Adidas)

SEDA DIUTURNAM SITIM.
Obey your thirst. (Sprite)

SANE POSSUMUS.
Yes We Can. (Barack Obama)

PETE OMNES!
Gotta catch them all! (Pokémon)

QUIDQUID INSCRIBITUR, EST.
Does exactly what it says on the tin. (Ronseal)

CEREVISIARUM PRINCEPS.
The king of beers. (Budweiser)

VITA BONA 'ST.
Life's Good. (LG)

ENITIMUR ENIXIUS.
We try harder. (Avis)

PENNAS TAURUS TIBI RUBER DAT.
Red Bull gives you wings. (Red Bull)

ADAMAS IN AETERNUM.
A diamond is forever. (De Beers)

SEE ALSO: Euphonic Words / Yoda Linguistics

❡ The *OED*'s first citation for the greeting **hello** is as late as 1853 in the *New York Clipper* ('Hello ole feller, how are yer?'), but the earliest evidence for any written 'hello' is 1823. Hunters **hallooed** their dogs in 1709, and someone was **hallooing** their misery in 1602, but 'hello' wasn't widespread until Thomas Edison promoted it as the recommended answer to a telephone call. (Alexander Graham Bell's preference, **ahoy**, never caught on.)

❡ 'Hello' evolved from **halloo** and **hallo**, words to attract attention from afar. These old forms are related to the German **hallo** and French **halle**, called by hunt riders to their dogs.

❡ Prior to 'hello', a Victorian 'good day' (or 'good morn', 'good morrow' and so on) would have sufficed. And for Shakespeare, 'hail', 'how now?' and 'well met' were much in evidence. But while 'hello', and the less formal **hi**, are the default greetings for much of the English-speaking world, there are plenty of options for anyone looking to change things up.

WORLD HELLO DAY

is held annually on 21 November. 'Anyone can participate in World Hello Day simply by greeting ten people,' its organisers say encouragingly, continuing: 'This demonstrates the importance of personal communication for preserving peace.'

ALOHA (HAWAIIAN)
Love and affection

AS-SALAMU ALAIKUM
(ARABIC)
Peace be upon you

CIAO (ITALIAN)
Hello, goodbye

KONNICHIWA (JAPANESE)
Hello

NAMASTE (SANSKRIT)
Bowing to you

¿QUÉ ONDA? (SPANISH)
What's up?

SALUDO AMIGO (SPANISH)
Greetings, friend

SALUT (FRENCH)
Hello

SHALOM (HEBREW)
Hello, goodbye, peace

———

Ayo	*Salutations*
Greetings, Gates	*Waz poppin'?*
H'roo	*Wha's da haps?*
Here I is	*Whassup?*
Hey beau	*What's knitten, kitten?*
Hey!	*What's shaking?*
How do?	*What's the score?*
Howdy	*Woddascoops?*
Howzit?	*Yo!*
My man	*Yo G*
Oop-pop-a-da	*Zappenin'*
S'up?	*Zup?*

SEE ALSO: *Goodbyes*

¶ Passengers passing through security at Milwaukee's General Mitchell International Airport might be surprised to see signs for the *Recombobulation Area*, where they can recover from the **discombobulation** of queues and x-ray machines. It's an unexpectedly humorous reference to a word that first appeared in American English in the nineteenth century – along with **absquatulate**, **exflunct** and **flusticated** – when there was a fad for inventing grandiose words with a faux-Latin hue.

¶ Although some disparaged the fashion (in his 1859 *Dictionary of Modern Slang*, John Camden Hotten called such creations 'vulgar corruscations' of an 'indulgent public'), the combination of onomatapoeic pop with an excess of syllables was a source of amusement even at the time. Sharing the joke in 1826, the humour column in Canadian weekly newspaper *The Casket* related this impenetrable conversation:

> *'Good-morrow friend, how do you feel to-day.'*
>
> *'Pretty well; how are you?'*
>
> *'Oh, sir, the intense frigidity of the circumambient atmosphere, combining with the porosity of the earth, and joined with the humidity of the climate has discomboborated my respiration and affected my theoreticks.'*

¶ The humorous creations continued into the twentieth century, becoming ever more of a mouthful. For instance, someone embarrassed might be **discomgollifusticated**, while someone 'astonished but pleased' could be **discumgalligumfricated**. And while many of these highfalutin words have since fallen out of fashion, **discombobulated** remains a perennial favourite among word lovers.

ABSQUATULATE (V.)
To abscond or make away.

BODACIOUSLY (ADJ.)
Completely or totally.

CALLITHUMPIAN (ADJ.)
Describing a musical group making a cacophonous racket.

CONBOBBERATION (N.)
A disturbance or disagreement.

DISCOMBOBULATED (V.)
To be confused, disturbed or disarrayed.

EXFLUNCTIFY (V.)
To cause something (or someone) to fail or be overcome.

EXPLIFICATION (N.)
An explanation. (Similarly, *to explanify* is to explain.)

EXPLATERATE (V.)
To ceaselessly talk to avoid answering a question.

FLUSTICATED (ADJ.)
Confused and befuddled, probably by drink.

HIGHFALUTIN (ADJ.)
Pompous or pretentious.

OBFLISTICATE (V.)
To wipe out (probably combining *obfuscate* and *obliterate*).

RAMBUNCTIOUS (ADJ.)
Uncontrollably exuberant, boisterous or wild.

SOCKDOLAGER (N.)
A knockdown blow or decisive point in an argument.

17

SEE ALSO: *Diner Slang / Funny Words*

SEE ALSO: Letters, Old and New / Printers' Marks

¶The **ampersand** – the squiggly symbol that means **and** – was found on a wall in Pompeii (*fig. 2*), which means it has been around since at least the eruption of Vesuvius in AD 79.

¶The Pompeiian ampersand was a **ligature**, meaning two letters combined to make one glyph (or character), in this case the **e** and **t** of the Latin **et**, meaning 'and'. In typography, ligatures are principally aesthetic. For instance, the ligature **fi** avoids the inelegant spacing of **f i**. But the Pompeiian scribbler wasn't being aesthetic, just efficient.

¶The ampersand wasn't the first time-saving glyph for 'and'. Around 50 BC, Tiro, secretary and scribe of the statesman and rhetorician Cicero, invented his own device (*fig. 1*), that came to be known as the **Tironian 'et'**. For a long time this symbol was used in the heavy Gothic script known as **blackletter**, the typeface used in Gutenberg's Bible.

¶But Tiro's creation was fighting a losing battle against the lithe ampersand. Blackletter was being used less frequently and, by the eighteenth century, the Tironian 'et' had all but vanished. Today, it only survives in Irish and Scottish Gaelic, where it is called the **agus** and **agusan** respectively.

¶For many years, folk etymology promoted the misleading claim that the ampersand was invented by, and named after, French physician André-Marie Ampère. It made sense (Ampère's 'and', yes?), but had not an amp of truth to it.

¶While the ampersand's true inventor will never be known, the word's origin is. It is a contraction of 'and per se and', a Latin-English hybrid that essentially means 'this symbol means **and**'.

¶Up to the nineteenth century, the alphabet was often taught with the ampersand as the twenty-seventh character. Children chanting their ABC would conclude with 'X, Y, Z, *and per se and*'; and when those last syllables were said quickly, they became 'ampersand'. But schoolchildren being schoolchildren, it went by other names too. In his *Dictionary of Slang and Colloquial English* (1905), John Farmer mentions a few variations, including **and-pussy-and**, **Ann Passy Ann**, **anpasty**, **anpazad**, **amsiam**, **amperzed**, **ampus-end**, and – a personal favourite – **zumzy-zan**. Farmer also notes that, being at the rear of the alphabet, 'ampersand' was also slang for the posterior.

¶But such schoolyard humour is beneath the ampersand. In his seminal work *A Brief History of the Ampersand* (1953), German typographer Jan Tschichold collected nineteen centuries' worth of them, describing them as 'enchanting', 'graceful', 'extravagant', 'lively' and 'feminine'. It is in this spirit that we celebrate English's most ostentatious mark.

THE TYRONIAN ET, AND THE EVOLUTION OF THE AMPERSAND

FIG. 1	FIG. 2	FIG. 3	FIG. 4	FIG. 5	FIG. 6	FIG. 7
c. 50 BC	pre-AD 79	mid-fourth century	c. AD 346	c. AD 509	seventh century	eighth century

AMPERSANDS BY DESIGN

ADAGE	*ALBERTUS*	*ARIAL*	*AVIANO DIDONE*	*ALTESSE*	*AMERICAN TYPEWRITER*
BASKERVILLE	*BLONDE FRAKTUR*	*BODONI*	*CINZEL*	*COOPER*	*COPPERPLATE*
DALLIANCE	*DIDONI*	*DIDOT ROMAN*	*DUNHILL*	*FLEUR*	*GOTHIQUE*
GARAMOND	*GRATITUDE*	*HOEFLER TEXT*	*KURALE*	*LIGHTFOOT*	*LUMINARI*
MODESTO	*MONARCH*	*MR DARCY*	*NAUTICA*	*ROSMATIKA*	*TIMES NEW ROMAN*

BRANDS AND AMPERSANDS

Which global brand does each ampersand belong to? (*Answers on page 214.*)

1   2   3   4   5   6

NEED A CLUE?

The brands are: Ben & Jerry's; Dolce & Gabbana; Johnson & Johnson; McKinsey & Company; Proctor & Gamble; Tiffany & Co.

¶ Anagrammatists – those who craft **anagrams** – have been rearranging letters since ancient Greece. Pythagoras is said to have used anagrams for divination, and a story is told of Alexander the Great's soothsayer using one to predict the sack of Tyre in 332 BC. While such tales are hard to verify, the long history of anagrams shows they're more than mere wordplay.

¶ Anagrams are a code to be deciphered, which explains their appeal in mysticism and religion. The ancient Jewish tradition of Kabbala uses anagrams to unlock the secrets of the Torah, while Platonists saw **anagrammatic virtues** hidden in the letters of one's name. Later, in the Middle Ages, church institutions across Europe exchanged religious anagrams in Latin, most famously this fictional exchange between Jesus and Pontius Pilate:

> **Pilate:** *Quid est veritas?*
> *('What is truth?')*
>
> **Jesus:** *Est vir qui adest.*
> *('It is the man before you.')*

¶ The popularity of anagrams grew in the seventeenth century when France's King Louis XIII appointed Thomas Billon as the first Royal Anagrammatist. As well as creating **anagrammatic prophecies**, Billon delighted the court with anagrams that were playful, topical or laudatory. His most popular turn was the transformation of a name into an apt and witty anagram.

ANAGRAM
A word or phrase formed by rearranging the letters of another.

Monday = dynamo
Below = elbow

ANANYM
(ALSO, ANADROME, SEMORDNILAP)

An anagram that, when reversed, makes a new word or phrase.

Semordnilap = palindromes
Robert = Trebor

APTAGRAM
An anagram that explains the original phrase.

The eyes = they see
Butterfly = flutter by

ANTIGRAM
An anagram that is an antonym (means the opposite) of the original phrase.

Santa = Satan
Filled = ill-fed

SYNANAGRAM
An anagram that is a synonym of the original phrase.

Angered = enraged
Astronomer = moon starer

TRIANAGRAM
A three-way anagram.

Listen = silent = tinsel
Earthlings = heartlings = slathering

> There is no one-word anagram for *anagram*, but if you google 'anagram', you'll see the message: 'Did you mean: nag a ram'.

¶ Anagrams have also been unexpectedly useful among scientists. Some of the greatest discoveries of the seventeenth century were accompanied by anagrams as *Establishment of Priority* (proof of a discovery). Wary about sharing findings too soon, scientists sent anagrams to their peers to prove they'd discovered *something*, but not revealing what. For instance, when Galileo discovered Saturn's rings in 1610, he sent an anagram to Johannes Kepler that hid the message:

> *I have observed the most distant planet to have a triple form.*

¶ Fifty years later, Robert Hooke published an anagram announcing his discovery of Hooke's Law which, when solved, read:

> *As the extension, so the force.*

¶ Elsewhere, nineteenth-century naturalists used anagrams for naming new species, a practice now incorporated into the *International Code of Nomenclature for algae, fungi, and plants*. Additionally, there are dozens of North American towns that are anagrams of people, places and things, from Saskatchewan's Adanac (Canada) to Windber, Pennsylvania (after mine owner Charles Berwind).

¶ More recently, **anagram maps** have appeared for transit systems around the world. These were inspired by the London Underground anagram map, incorporating Anger Perk (Regent's Park), Burst Racoon (Barons Court) and No Suet (Euston).

ANAGRAMS OF NOTE

IMPRESSIVELY LONG ANAGRAMS
refragmentation = antiferromagnet
undefinability = unidentifiably
incorporate = procreation

A RARE ANAGRAM EQUATION
eleven + two = twelve + one

ANAGRAM PSEUDONYMS
Damon Albarn = Dan Abnormal
Edward Gorey = Ogdred Weary (also, Regera Dowdy, E. G. Deadworry and more)
François Rabelais = Alcofribas Nasier
(George) Bernard Shaw = Redbarn Wash
Vladimir Nabokov = Vivian Darkbloom

LEWIS CARROLL ANAGRAMS
Florence Nightingale = flit on, cheering angel
Disraeli = I lead, Sir

ANAGRAM COMEDY
Anagrams of the Fawlty Towers sign seen at the start of each episode:
Fatty Owls; Fawty Toer; Flay Otters; Flowery Twats; Warty Towels; Watery Fowls.

ANAGRAM AS PLOT DEVICE
Louis Friend = Iron Sulfide
(Silence of the Lambs)

Tom Marvolo Riddle = I am Lord Voldemort
(Harry Potter and the Chamber of Secrets)

Redrum = murder
(The Shining)

O, Draconian devil = Leonardo da Vinci
(The Da Vinci Code)

LEXICON FAVOURITES
Elvis = lives
Fire of London = inferno of old
Gin and vermouth = hungover, damn it!

ANIMAL ADJECTIVES

SEE ALSO: Animal Verbs

22

ANT
Formicine

BEAR
Ursine

BISON
Bisontine

BUFFALO
Bubaline

BULL
Taurine

CAMEL
Cameline

CAT
Feline

CHICKEN
Galline

COW
Bovine

CRAB
Cancrine

CROW
Corvine

DODO
Didine

DOG
Canine

DOLPHIN
Delphine

DONKEY
Asinine

DOVE
Columbine

DRAGON
Draconine

EAGLE
Aquiline

ELEPHANT
Elephantine

FISH
Piscine

FROG
Ranine

GAZELLE
Gazelline

GIRAFFE
Giraffine

GOOSE
Anserine

GUINEA PIG
Cavine

HARE
Lapine

HIPPOPOTAMUS
Hippopotamine

HORSE
Equine

HUMAN
Hominine

HYENA
Hyenine

KANGAROO
Macropodine

KILLER WHALE
Orcine

LEMMING
Microtine

LION
Leonine

MANATEE
Manatine

MOSQUITO
Aedine

MOUSE
Murine

OCTOPUS
Octopine

ORANGUTAN
Pongine

PANTHER
Pantherine

PIG
Porcine

PORCUPINE
Hystricine

PYTHON
Pythonine

RABBIT
Leporine

RAM
Arietine

RHINOCEROS
Rhinocerine

SEAGULL
Larine

SHEEP
Ovine

SNAKE
Serpentine

TERMITE
Termitine

TICK
Acarine

TIGER
Tigrine

TORTOISE
Geochine

TURTLE
Terrapine

VULTURE
Vulturine

WASP
Vespine

WOLF
Lupine

WORM
Lumbricine

ANIMAL VERBS

APING (*me*)
BADGERING (*someone*)
BEARING (*with*)
BEAVERING (*away*)
BEETLING (*off*)
BUCKING (*up*)
BUGGING (*someone*)
CARPING (*on*)
CHICKENING (*out*)
CLAMMING (*up*)
COCKING (*up*)
CRANING (*your neck*)
CROWING (*about*)

DOGGING (*don't ask!*)
DUCKING (*the issue*)
EARWIGGING (*neighbours*)
FERRETING (*about*)
FISHING (*for compliments*)
FLOUNDERING (*around*)
FOXING (*the police*)
HOGGING (*the limelight*)
HORSING (*around*)
LARKING (*around*)
LEECHING (*off*)
MONKEYING (*around*)
PARROTING (*the teacher*)

PIGGING (*out*)
PONYING (*up*)
RABBITING (*on*)
RATTING (*on*)
SLOTHING (*around*)
SLUGGING (*away*)
SNIPING (*at*)
SQUIRRELLING (*away*)
SWANNING (*off*)
TITTING (*about*)
WEASLING (*out*)
WOLFING (*down*)
WORMING (*away*)

SEE ALSO: *Animal Adjectives* ☞ 📖

📖 SEE ALSO: *Charles Dickens' Characters*

APTRONYMS

¶ When someone's name seems curiously fitting to their job, it's an ***aptronym*** (also called a ***euonym***). While aptronyms can be a source of mirth, some psychologists believe one's name can also influence life choices, a theory known as ***nominative determinism***. Seventeenth-century Puritans who named children after the cardinal virtues – Hope, Charity, Faith and so on – believed this too, and there's now evidence that, sometimes, it can happen.

¶ When 313,445 surnames in the General Medical Council's register were analysed in 2013, researchers found a greater correlation between name and medical specialism than chance alone would explain. Was Laura Hamm destined for the deli counter? Perhaps not. But Dr Docktor *might* have felt powerfully drawn towards the medical profession.

ANGEL COLON	*Gastroenterologist*
BRAD SLAUGHTER	*Meat manager*
CHRISTOPHER COKE	*Cocaine smuggler*
DAVID BIRD	*Ornithologist*
DAVID DOLLAR	*Economist*
DOUGLAS HART	*Cardiologist*
DR ALEXANDER PHILPOTT	*Urologist*
ED CURRIE	*Chilli pepper farmer*
IGOR JUDGE	*Lord Chief Justice*
JACQUELINE HOTT	*Sex therapist*
JOHN BLOW	*Organist*
KATIE VOLYNETS	*Tennis player*
LAURA HAMM	*Deli manager*
MARGARET SPELLINGS	*Secretary for Education*
ROBERT CASHDOLLAR	*Lobbyist*
SARA BLIZZARD	*Weather presenter*
SCOTT SPEED	*Racing driver*
SUE YOO	*Lawyer*
USAIN BOLT	*Sprinter*

AUSSIE ABBREVIATIONS

¶ Abbreviated words are a distinctive feature of Australian English. Although every English-speaking country uses them, none have so many, nor use them so often. These *diminutives* are baked in to Australian English in a process that started in the nineteenth century. Today there are estimated to be over 5,000 diminutives in the Australian lexicon, or ***Aussie lexo***.

AGGRO	*aggressive*	COLDIE	*cold beer*	SALVOS	*Salvation army*
AMBO	*ambulance*	DEFO	*definitely*	SAMBO	*sandwich*
ARVO	*afternoon*	DOCCO	*documentary*	SANNY	*hand sanitiser*
AVO	*avocado*	GARBO	*garbage collector*	SCRATCHIE	*scratchcard*
BARBIE	*barbecue*	HOSPO	*hospitality*	SERVO	*service station*
BICCIE	*biscuit*	JARMIES	*pyjamas*	SMOKO	*cigarette break*
BLOWIE	*blowfly*	LOCKO	*covid lockdown*	STUBBY	*small bottle of beer*
BREKKIE	*breakfast*	MILKO	*milkman*	SUNNIES	*sunglasses*
BUSHIE	*bushranger*	POKEY	*poker machine*	TANTY	*tantrum*
CHEWY	*chewing gum*	PREGGO	*pregnant*	TRAINO	*train station*
CHOCCY	*chocolate*	REGO	*car registration*	VEGGO	*vegetarian*
CHRISSIE	*Christmas*	RELLIE	*relative*	WOMBIE	*wombat*

SEE ALSO: *Americanisms / Strine*

24

SEE ALSO: *Here's Johnny*

AVERAGE JOE

¶ ***Average Joe*** is the personification of normal, a statistical mean given human form. Although the term was coined in 1940, Joe – 'an imaginary nobody' – is cited as far back as 1846 (along with other faceless fellows in the dictionary, like John, Jack, Tom and Roger).

¶ But Average Joe isn't an anonymous nobody so much as the average everybody.

Partner to ***Average Jane*** and acquaintance of ***John Q Public***, Average Joe is the man statisticians, politicians and journalists need to reach.

¶ Given this valuable role, Average Joe has ordinary cousins around the world: the placeholder names designated for ***Mr Everyman***. (There are Everywomen too, but not so many.)

Aam Aadmi (*India*)	Israel Israeli (*Israel*)	Max Mustermann (*Germany*)
Anders Andersen (*Denmark*)	Jan Kowalski (*Poland*)	Monsieur Toulemonde (*France*)
Fred Nurk (*Australia*)	Joe Bloggs (*Britain*)	Nanashi No Gonbee (*Japan*)
Fulan Alfulani (*Arab countries*)	Jón Jónsson (*Iceland*)	Piet Pompies (*South Africa*)
Hong Gildong (*Korea*)	Marko Marković (*Bosnia*)	Sven Svensson (*Sweden*)

B.

¶ Australian comedian Barry Humphries contributed so prolifically to the nation's slang lexicon that he is referenced over 125 times in the *Australian National Dictionary*, with twenty-four first citations.

¶ A self-confessed bibliomaniac (his library contained over 20,000 works), Humphries had a keen appreciation of language, particularly the vernacular within Australian English. Through his comic creations (Dame Edna Everage, Sir Les, Barry McKenzie and, in his final years, Sandy Stone) Humphries coined and popularised dozens of slang terms, many of which are still used.

¶ Slang being slang, and Humphries being Humphries, the glossary below contains plenty of sex and excreta. (His material could be racist, sexist and homophobic too, but these terms have been omitted.) Even with this self-censorship, however, readers of a sensitive disposition are advised to skip this page for something more wholesome.

BLOW THE BEEF BUGLE
Fellate
(also: gnaw the 'nana)

BRITSVILLE
England

BUGLE DUSTER
A handkerchief

BUSH BUZZER
A vibrator

CALL CHARLES
Vomit
(also: technicolour yawn, throw one's voice, cry Ruth, liquid laugh, make love to the lav, go [for] the big spit)

CHUG-A-LUG
An alcoholic beverage

DIP THE DAGGER
Have sex
(also: exercise the ferret)

DONGER
Penis
(also: pyjama python)

DROP OFF THE TWIG
Die

DRY AS A DEAD DINGO'S DONGER
Thirsty
(also: dry as a kookaburra's khyber)

FANG FACTORY
Dental surgery

FLOG THE LIZARD
Urinate
(also: aim Archie at the Armitage, shake hands with the unemployed, siphon the python, strain the potatoes, splash the boots, drain the dragon)

FURRY HOOP
Vagina

HORNBAG
An attractive woman

OPEN MY LUNCHBOX
Fart

PUNISH PERCY WITH THE PALM
Masturbate
(also: jerk the gherkin, twang the wire)

NUNGA MUNCHER
Cunnilingus

NUT CHOKERS
Male underwear
(also: thunderbags)

TOP BOLLOCKS
Female breasts

NUDGE THE TURPS
To drink heavily

STONKERED
Drunk

SUGAR-BAG
Bribe

THROTTLING PIT
The toilet

UGLY AS A HATFUL OF ARSEHOLES
Unattractive

25

SEE ALSO: *Farts / Fuck / Strine*

¶ The first **bastard** appeared in the early fourteenth century, although back then it was a neutral word for a child born outside of marriage. Put a 'the' before it (for example '*the* bastard of Flanders') and it suggested someone illegitimate but highborn, such as the son of a nobleman.

¶ It didn't take long for the word to become, well, **bastardised**. It soon came to mean anything that had been adulterated or weakened, and by the seventeenth century it was an abusive term for someone wicked or cruel.

¶ Curiously for a word that can be used so offensively, it can also be quite innocent, as the following collection of bastards demonstrates. Incidentally, the collective terms for a group of bastards are a **bagful** or **shower of**.

BASTARDA
a cursive Gothic script

BASTARD BALM
an aromatic flowering plant

BASTARD CANNON
a large-bore cannon

BASTARD CANOE
a birchbark canoe

BASTARD MOULD
a mould for draining sugar

BASTARD PLOVER
a lapwing

BASTARD RHUBARB
a variety of rhubarb

BASTARD SECRETARY
a cursive script

BASTARD SUGAR
impure coarse brown sugar

BASTARD SWORD
a short sword

BASTARD TITLE
the page before a title page

BASTARD-TOOTHED
a type of toothed file

BASTARD WING
feathers found on a bird's wing

BASTARDS ON A RAFT
poached eggs on toast

BROWN BASTARD
a sweet wine from Spain

SEE ALSO: *Changed Meanings*

SEE ALSO: *Printers' Marks*

26

BEATRICE WARDE

¶ Beatrice L. Warde (d. 1969), known as The First Lady of Typography, was a writer, educator and typography expert who worked at the Monotype Corporation. Warde entered the male-dominated world of printing in 1927 when Monotype offered a job to her pseudonym, Paul Beaujon. Although her employer was taken aback when Beaujon turned out to be Beatrice, she became editor of the *Monotype Reader*, in which she was a prominent advocate of the printer's craft.

¶ A recurring theme of Warde's writing was the reminder that typography should be a purposeful tool rather than a decorative indulgence. She challenged typographers to use 'invisible typography' that, like a 'crystal goblet' – the title of a famous essay she wrote in 1930 – would perfectly reveal its contents. For Warde, the reader should focus 'through type and not upon it' to appreciate the ideas and thoughts of the author.

¶ But it's Warde's 1932 'manifesto', *This is a printing office*, that she is best known for. Written to showcase Eric Gill's Perpetua typeface, Warde expressed in seventy perfect words the purpose of the print-maker. Today, her manifesto can be found in print-works and type foundries the world over. The declaration can also be seen on a brass plaque outside the United States Government Publishing Office in Washington, D.C.

THIS IS
A PRINTING
OFFICE

CROSS-ROADS OF CIVILIZATION

REFUGE OF ALL THE ARTS
AGAINST THE RAVAGES OF TIME

ARMORY OF FEARLESS TRUTH
AGAINST WHISPERING RUMOUR

INCESSANT TRUMPET OF TRADE

FROM THIS PLACE WORDS MAY FLY ABROAD

NOT TO PERISH ON WAVES OF SOUND, NOT TO VARY WITH THE WRITER'S HAND
BUT FIXED IN TIME, HAVING BEEN VERIFIED BY PROOF

FRIEND, YOU STAND ON SACRED GROUND

THIS IS A PRINTING OFFICE

BEE'S KNEES

¶ **The bee's knees** is an expression associated with flappers from the Jazz Age to describe something excellent. The phrase first appeared in 1797, but meant something small and insubstantial. It then became a nonsense item, like *a bag of holes*. Only in the 1920s did it come to mean 'the acme of perfection'.

¶ The phrase entered flapper culture amid a fad for combining animal names – such as gnat, owl or tiger – with something else, to indicate the utmost approval. Most of these nonsense formations were short-lived, with the exception of *the bee's knees*, *the cat's pyjamas* and *the duck's quack*, all of which continue to delight. (And the answer to the inevitable question is *no*; bees don't have knees, but knee-like joints.)

THE FLAPPER MENAGERIE

THE BEE'S KNEES
(also: ankles)

THE BULLFROG'S BEARD

THE BULLOCK'S BOLLOCKS

THE BUTTERFLY'S BOOK

THE CAT'S PYJAMAS
(also: canary, cuffs, eye, eyebrows, kimono, miaow, underwear, whiskers)

THE CLAM'S GARTERS

THE DUCK'S QUACK
(also: nuts)

THE EEL'S ANKLE
(also: hips)

THE ELEPHANT'S ARCHES
(also: adenoids, hips, instep, manicure, wrist)

THE FROG'S ANKLES
(also: eyebrows)

THE GNAT'S ELBOW

THE GRASSHOPPER'S KNEES

THE HEN'S EYEBROWS

THE KIPPER'S KNICKERS

THE LEOPARD'S STRIPES

THE BEE'S KNEES
COCKTAIL (1920S)

60ml gin
22.5ml lemon juice
15ml honey syrup
10ml orange juice
Orange twist for garnish

Shake ingredients with ice
in a cocktail shaker.

Strain into a chilled coupe glass and
garnish with an orange-zest twist.

THE CAT'S WHISKERS
COCKTAIL (2010S)

30ml honey schnapps
25ml dry gin
25ml simple syrup
25ml lemon juice
Bee pollen for garnish

Shake ingredients with ice
in a cocktail shaker.

Strain into a chilled coupe glass
and garnish with bee pollen.

SEE ALSO: *Animal Verbs / Dictionary of Small Things*

28

❡ 'Hereafter I shall estimate the force of the wind according to the following scale', wrote the captain of HMS *Woolwich*, Sir Francis Beaufort, in his private log on 13 January 1806. He could scarcely have imagined that this simple 0–12 scale would evolve into the **international standard for the measurement of wind force**.

❡ Describing wind conditions was essential in the age of sail. Although Beaufort wasn't the first to attempt it, his scale was unusual for describing the *effect* of the wind, not the wind alone. But what cemented its place in history was its adoption by the Royal Navy in 1838 and its acceptance at the First International Meteorological Conference in 1853.

❡ The **Beaufort Scale** is an empirical scale, with wind-speed measurements only added in 1906. But what the Beaufort Scale describes has changed. Beaufort's 1838 version described the wind's effect on a ship's rigging, specifically a *man-of-war*, the warship of the day. The scale went from the calm of 0 to the hurricane of 12: 'That which no canvas can withstand'. Later, when sail gave way to steam, the scale focused on the condition of the sea. The famous land-based observations were added in 1906 by meteorologist Sir George Simpson, who also introduced the wind-speed measurements.

❡ For sailors, the Beaufort Scale could be life-saving. But for landlubbers who've never seen a hurricane, it's become poetry. Scott Huler, author of *Defining the Wind*, called the land-based Beaufort 'the apex of descriptive nonfiction in English.' That's an unusual accolade for a scientific scale (although the **Schmidt Sting Pain Index** makes for a gripping read too).

29

SEE ALSO: *Weights and Measures*

THE BEAUFORT SCALE

Calm; smoke rises vertically.

Smoke drifts with air; weather vanes inactive.

Wind felt on face; leaves rustle; ordinary vane moved by wind.

Leaves and small twigs in constant motion; wind extends light flag.

Small branches sway; dust and loose paper blows about.

Small trees in leaf begin to sway; crested wavelets form on inland waters.

Large branches sway; telegraph wires whistle; umbrellas used with difficulty.

Whole trees in motion; difficult to walk against wind.

Twigs break off trees; generally impedes progress.

Slight damage to buildings; chimney pots and slates removed.

Trees uprooted; considerable damage to buildings.

Widespread damage; very rarely experienced.

Devastation.

¶ The *Wycliffe Bible* of 1382 was the first complete translation of the Old and New Testaments into English. It was immediately condemned as heretical, as were those who read it.

¶ Although it's not known how much of the *Wycliffe Bible* was the work of its instigator, John Wycliffe, his name remains indelibly associated with the mission to translate the Bible into the vernacular. And while Wycliffe was posthumously excommunicated – and his remains exhumed, burned and tossed into the River Swift – his legacy was harder to erase.

¶ Today, according to the Wycliffe Global Alliance, the Bible has been fully translated into 736 languages, and partially into a further 2,922. Within English alone, there are over 900 bible translations to choose from.

¶ Historically, translations aimed to be accurate and intelligible, but many wanted to make the Bible more relevant, with ***idiomatic*** and ***paraphrase*** versions. Black Americans have a long tradition of Bible adaptation, and the last few decades have seen the *Black Bible Chronicles, Rappin' With Jesus, Hood Bible: King Pin Version* and *The Ghetto Bible*. Other communities can also find their Bible: gay Christians can read the *Queen James Bible*, kids have *The Action Bible* ('230 fast-paced narratives in chronological order') and social activists can choose between *The Inclusive Bible* and the *Green Bible*.

¶ Although Wycliffe would have approved of the spirit of this work, he might have been perplexed by Bibles translated into *Star Trek* Klingon, *Avatar* Na'vi, or the constructed language Toki Pona.

30

SEE ALSO: *Index of Forbidden Books*

SEVEN BOOKS OF GENESIS

Below are seven verses from Genesis taken from different published versions of the Bible.

SMS BIBLE
(GENESIS 1:1)

In da Bginnin God cre8d da heavens & da earth.

LOLCAT BIBLE
(GENESIS 1:2)

Teh Urfs no has shayps an has darwk fase, an Ceiling Cat roed invisible bike oval teh wawters.

GEN Z BIBLE
(GENESIS 1:3)

Then God was like, 'Yo, let there be light,' and boom, there was light.

LEET BIBLE
(GENESIS 1:4)

4nd God 54w 7h7 7h3 l1gh7 w45 g00d. 4nd God 53p4r8d 7h3 l1gh7 from 7h3 d4rkn355.

EMOJI BIBLE
(GENESIS 1:5)

God called the light 'Day' and the darkness 'Night.' And just like that, the first day was wrapped. ⚙ 🌙

THE PIRATE BIBLE
(GENESIS 1:6)

Arrrr, God said, Let there be a sky in the midst of th'drink, and let it divide th'drink from th'drink!

THE GHETTO BIBLE
(GENESIS 1:7)

And Big Daddy made da earth it divided da water which wuz under da earth from the water which wuz above the earth an' it wuz bangin'.

THE POLARI BIBLE
(GENESIS 1:8)

And Gloria screeched the firmament Heaven. And the bijou nochy and the morning were the second journo.

BINGO CALLS

¶ Versions of **bingo** have been played since the sixteenth century, derived from the Italian game **Lo Giuoco del Lotto**. But the popularity of the modern game is widely credited to Hugh J. Ward, who spotted Canadian soldiers playing **Housey-House** in 1916. Ward started touring the game as **Beano** (because beans were placed on the numbers) in carnivals across America from 1924, where it was discovered by Edwin S. Lowe, who turned it into a boxed game around 1930. Although Beano was renamed Bingo, a similar game was being played in Europe as **Lotto**, **Housey** and **Tombola**, but the Bingo takeover was coming.

¶ The **bingo lingo** used by callers for the 90 numbers on the game cards originated in the Service messes during WWII, and was infused with military slang. The language continues to be updated, but many calls remain timeless. So, eyes down – look in!

1. - blind one
2. - one little duck
3. - you and me
4. - knock at the door
5. - man alive
6. - Tom's tricks
7. - God's in heaven
8. - one fat lady
9. - doctor's orders
10. - one oh, number ten
11. - legs eleven
12. - a monkey's cousin
13. - unlucky for some
14. - Valentine's day
15. - young and keen
16. - sweet sixteen
17. - dancing queen
18. - coming of age
19. - goodbye teens
20. - blind twenty
21. - key of the door
22. - two little ducks
23. - thee and me
24. - two dozen
25. - duck and dive
26. - pick and mix
27. - little duck with a crutch
28. - overweight
29. - you're doing fine
30. - dirty gertie

31. - get up and run
32. - buckle my shoe
33. - two little fleas
34. - ask for more
35. - jump and jive
36. - three dozen
37. - a flea in heaven
38. - Christmas cake
39. - those famous steps
40. - naughty forty
41. - time for fun
42. - Winnie the Pooh
43. - down on your knees
44. - droopy drawers
45. - halfway there
46. - up to tricks
47. - four and seven
48. - four dozen
49. - nick nick
50. - bull's eye
51. - tweak of the thumb
52. - weeks in a year
53. - stuck in the tree
54. - clean the floor
55. - snakes alive
56. - was she worth it?
57. - Heinz varieties
58. - make them wait
59. - Brighton line
60. - five dozen

61. - baker's bun
62. - turn on the screw
63. - des eerie
64. - red raw
65. - old age pension
66. - clickety click
67. - made in heaven
68. - saving grace
69. - either way up
70. - three score and ten
71. - bang on the drum
72. - Danny La Rue
73. - a crutch and a flea
74. - hit the floor
75. - strive and strive
76. - trombones
77. - two little crutches
78. - heaven's gate
79. - one more time
80. - Gandhi's breakfast
81. - fat lady and a little wee
82. - fat lady with a duck
83. - fat lady with a flea
84. - seven dozen
85. - staying alive
86. - between the sticks
87. - Torquay in Devon
88. - two fat ladies
89. - all but one
90. - end of the line

SEE ALSO: *Funny Words / Origins of Nonsense*

BREASTS

Alpine mountains	Cans	Groceries	Nungers
Apple-dumplings	Cats and kitties	Headlamps	Puppies
Baby bumpers	Chalubbies	Honkers	Rack
Bazongas	Chesticles	Howitzers	Shock absorbers
Bazookas	Chichibangas	Jabongoes	Tale of two cities
Bing-bongs	Chubblies	Jemimas	Thingumabobs
Bongoes	Clackers	Kaboolies	Tipperary fortune
Cajooblies	Dairy queen	Kahoonas	Tooraloorals
	Dubbies	Knockers	Wallpies
	Duckies	Maracas	Wembleys
	Equipment	Melons	Whamdanglers
	Flight deck	Mary Ellens	Whim-whams
	Funbags	Ninnies	Wobblers
	Gazongas	Num-nums	Zogs

SEE ALSO: *Testicles*

SEE ALSO: *Etymology Mysteries / Obsolete Occupations*

BRITISH PLACE NAMES

❡ British place names can be a delight. But while the likes of **Giggleswick**, **Pratt's Bottom**, **Great Heck** and **North Piddle** might raise a laugh, they are also extraordinary linguistic fossils. Under the microscope, these names reveal ancient words from Old English, Old Norse, Cornish, Norman French and the Celtic languages that are highly descriptive.

❡ Some names tell of who was in charge, like Essex – '(land of the) East Saxons (East Seaxe)' – or Norfolk – '(land of the) northern people (Nordfolc)'. Landowners and bigwigs are similarly remembered, as in Banbury (Banna's stronghold) and Fakenham (Facca's homestead). In fact, many of Britain's most unusual names – like **Cocking**, **Muckton**, **Ogle** and **Great Snoring** – merely derive from family names.

❡ The majority of placenames are either **habitative** (indicating habitations or buildings) or **topographical** (reflecting physical features of the landscape). The former can be seen in names containing words like **burh** (stronghold), **ham** (homestead), **minster** (church) and **worth** (enclosure), as in Edinburgh, Nottingham, Westminster and Wandsworth. The latter feature words like **cofa** (tree), **ford** (river-crossing), **mond** (mound) and **mor** (marshy ground), all found in Coventry, Ashford, Richmond and Blackmore.

❡ Many names combine a few descriptive features. **Chesham**, for instance, means something like 'river-meadow by a heap of stones', while **Cheswick** is the 'farm where cheese is made'. **Gotham** might today be associated with Batman, but the first Gotham, near Nottingham, comes from Old English meaning 'homestead where goats are kept'.

¶ With help from etymologists, these placenames turn out to make perfect literal sense, almost as if one were receiving directions. For those living at the time of the Domesday Book, the survey of England and Wales completed in 1086, it would have been helpful to know that *Itching-*ton* was 'the farmstead by the river Itch', that *Ugley* was 'Ugga's woodland clearing', or that *Wormwood Scrubbs* was 'a wood infested with snakes'. It is only now, when the names are said in modern English, that they seem funny. But there's nothing funny about *Fingrinhoe* or *Six Mile Bottom*.

AN ETYMOLOGICAL TOUR OF BRITAIN

BITCHFIELD, LANCASHIRE
In the Domesday Book as Billesfelt, this either pertains to a person – 'open land of a man called Bill' – or a figurative use of the Old English for sword, bill.

CHEDDAR GORGE, SOMERSET
'Cheddar' is from Old English ceodor, meaning 'ravine', making the name equivalent to Ravine Gorge.

GREAT SNORING, NORFOLK
In the Domesday Book as Snaringes, which means '(settlement of) the family of a man called Snear'. Little Snoring is but a short distance away.

HASLEMERE, SURREY
From Old English hæsel + mere, meaning 'pool where hazels grow'.

LOWER SWELL, GLOUCESTERSHIRE
From Old English swell, meaning 'rising ground or hill'. Also found in Upper Swell.

LOOSE, KENT
Listed as Hlose in the eleventh century. From Old English hlōse, meaning 'place by the pigsty'.

LOUDWATER, BUCKINGHAMSHIRE
As it sounds; 'the noisy stream', from Old English hlūd + wœter.

NOBOTTLE, NORTHAMPTONSHIRE
In the Domesday Book as Nuebote, from Old English words meaning 'new building'.

OGLE, NORTHUMBERLAND
Probably 'Ocga's hill'.

PRATT'S BOTTOM, GREATER LONDON
'Bottom' is from Old English botm, meaning the bottom of a valley, and Pratt was a family name, so: 'valley bottom of the Pratt family'.

SCUNTHORPE, NORTH LINCOLNSHIRE
In the Domesday Book as Escumetorp, meaning 'farm of a man named Skúma'.

SEETHING, NORFOLK
In the Domesday Book as Sithinges, probably 'place of the family of a man called Sitha'.

SWILLINGTON, LEEDS
In the Domesday Book as Suillintune, from Old English 'farm near the pig hill'.

WETWANG, YORKSHIRE
In the Domesday Book as Wetuuangha, probably from Old Scandinavian vœtt-vangr, meaning 'field for the trial of legal action'.

¶ One area of humour that doesn't get the recognition it deserves is the niche occupied by punning business names, such as the computer shop **Bits and PCs**, or **Tiecoon**, the tie shop formerly in New York's Penn Station.

¶ Some people think they're too good for puns, treating them as entry-level humour for children and Christmas crackers. But such people are snobs. Whoever came up with **Chance & Counters** for their board game cafe was clearly a genius, as was the owner of **Get Stuffed**, the legendary taxidermy shop on London's Essex Road. Such names don't just bring joy to those who see them, but provide an endless source of free marketing.

¶ This directory includes some exceptional puns. Although space doesn't allow for some of the equally ingenious straplines, an exception must be made for the camping shop in Leicester, UK, that promotes its seasonal sale with the slogan, 'Now is the winter of our discount tents'. Please, take a bow.

SEE ALSO: *Goodbyes*

AUTO REPAIR
Dire Scrapes
Wreck-a-mended

BARS
Pour Judgement
Tequila Mockingbird
U Otter Stop In

BICYCLE REPAIR
Cycloanalysts
Cycology
The Old Spokes Home

BUILDERS & DECORATORS
Bonny Tiler
Chisel Me Timbers
Completely Plastered
George Floorman
Grout of this World
Overcome with Emulsion
Slates and Ladders
William the Concreter
Woodfellas

CHEESE SHOPS
C'est Cheese
Fond Ewe Fine Cheeses

CLEANING SERVICES
Spruce Springclean
Sweeping Beauty

COFFEE SHOPS
Brewed Awakening
Brew Ha Ha
C U Latte
Cup-A-Cabana
Espresso Yourself
Fuckoffee
Higher Grounds Cafe
Pony Espresso
Thanks a Latte

DRIVING LESSONS
El Passo
Samuel 'L' Jackson

FISH & CHIPS
A Salt and Battery
Battersea Cod's Home
Frying Nemo
Jack the Chipper
New Cod on the Block
Oh My Cod
Starchip Enterprise
The Arch Fishshop
of Canterbury
The Codfather

FLORISTS
Dark Side of the Bloom
Floral 'n' Hardy
Florist Gump
Thanks a Bunch

FIREPLACES
Alexander the Grate
Grate Expectations

FISHMONGERS
The Prawnbrokers

FURNITURE
Sofa So Good
Suite Deal

GARDENING
Back to the Fuschia
Easy Lay Landscaping
The Lawn Ranger
Rough around the Hedges
Lawn-N-Order
The Dirty Hoe

HAIRDRESSERS
British Hairways
Curl up and Dye
Deb'n'Hair
From Hair to Eternity

Hair Force One
Herr Kutz
Hair Razors
Hair-O-Dyenamix
Hairs Johnny
Sherlock Combs

KEBABS
Abra Kebabra
Prima Donner
Jason Doner Van

LAUNDRY SERVICES
All Washed Up
Wish You Wash Here
Iron Maiden

MAN WITH VAN
He-Van Movers of the Universe
Jean Claude Van Man

OPTICIANS
Eye Carumba
Spex in the City
Optom-Eyes

PET GROOMING
Short Bark and Sides
Doggy Style
The Laundromutt
Hairy Poppins

PLUMBING
Napoleon Boiler Parts
Pipe Down
Flush Gordon
All Cisterns Go

RECORD STORES
Vinyl Frontier

RESTAURANTS
Mustard's Last Stand
Pete's A Place
Men At Wok
Ho-Lee-Chow
Franks A Lot
Burger Off
Lord of the Fries

WINDOWS
Pane in the Glass

SANDWICH SHOPS
Bread Pitt
Hansel and Pretzel
Goodfillas
Top Bun
Baguette Me Not
Baguetteaboutit
In Bread

SHOE SHOPS
Sole Man
R. Soles

SEPTIC TANKS
Suck Cess
Dr Pumper

SPORTING GOODS
The Merchant of
Tennis

TAILORING
Sew It Seams
Sew What?

TREE SURGEONS
Tree Wise Men
Morgan Treeman
Out on a Limb

VW AUTO REPAIR
Old Volk's Home

WASTE SERVICES
Dumponus
What a Load of Rubbish
Junk and Disorderly
Lord of the Bins

TRIBUTE BANDS

Tribute acts have their own variety of punning names. 1990s popsters Take That has Fake That, Take This and Retake That; and Oasish, Noasis and Definitely Might Be honour Britpop legends Oasis. Other well-known tribute bands include:

AMY HOUSEWINE
(Amy Winehouse)

BEACHED BOYS
(Beach Boys)

BY JOVI
(Bon Jovi)

DAVID BLOWIE
(David Bowie)

EARTH, WIND FOR HIRE
(Earth, Wind & Fire)

HAYSEED DIXI
(AC/DC)

IRN-MAIDEN
(Iron Maiden)

NO
(Yes)

PHONEY M
(Boney M)

PIG FLOYD
(Pink Floyd)

THE CLONE ROSES
(The Stone Roses)

THE FILLERS
(The Killers)

THE FAUX FIGHTERS
(The Foo Fighters)

THE ROLLING CLONES
(The Rolling Stones)

C.

CHANGED MEANINGS

¶ Language purists like to remind anyone who will listen that ***decimation*** actually means the slaughter of one in ten people, and was the military punishment wielded by the Roman army against deserters and mutineers. The same people are also happy to clarify that, strictly speaking, a ***myriad*** is 10,000, and not the indeterminably large number most people think. Both claims are correct; that is what the words *originally* meant. But language is always evolving, and these meanings fell out of use long ago.

¶ This evolution can be a source of frustration, even confusion, when the meaning of words is lost, altered or inverted. But there's no stopping this tide of change, and never has been. Even a comparison of words pre- and post-internet, such as ***ping***, ***swipe***, ***text***, ***follow***, ***cloud***, ***troll***, ***sandbox*** and countless more, shows how they can acquire new senses far removed from their original meanings.

¶ Those who object to these newfangled meanings should reflect on how many commonplace words have been similarly altered *without* their knowledge. To give them an idea, the following dictionary of changed meanings should help. It is, dare one say, ***terrific***.

A SMALL DICTIONARY OF CHANGED MEANINGS

AWFUL (ADJ.) (C. 1175)
Filled with awe.

BLOCKBUSTER (N.) (1942)
A large bomb capable of destroying
a block of buildings.

BRAVE (V.) (1619)
To threaten.

BUXOM (ADJ.) (C. 1175)
Compliant, obedient,
easy to influence.

BULLY (N.) (1548)
A term of endearment between
close friends, similar to dear
or darling. Later used between
men to indicate a good chap.

CARTOON (N.) (1684)
A design sketch for a large work of art
(such as a fresco, tapestry or stained
glass) done on heavy paper.

CHEAT (V.) (C. 1440)
To confiscate. From escheat, the
legal forfeiture of property.

CLOUT (N.) (OLD ENGLISH)
A patch of metal, cloth or leather
used to mend something.

CLUE (N.) (1393)
A ball of yarn.

FIG.1 *A clue of yarn*

DEADLINE (N.) (1863)
From the American Civil
War; the boundary line in a
military prison beyond which
a prisoner might be shot.

EGREGIOUS (ADJ.) (C. 1550)
Remarkable, distinguished,
of great renown.

DIGITAL (N.) (1450)
A whole number less than ten.

DISAPPOINT (V.) (1434)
To remove someone from their appointed
office, to dismiss them from authority.

EXPLODE (V.) (1552)
To reject or replace something, like
a custom or tradition. A later, second
meaning was to condemn, banish or drive
away. By 1614, audiences might explode a
performer from the stage with jeering.

FIZZLE (N.) (1533)
A noiseless fart.

FLIRT (V.) (1532)
To make a sudden movement; to flick, dart
or bound. Typically associated with birds.

GARBAGE (N.) (1422)
Animal offal or entrails used for food.

FIG. 2 *A plate of garbage*

GIRL (N.) (C. 1300)
A child or young person, regardless of sex.

HUSSY (N.) (1470)
A Scottish word for a housekeeper
or mistress of the house. Also, the
female head of the family.

LUXURY (N.) (1340)
Lust, lechery, lasciviousness.

MAGAZINE (N.) (1451)
A storehouse or depot for merchandise.

MEAT (N.) (OLD ENGLISH)
Food of any variety, whether
consumed by humans or animals.

NAUGHTY (ADJ.) (C. 1400)
Having nothing – naught. Poor.

NICE (ADJ.) (C. 1300)
A foolish or simple person.

OVATION (N.) (1533)
A historical word for the processional entrance
given to a military commander in ancient
Rome who had fallen short of a triumph and
therefore received a more modest reception.

PRESTIGE (N.) (1656)
A magic trick, an illusion. From fourteenth-
century French word for a conjuror's illusion.

FIG. 3 *Prestige with a deck of cards*

PRETTY (ADJ.) (OLD ENGLISH)
Skillful, crafty or cunning. Also,
archaic Scottish word for brave.

RADICAL (ADJ.) (1398)
Relating to the roots of a plant.

QUIZ (N.) (1780)
An eccentric person; someone
who looks ridiculous.

SECRETARY (N.) (1387)
A confidant, or one trusted with secrets.

SILLY (ADJ.) (1450)
A Scottish word meaning worthy or pious.

STILETTO (N.) (1611)
A short dagger with a slender, thin
blade designed to penetrate armour.
From Italian for 'little steel'.

SLY (ADJ.) (1175)
Clever, wise or skillful with one's hands.

TABLOID (N.) (1884)
A small compressed substance, like
a medical pill or block of tea.

TERRIFIC (ADJ.) (1667)
Inspiring terror, frightful, awful.

¶ Charles Dickens started his *Book of Memoranda* in January 1855. It's only a small notebook, but it would be hard to imagine a more extraordinary literary artefact. His jottings include observations, character notes, scene descriptions, book ideas ('How as to a story in two periods – with a lapse of time between, like a French Drama?' was the seed from which *Tale of Two Cities* sprouted), and long lists of names. Among these are names he would later breathe life into: **Pumblechook**, **Meagles**, **Podsnap**, **Magwitch** and more. But more tantalising are the names that never escaped the *Memoranda*: **Topwash**, **Jiggins**, **Zephaniah Fury** and **William Why**. What stories they could have told.

¶ Over twenty-one novels, more than fifty short stories, seven plays and numerous collaborations, Dickens created over 1,500 characters – enough for a small village. The *Memoranda* gives a glimpse into how these characters came to be. Some names, for instance, he borrowed from the *Privy Council Education Lists*; others evolved, like Stiltington, who became Stiltwalk, then Stiltingstalk, and finally, **Lord Lancaster Stiltingstalking**. John Forster, Dickens' closest friend, and later his biographer, described how, before **Martin Chuzzlewit**, Dickens considered Martin Sweezleden, Sweezleback, Sweezlewag, Chuzzletoe Chuzzleboy, Chublewig and Chuzzlewig.

¶ Punning or descriptive names were a favourite for Dickens because they introduced characters so efficiently. There are the lawyers, **Brass** and **Tangle**, schools ruled by **Mrs Wackles** and **Dr Strong**, and families of varying fortunes, from the destitute **Mr Landless** to the wealthy **Mr Richland**. Names often described a character's personality too, from the talkative **Mr Gusher** to the sanctimonious **Mr Pecksniff**, and those dreadful **Veneerings**, with their new money. One can picture Dickens chuckling to himself while creating these names. **Count Smorltork** and **Lord Mutanhead**? Wonderful.

¶ Dickens had other tricks, such as *portmanteaus* (**Miss Creeble**, combining creep and feeble) and *onomatopoeias* (**Mr Tinkling** and **Mr Toots**) – but he also drew from real life. **Edwin Drood**, for instance, was inspired by the publican landlord Edwin Trood, while **Bob Fagin** had in real life looked after Dickens when he was a young boy working in a blacking factory.

¶ Some people may find Dickens' names a bit too pantomime. He did 'normal' too – like Edward Chester or Bob Sawyer – and they're always decent coves. But most people want more **Crispsparkle** in their lives.

FIG.1 *Sergeant Buzfuz*, The Pickwick Papers

SEE ALSO: *Medical Conditions that Make Nice Names*

DICKENS CHARACTERS IN THE DICTIONARY

GAMP (N.): an unqualified, sometimes drunken, nurse or carer. Also, a GAMP UMBRELLA (N.), a large, loosely-tied umbrella. (*Sarah Gamp, Martin Chuzzlewit*)

GRADGRIND (N.): someone hard and unsympathetic – like Gradgrind himself, 'a man of facts and calculations'. (*Thomas Gradgrind, Hard Times*)

HAVISHAM SYNDROME (N.): a disorder where a traumatic event causes one to be socially withdrawn and to neglect personal care. (*Miss Havisham, Great Expectations*)

MICAWBER (N.): an irresponsible optimist; one who lives in naive expectation of improved fortunes. (*Wilkins Micawber, David Copperfield*)

PODSNAP (N.): someone complacent and unwilling to face unpalatable facts. Also, PODSNAPPERY (ADJ.). (*John Podsnap, Our Mutual Friend*)

PECKSNIFF (N.): a sanctimonious hypocrite. (*Seth Pecksniff, Martin Chuzzlewit*)

SCROOGE (N.): a tightfisted miser. (*Ebeneezer Scrooge, A Christmas Carol*)

TURVYDROP (N.): one who presents as a model of deportment. (*Mr Turvydrop, Bleak House*)

MINOR CHARACTERS WITH GLORIOUS NAMES

Anne Chickenstalker
Belinda Pocket
Dick Datchery
Dick Swiveller
Dolge Orlick
Dr Slammer
Fascination Fledgby
Inspector Bucket
Jefferson Brick
Jerry Cruncher
John Peerybingle
Josiah Bounderby

Kit Nubbles
Lady Honoria Dedlock
Luke Honeythunder
M'Choakumchild
Mr Bumple
Mr Feeder
Mr Fezziwig
Mr Pumblechook
Mr Sleary
Mr Smallweed
Mr Snagsby
Mr Sowerberry

Mr Stryver
Mr Wopsel
Mrs Crummles
Miss Twinkleton
Mrs Todgers
Nicodemus Boffin
Paul Sweedlepipe
Pleasant Riderhood
Samuel Slumkey
Tilly Slowboy
Wackford Squeers Jr

NAMES DICKENS DECIDED NOT TO USE

Susan Goldring
Matilda Rainbird
Catherine Two
Ambrosia Events
Walter Ashes
Robert Ladle

Henry Ghost
Thomas Fatherly
Joey Stick
Sophia Doomesday
Rosetta Dust
Birdie Nash

Sarah Goldsacks
Alice Thorneywork
Silas Blodget
Robert Gospel
George Muzzle

NICKNAMES DICKENS GAVE HIS CHILDREN

Lucifer Box (Katy)
Mild Glo'ster (Mary)

Master Floby (Charley)
Young Skull (Walter)

Chickenstalker (Francis)
Plornish (Edward)

¶ The **Cherokee Syllabary**, the writing system of the Cherokee Nation, was the work of one man: a Cherokee named Sequoyah (d. 1843). His achievement is particularly remarkable because he is thought to have been illiterate, making it a rare instance of a writing system created by someone who couldn't read or write. (**Pahawh Hmong**, invented by Shong Lue Yang in 1959, is another.)

¶ Sequoyah was a silversmith, blacksmith and warrior. In an 1828 interview, he described how a letter taken from a prisoner left a hunting party mystified by how white men could 'put talk on a piece of paper, send it any distance, and have it understood by others'. But to Sequoyah, who grasped the power of written language, there was no magic in these 'talking leaves'. He recognised the general principles of written language and knew one could be created for Cherokee.

¶ Around 1810 Sequoyah began working on his system. The task would consume his life for over a decade and leave many wondering whether he'd lost his mind. Friends pleaded with him to abandon his project, but Sequoyah refused. 'They did not cause me to begin and they shall not cause me to give up', he reportedly said.

¶ His early attempts were **logographic**, first representing words, then whole sentences, with symbols. When he realised this would be unmanageable, he began observing the sounds of the Cherokee language, identifying 86 unique syllables. He then created symbols for each, some derived from the Latin alphabet (though unrelated to their English sounds), with many more he designed himself.

¶ Having tested the syllabary with his daughter and neighbours, who found it easy to learn and use, Sequoyah began introducing others to his system.

¶ In 1821 Sequoyah brought his syllabary to a tribal council meeting, demonstrating how it worked with his daughter. Although many remained suspicious, fearing it was witchcraft or doubting its usefulness, Sequoyah persisted with such demonstrations. When he received a letter written in his system from friends in the Arkansas Territory, tribal elders finally appreciated that Sequoyah had given the Cherokee their own 'talking leaves'.

¶ As the syllabary was accepted, it spread. It was formally adopted by the Cherokee Nation in 1825, and in 1828, *The Cherokee Phoenix*, America's first bilingual newspaper, was printed. By the 1830s around 90 per cent of the Cherokee could use the syllabary. Even amid the tragedy of the forced migration of the Cherokee by the US government on the Trail of Tears in 1830, Sequoyah's syllabary had become a priceless cultural possession.

¶ While the number of Cherokee speakers plummeted in the twentieth century, efforts to revive the language have relied on Sequoyah's work. Cherokee immersion schools, keyboard pads, fonts, language apps and the revival of *The Cherokee Phoenix* are helping to rescue the language from extinction. But none of this would be possible without the astonishing efforts of this remarkable man: Ꮝꭱꮹ (*se quo yah*).

SEE ALSO: *Dictionaries of Interest*

The Cherokee Syllabary

	a	e	i	o	u	v [ə]
	D a	R e	T i	Ꮺ o	O u	i v [ə]
	Ꮝ ga Ꮙ ka	Ꭼ ge	Ꭹ gi	A go	J gu	E gv
	Ꮀ ha	Ꭾ he	Ꮂ hi	Ꮉ ho	Ꮗ hu	Ꮌ hv
	W la	Ꮄ le	Ꮅ li	Ꮆ lo	M lu	Ꮈ lv
	Ꮉ ma	Ꮊ me	H mi	Ꮏ mo	Ꮊ mu	
	Ꮎ na Ꮏ hna Ꮐ nah	Ꮑ ne	Ꮒ ni	Z no	Ꮔ nu	Ꮕ nv
	Ꮖ qua	Ꮗ que	Ꮘ qui	Ꮙ quo	Ꮚ quu	Ꮛ quv
	Ꮜ sa Ꮞ s	Ꮞ se	Ꮟ si	Ꮠ so	Ꮡ su	Ꮢ sv
	Ꮣ da Ꮤ ta	Ꮥ de Ꮦ te	Ꮧ di Ꮨ ti	Ꮩ do	Ꮪ du	Ꮫ dv
	Ꮬ dla Ꮭ tla	Ꮭ tle	Ꮯ tli	Ꮰ tlo	Ꮱ tlu	Ꮲ tlv
	Ꮳ tsa	Ꮴ tse	Ꮵ tsi	Ꮶ tso	Ꮷ tsu	Ꮸ tsv
	Ꮹ wa	Ꮺ we	Ꮻ wi	Ꮼ wo	Ꮽ wu	Ꮾ wv
	Ꮿ ya	Ᏸ ye	Ᏹ yi	Ᏺ yo	Ᏻ yu	Ᏼ yv

YESTERDAY	TODAY	TOMORROW
Ꮢ Ꭿ	A Ꭿ T Ꮝ	Ꮡ Ꮎ Ꮄ T
sv hi	go hi i ga	su na le i

-CIDE

¶ Homicide, the killing of another person, was first mentioned in the thirteenth century. **Murder** came from Old English, as did **slay** and, possibly, **kill**. Bloody words like **aquell**, **fordo** and **spill** have all been lost, but are curiously evocative.

¶ Homicide, on the other hand, is a borrowing from classical Latin via French. The **-cide** root is Latin for killing. Although the Romans were well acquainted with **matricidium** and **patricida**, most of the other **-cide** constructions date from the seventeenth century

AMICICIDE
Killing of one's friend.

AUTOCIDE
Suicide by crashing one's car.

AVUNCULICIDE
Killing of one's uncle.

BOVICIDE
Killing of oxen, also: butcher.

DEICIDE
Killing of a god.

DEMOCIDE (OR POPULICIDE)
Killing of a population by its government.

DOMICIDE
Systematic destruction of homes.

ELITICIDE
Killing of a nation's elite.

FEMICIDE
Killing of a woman because of her gender.

FILICIDE
A parent's killing of a child.

FRATRICIDE
A sibling's killing of a brother.

GENOCIDE
Systematic killing of a national, racial, religious or ethnic group.

GERONTICIDE (OR SENICIDE)
Killing of the elderly.

INFANTICIDE
Killing of a child under one.

MAGISTRICIDE
Killing of a teacher or master.

MAGNICIDE
Killing of a major political figure.

MARITICIDE
Killing of one's husband.

MATRICIDE
Killing of one's mother.

MEDICIDE
Suicide assisted by a doctor.

NEPOTICIDE
Killing of one's nephew.

OMNICIDE
Destruction of all human life.

PAPICIDE
Killing of a pope.

PARRICIDE
Killing of one's mother or father.

PATRICIDE
Killing of one's father.

PEDICIDE
Killing of children.

PROLICIDE
Killing of one's own children.

REGICIDE
Killing of a monarch.

SORORICIDE
Killing of one's sister.

TYRANNICIDE
Killing of a tyrant.

UXORICIDE
Killing of one's wife.

VATICIDE
Killing of a prophet.

XENOCIDE
Killing of an alien species.

SEE ALSO: *Euphemisms for Death*

COLLECTIVE NOUNS

❡ English contains hundreds of *collective nouns*, for animals, humans and things. Some, like a *swarm of bees* or *herd of cows*, are commonplace, while others are more novel. Most people have heard of a *parliament of owls* and a *murder of crows*, but might be less familiar with a *sloth of bears*, an *unkindness of ravens* or a *shrewdness of apes*.

❡ Many of these collective nouns appeared in a remarkable fifteenth-century work called *The Boke of Seynt Albans* (*The Book of Saint Albans*) by Juliana Berners, an enigmatic author who certainly existed – or possibly didn't.

❡ The book has sections on Hawking, Hunting and Heraldry, but at the back is a list of 164 collective nouns, starting with a *herd of harts* and ending with a *dishonour of Scotts*.

❡ Even more curious are the author's collective nouns for people: a *fighting of beggars*, a *rascal of boys*, a *cowardness of curs* and a *laughter of hostelers*. Berners clearly enjoyed her list, which you can read for yourself in Appendix 1.

❡ In truth, many collective terms can feel rather contrived and often go unused, but there are many we use instinctively. People just know that cash comes in *wads*, savages in *hordes* and emotions in a *gush*. Since there's no record of a collective noun for collective nouns, the following is humbly suggested...

SEE ALSO: *Animal Adjectives*

A NUMERATION OF COLLECTIVE NOUNS*

An army of lawyers

A barrage of questions

A barrel of laughs

A bevvy of beauties

A box of tricks

A bunch of idiots

A bundle of nerves

A can of worms

A cornucopia of delights

An embarassment of riches

A flood of emotions

A horde of zombies

A host of reasons

A litany of crimes

A litany of complaints

A load of bollocks

A load of old cobblers

A load of rubbish

A month of Sundays

A mountain of bills

A myriad of reasons

A nest of rumours

FIG.1 *A hill of beans*

An ocean of knowledge

A pack of lies

A phalanx of lawyers

A pit of vipers

A pack of journalists

A plethora of reasons

A riot of colours

A sea of faces

A shower of bastards

A slew of problems

A spate of attacks

A tissue of lies

A torrent of abuse

A wealth of experience

---

*Strictly speaking, collective nouns are used for **countable** nouns. This list also includes some uncountable nouns because they can still mount up, even if they can't be numbered.*

❡ *Visual sound effects* became a regular feature of comics just before the 'talkies' arrived in movie theatres in 1927. Credit for this innovation is widely given to American cartoonist Roy Crane. Although Crane wasn't the first to write sounds in comics, he made them a prominent feature of his work, starting with his *Wash Tubbs* strip in 1924. As well as a host of regulars like *BAM!*, *PLUNK!* and *WHACK!*, Crane would drop in the occasional *BAM-BOOIE!* and *SOCKO!* to liven things up.

❡ People who don't read comics or graphic novels may think these onomatopoeic effects are childish, particularly if all they remember are the cartoony *KA-POW*s from the *Batman* TV show. But comic aficionados appreciate the ingenuity involved with crafting these sounds, and know how important they've become to the comic artform.

❡ Consider, for instance, the sound of gunfire. The difference between the *BLAM!* of a shotgun, the *CRACK!* of a rifle and the *RA-TA-TAT!* of a machine gun is clear. But what is the sound of an atomic machine gun? Or a bullet ricocheting off steel, or stone, or just going through the air? How does a Nazi's Schmeisser sound different from an M-16 machine gun, or an M230 chain gun? And how does a bullet shot into the back sound different from one in the head?* Because these things matter.

❡ Linguists question whether these words – sometimes known as *onomatopemes* – are mimicking the sound of a thing, or simply the idea of it. Does someone impaled by a sword really go *nnghh*? Is the sound of cracking ice really *kkkk*? And how should 'nnghh' and 'kkkk' be pronounced? The answers to these questions are 'no', 'no' and 'not known', but it isn't a problem for

readers, who appreciate the instant get-ability of these sounds.

❡ Some comic book sounds are so iconic that they're strictly associated with one character alone, like Spiderman's *thwip*. In Spiderman's early days, his web-slinging was silent. Then it started to make a noise. Then, it went 'thwip'. The word was created by Spiderman's co-creator, Steve Ditko, and is particularly pleasing to say. It's also synonymous with Spiderman, so it would take a brave cartoonist to put a thwip into a non-Spiderman story.

❡ Similarly iconic are *snikt* and *snakt*, the unmistakable sound of Wolverine's adamantine claws extending and retracting. And also, *bamf* – the sound of teleportation that signals Nightcrawler has arrived. Or left. Or gone to the other side of the room.

❡ Marvel's Scourge of the Underworld isn't in the same league as Spiderman or Wolverine, but in his quest to rid the world of villains, he uses a gun that goes *pum* when fired, and *spak* when a bullet hit its mark.

FIG.1 Wash Tubbs and Captain Easy, *Roy Crane (1926)*

SEE ALSO: *Euphonic words / Maluma and Takete*

See page 214 to find out how these sounds are written.

So, **pum-spak** became Scourge's signature sound (followed by his cry of 'Justice is served!' as a body hit the floor).

¶ Some sound effects are memorable in other ways. Marvel's *Incredible Hercules* series had its own distinctive sound library, with fight scenes featuring such bone-crunching gems as **MACEINDAFACE! THRAKADOOM! CRACKAJAMMA!** and the unstoppable **SUKKAAPUNCH!** Sounds could also be highly specific, like the pain of being kicked in the testicles – **NUH-HKKRACK!** – or the unmistakable sound of Hercules' nipples being twisted: **NURP!**

¶ What makes a comic sound effect work isn't always clear. **SPLOIT!**, the sound of food being flung with a spoon, makes a kind of sense. But it could just as easily be the sound of a knife plunging into flesh, a soufflé collapsing or a firework that fails to go off. As linguists like to remind us, the associations we have with different sound words are mainly arbitrary. After all, **RA-TA-TA-TA-TAT** in no way sounds like a machine gun, it's just the representation everyone understands.

¶ To experience sound effects without any associations, browse a comic in a language you don't know. Asterix in its original French is full of sound effects that bewilder English speakers, like the sound of a fight – **SCHTIAF!** – or the cry of pain – **OUAPP!** Japanese manga – which is full of onomatopoeic effects like **kusha-kusha** (paper crumpling), **gobo-gobo** (gurgling) and **peko-peko** (stomach grumbling) – adds an additional poetic dimension with words like **kyun-kyun** (heart-wrenching) and **guzu-guzu** (procrastinating). Even if you don't know your **doki-doki** from your **gishi-gishi**, the sound of the words is enough to bring the pictures to life.

EXPLOSIVE SOUNDS

BARRRROOOOMM!	atomic weapon
BHWOOOOM!	grenade thrown into hideout
BLA-AAAAAMMM!	car collision
BLAM-WHEEE!	mortar round
BOOMER-ROOM!	explosive bowels
BUH-BOOM!	50 cal. nitro express shell
CHAT-CHOOOOM!	ammunition store
FOOSH!	flame-shooting
FTOOM!	sidewinder missile
HAUUGGGHHHHHHH!	volcanic eruption
KABOOOMM!	grenade inside tank
KATRANG!	high-impact collision
KATOOOSH!	energy beam
PH-SHOOSH!	flame thrower
VA-THROOOM!	missile
VOOSH!	missile launch
WAAAHOOM!	artillery shell
WHAM!	fuel tank
WHOOM!	dynamite
WROOOOOOOOM!	atomic reactor

SOUND EFFECT QUIZ

Match the sound effects with their descriptions.

WHRRRRR-TCHAK	breaking glass
TCHIKIT	a lock being picked
TPTPTP	belching
PLURP	coughing up hairball
GAGGAK-THOOF	putting in contact lens
GAK	a bird pooing
VIP	spitting out beetle
SKLANG	spinning revolver cylinder
SCHLUCK	feet running quickly
BRAP	a bullet passing by
SLRRRK	a card deck being riffled
FERRIP	drinking soup

(Answers on page 215)

¶ In the criminal cant of the sixteenth century, the **cony-catcher** was a con man – a cony being a tame rabbit, fattened for the dinner table. Early collections of slang promised to inform readers about the scammers looking for a quick grote. And there were many, with names that reflected their criminal penchant. There was the **verser**, the cheat's accomplice, the **gull-groper**, who offered dodgy loans, and the **low-gagger**, who pretended to be sick. The **pot-hunters** feigned drunkenness, the **rum-gaggers** told tales of nautical woe, and the **Jack in a box** duped tradesmen. Anyone who didn't want to be the kind of **cod's head** to fall for such tricks would learn the schemes of these smooth-talking **tongue pads**. Here are just some of the canters they had to look out for.

BLACKLEG	*a racecourse swindler*
CADATOR	*a 'gentleman' swindler*
CAPPER	*a swindler's accomplice*
CROSSBITER	*a cardsharp*
FATER	*a duplicitous fortune-teller*
FALCONER	*a swindler posing as a poor scholar*
FOISTER	*a dice cheat*
GAGGER	*a swindler who uses sob stories*
GOUGER	*a swindler*
HIGH-FLYER	*a swindling beggar*
HUMMER	*an imposter*
NICKER	*a cheat*
SWINDLING GLOAK	*a confidence trickster*
OLD COLE	*an experienced dice cheat*
RING CHOPPER	*a seller of counterfeit gold*
SKIRT-FOIST	*a female cheat*

D.

DEWEY DECIMAL CLASSIFICATION SYSTEM

¶ The **Dewey Decimal Classification** is the most widely used library classification system in the world. It was invented by American librarian 'Melvil' Dewey (d. 1931), who published and copyrighted his system in 1876. The first index was detailed in a forty-four-page pamphlet; in 2023, the index was over 4,300 pages, with new classifications added annually.

¶ Before Dewey, there was no common system for organising books in libraries. Librarians might place works based on date of acquisition, volume height, alphabetical order, theme or personal whim. As such, libraries were hard to browse, although few allowed readers to browse in the first place.

¶ Dewey's system provided an elegant and logical approach for placing any book in any library. First, a work would be assigned one of ten **main classes**, encompassing the world of knowledge. Today, these are:

- **000** *Computer science, information & general works*
- **100** *Philosophy & psychology*
- **200** *Religion*
- **300** *Social sciences*
- **400** *Language*
- **500** *Science*
- **600** *Technology*
- **700** *Arts & recreation*
- **800** *Literature*
- **900** *History & geography*

¶ These are then divided into ten *divisions*, each dividing again into ten further *sections*. Through the divisions and sections, the index spreads out like the branches of a tree. To take an example, *Quantum Physics for Dummies* has the Dewey Classification 539 because it is:

> (main class) **500** *Science*
> (division) **530** *Physics*
> (section) **539** *Modern physics*

¶ When more detail is required, a decimal point is added after the 3-digit number, then further numbers are used. *Chess for Dummies*, for instance, is located thus:

> **700** *Arts & recreation*
> **790** *Sports, games and entertainment*
> **794** *Indoor games of skill*
> **794.1** *Chess*
> **794.12** *Theory and instruction*

¶ In theory there's no limit to the length of a Dewey number. One of the longest is a twenty-seven-digit classification registered by Library and Archives Canada for tractor numbers in Winnipeg. Although probably registered as a joke, it shows how pinpoint accurate the Dewey system can be.

¶ What makes the Dewey Decimal Classification so astonishing is the underlying ambition to find the right place for any printed work. In so doing, Melvil Dewey sparked a revolution in how libraries were organised that is still felt today. Within fifty years of its release, it had been adopted by 95 per cent of US public libraries; and in 1905, Dewey principles were incorporated into the international Universal Decimal Classification (UDC) found in libraries around the world. It was, in other words, a genuinely world-changing idea.

¶ Unfortunately, however, Dewey's personal life was less glorious. As well as having, as one biographer put it, 'a persistent inability to control himself around women', Dewey was openly racist and anti-semitic. Indeed, he was forced to resign as New York State Librarian because of this.

¶ Both as a consequence of his prejudice and the context of his time, the early editions of the Dewey Classification System contained some bigoted choices. The most systemic problem was described by librarian Dorothy Porter, who, during the 1930s and 1940s, described how any work by a Black author would routinely be indexed under **326 Slavery**. By 1942, Black writers had at least made their way to **800 Literature**, but only so far as **809.8 History of literatures of special racial groups: Jews, negroes, etc**.

¶ Another prominent bias still present today was baked into the ten divisions of **200 Religion**. Within this section, Christianity is expansively represented across six divisions while every other faith is slotted in just one: **290 Other religions**. Although it doesn't affect whether a book will be found in a library, the system's skew towards Christianity feels dated, but is now too embedded to rectify.

¶ Today, the DDC is principally accessed through WebDewey, where it remains the most-used library cataloguing system in the world. Partly based at the US Library of Congress, it continues to be the foundation of US public libraries. Dewey himself might have been a flawed man, but his creation remains a towering achievement that continues to make the world's knowledge more accessible.

DICTIONARIES OF INTEREST

A TABLE ALPHABETICALL

(Robert Cawdrey, 1604)

Widely acknowledged to be English's first monolingual dictionary.

A NEW DICTIONARY OF THE TERMS ANCIENT AND MODERN OF THE CANTING CREW

(B. E. Gent, c. 1698)

At the time, Gent's dictionary was the largest collection of criminal cant (slang) yet published.

THE GENTLEMAN'S DICTIONARY

(Georges Guillet de Saint-Georges, 1705)

A three-part dictionary concerned with horse riding, warfare and navigation.

THE COOK'S AND CONFECTIONER'S DICTIONARY

(John Nott, 1723)

A cookbook alphabetised in dictionary form, from ale to zest.

DICTIONARIUM DOMESTICUM

(Nathan Bailey, 1736)

A household dictionary to help the mistress of the house ensure provisions are 'frugally and housewifely ordered.'

DICTIONARY OF LOVE, OR THE LANGUAGE OF GALLANTRY EXPLAINED

(Anonymous, 1754)

A surprisingly cynical dictionary of romantic language. For example: 'Most of the present Love is what our blunt ancestors called … Sordid Interest.'

THE FARRIER'S AND HORSEMAN'S COMPLETE DICTIONARY

(Thomas Wallis, 1759)

An influential guide to eighteenth-century farriery.

THE POLITICIAN'S DICTIONARY

(Pub. Geo Allen, 1775)

A revealing snapshot of how Britain saw the world and its commanding role within it. Published the same year as the start of the American War of Independence.

A CLASSICAL DICTIONARY OF THE VULGAR TONGUE

(Francis Grose, 1785)

The seminal dictionary of British slang, authored by a contemporary of Samuel Johnson.

THE BRITISH SPORTSMAN, OR, NOBLEMAN, GENTLEMAN AND FARMERS' DICTIONARY, RECREATION AND AMUSEMENT

(William Augustus Osbaldiston, 1792)

One of the first sporting dictionaries, 'with particular Instructions for Riding, Racing, Hunting, Coursing, Hawking, Shooting, Setting, & Fishing'.

BLACKGUARDIANA: OR, A DICTIONARY OF ROGUES, BAWDS, PIMPS, WHORES, PICKPOCKETS, SHOPLIFTERS

(James Caulfield, 1793)

A dictionary of cant language and 'burlesque' terms, much repurposed from Grose's 1785 dictionary.

A DICTIONARY OF TERMS, ACADEMICAL AND COLLOQUIAL, OR CANT, WHICH ARE USED AT THE UNIVERSITY OF CAMBRIDGE

(Pub. W. J. Richardson, 1803)

Properly titled *Gradus ad Cantabrigiam*, this is an illuminating dictionary of Cambridge lingo.

A BIOGRAPHICAL DICTIONARY OF THE CELEBRATED WOMEN OF EVERY AGE AND COUNTRY

(Mary Matilda, 1804)

An important biographical dictionary by an early champion of women's rights.

———

THE DICTIONARY OF DISTINCTIONS

(John Murdoch, 1811)

An intriguing dictionary with three alphabetised lists: one for homophones; one for pronunciation; and one for the effect of adding an E to the end of words.

———

DICTIONNAIRE INFERNAL

(Jacques Collin de Plancy, 1818)

A dictionary of demonology.

———

A VOCABULARY OF THE FLASH LANGUAGE

(James Hardy Vaux, 1819)

A dictionary of criminal slang written while Vaux was confined at Newcastle Penal Settlement in New South Wales, Australia, and to whose warden the book is dedicated. This was the first dictionary to be written in Australia.

———

THE DICTIONARY OF DAINTY BREAKFASTS

(Phillis Browne, 1898)

An alphabetised list of breakfast recipes, although **brains fried in batter** and **game pie made in a dish and covered with pastry** seem neither 'dainty' nor breakfasty.

———

A DICTIONARY OF MIRACLES, IMITATIVE, REALISTIC, AND DOGMATIC

(E. Cobham Brewer, 1901)

As well as a comprehensive collection of miracles, Brewer's dictionary included detailed information about child martyrs and a well-illustrated section on instruments of torture.

———

THE DEVIL'S DICTIONARY

(Ambrose Bierce, 1911)

First published as *The Cynic's Word Book* in 1906, Bierce's *Devil's Dictionary* was the first humorous dictionary, with satirical definitions and wry observations. For instance: 'DICTIONARY (N.) A malevolent literary device for cramping the growth of a language and making it hard and inelastic'.

———

BBC PRONOUNCING DICTIONARY OF BRITISH NAMES

(G. E. Pointon, 1971)

Published by the BBC's Pronunciation Unit, the *Pronouncing Dictionary* was initially made for BBC staff before being with a wider readership. The book doesn't promote BBC English; instead, it advises how proper nouns should be pronounced (for example **Llanbedrycennin** in Wales).

———

BERNSTEIN'S REVERSE DICTIONARY

(Bernstein et al, 1976)

An unusual dictionary in which it is the definitions, not the headwords, that are arranged alphabetically. It might seem strange, but it works.

———

THE DICTIONARY OF PLAYGROUND SLANG

(Chris Lewis, 2003)

A collection of British playground slang that's every bit as puerile and offensive as would be expected.

———

DICTIONARY OF IMPROBABLE WORDS: ALL-CONSONANT & ALL-VOWEL WORDS

(Craig Conley, 2018)

A humorous dictionary primarily containing onomatopoeic words, from **ai-eee ai-eee** to **zzzzzzzz/jjjj**: (N.) 'an enlivening sound explored in Continuum therapy.'

———

AGLET

The metal or plastic tip at the end of a shoelace.

AWL

The slender, sharp-pointed blade on a Swiss Army knife that nobody knows what it's for. Traditionally used for making holes in leather.

BARM

The foamy head on beer.

BASKET

The disc-shaped attachment at the base of a ski pole that stops it pushing too far into snow.

CHAD

The small discs of paper ejected by a hole punch.

CHANKINGS

The bits of food one spits out, like pips, pith and fruit stones.

CHEEK

The side of a hammer. (The side opposite the head is the peen.)

CORNICIONE

The raised crust on a pizza.

CUPULE

The cup (or involucre) around an acorn.

FIG.1 *An acorn, showing the nut inside the cupule*

DOTTLE

The residue of ash or half-burnt tobacco left in a smoking pipe.

DOUBLET

A domino with the same number of pips at either end.

ESCUTCHEON

A key-hole plate found on doors.

FERRULE

The protective cap at the tip of a stick or umbrella. Also, the metal sleeve at the top of a pencil that holds the rubber.

FIPPLE

The plug at the mouth of a recorder, whistle or flute through which one blows.

FROG

The button and loop fastening found on duffle coats.

FURCULA

The 'wishbone' on a bird, found below the neck.

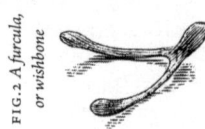

FIG.2 *A furcula, or wishbone*

GELASIN

Another word for the cheek dimples formed by smiling.

GINGLYMUS

A hinge joint between two bones.

GNOMON

The bit that sticks up on a sundial that casts its shadow.

GRAWLIX

The string of typographic symbols used in cartoons to indicate strong language (*@%#!).

HOMING BARS

The small bumps on the F and J keys on a keyboard to guide finger placement.

JINGLES

The small jangling discs found in the frame of a tambourine.

SEE ALSO: *Pedantry / Spelling Bee Winners*

KEEPER

The loop on a belt that holds the end in position after the buckle.

KNURLING

The indentations on a thimble.

LAGNIAPPE

A small gift or bonus given to a customer having purchased a product, such as a lollipop or bookmark.

OBELUS

The division symbol (÷).

OCTOTHORPE

The hash sign (#).

PEDICEL

The plant stalk that supports fruit.

PIPS

The dots on a die, playing card or domino.

PUNT

The concave bottom of a glass bottle.

PYRAMID SPOT

The spot on a snooker table where the pink ball is placed (centred either side and 23 inches from the foot rail).

RETICLE

The grid, crosshairs or other pattern in the eyepiece of an optical instrument (such as a microscope or gunsight).

FIG. 3 *Reticle in telescopic sight*

SHIVE

A thin, flat cork for stopping a wide-mouthed bottle.

SNOOT

The nose of an aircraft.

STOP

The metal stop at the bottom of a zipper.

SOUFFLE CUP

The small paper cup used by restaurants for small servings of condiments.

FIG. 4 *Souffle cup*

TABLE

The flat upper surface of such a gemstone.

TANG

The tongue of a serpent (also, the sting of an insect, and the end of a tape measure).

THROAT

The triangle-shaped section in the middle of the tennis racket between head and handle.

THRUST TUBE

The mechanism that releases the ink chamber in a ballpoint pen.

TITTLE

The dot above a lowercase i or j.

TUCK

The end of a cigar (also known as the foot).

51

VAMP

The part of a boot or shoe that covers the front of the foot.

VIBRASSAE

Zoological term for a cat's whiskers, or other bristly hairs that grow around an animal's mouth.

WATCH POCKET

The small pocket on a pair of jeans (also known as a coin pocket or frontier pocket).

ZARF

The protective sleeve on a takeaway coffee cup.

¶ Dieting might seem to be a modern obsession, but the word has a long history that reflects an ancient concern with food, physique and general health.

¶ The word *diet* comes to English, via French and Latin, from the ancient Greek *diaita*, meaning 'way of living' or 'prescribed course of food'. This sense was reflected by the Greek physician Galen, writing in the second century BC, who regarded food as a therapeutic tool and argued that a good doctor should be a good cook too.

¶ Early Christians were also preoccupied with food, although their concern was the temptation it presented rather than 'getting in shape'. From the Christian ascetics of the fourth century to the accounts of *anorexia mirabilis* (miraculously inspired loss of appetite) in medieval Europe, and the '*fasting girls*' of the Victorian era, Christianity has a tradition of associating food with sinfulness. This sense of guilt continues to affect attitudes to eating, particularly in the Christian diet industry, with books like *Fasting for Spiritual Breakthrough* (2017) and *Help Lord – The Devil Wants Me Fat!* (1980).

¶ The progenitor to the modern diet book was *Discourses on a Sober Life* (1558) by Luigi Cornaro, a Venetian nobleman. Later published as *How to Live for a Hundred Years and Avoid Disease*, it deals with diet and lifestyle, advising what would now be described as a calorie restricted plan.

¶ The tone of diet books started to change in the nineteenth century (which is also when the phrase *on a diet* first appears in the *OED*). Most noticeable was a new

directness in the title of works, like *Letter on Corpulence* (1863), *Advice to Stout People* (1898) and *Food for the Fat* (1889). Print advertisements also started using a loud, on-the-chin style. '*Are You Too Fat? Get Thin!*' exhorted the ad for Tibbett's Hydridic Obesity Pills in 1882, while Dr Gordon's Elegant Pills snared readers in 1890 with the uncompromising message: '*TOO FAT!!*'

¶ Where the ancient Greeks were interested in holistic health, and Christians were resisting the Devil, dieters in the nineteenth and twentieth century were told in no uncertain terms to 'lose ugly fat', 'streamline your figure' and 'be slimmer in just 1 week'. People were being sold the promise of dramatic results in the shortest of times, and nothing sheds pounds faster than a hot fad diet.

¶ The trailblazer of fad diets was Horace Fletcher, 'The Great Masticator'. His best-selling book *Fletcherism* (1913) promoted a system of slow, prolonged chewing – *Fletcherising* – in which food was only swallowed 'when it practically swallows itself' (typically five minutes per mouthful, although Fletcher once chewed on a green onion for twelve). Fletcherism became a craze, with people organising *Munching Parties* and public figures enthusing about his system. Fletcherism also possessed many of the signature qualities of future fad diets, including the suggestion of science, the promise of dramatic effects, the spirit of radical novelty and the interest of celebrities. Most importantly, however, there was a book to explain the system.

¶ Fletcherism faded soon after its inventor's death in 1919, but it had created an appetite for fad diets that has never been sated. There was the **Lambchop and Pineapple diet** (1920s); the 18-day **Grapefruit diet** (1930s); the **Cabbage Soup diet** (1950s); the **Scarsdale diet** (1970s), that would later inspire the **Atkins** and **Southbeach** diets; the **Russian Air Force diet**; the **Caveman diet** (known also as **Paleo**); the **Halleluja diet**; and the **Mediterranean**, **Indian**, **Italian**, **Natural**, **Hypno-**, **Zone**, **Reverse** and **Prism** diets. In today's social media, it seems there is no idea too strange, or too inadvisable, for a fad diet, as exemplified by the **Cotton Wool diet** (2010s), with its programme of juice-dipped cotton wool balls.

❡ Such diets have brought with them a new language for how people talk about food, health and the human body. In an interesting twist, however, one of the most popular diets today is the Mediterranean diet, suggesting a return, after 2,000 years, to the **diaita** of ancient Greece.

53

DINER SLANG

¶ The precursor of the iconic US diner was the nineteenth-century horse-drawn lunch wagon that brought workers affordable and well-cooked fare. These wagons, or **lunch cars**, grew in size and comfort, and by the 1910s hundreds were being built each year. As lunch cars started to establish permanent premises from the 1920s, they became known as **diners** or **luncheonettes**, offering a familiar menu of griddle dishes, lunch specials and desserts.

¶ To deal with the rapid flow of orders, and also because it was fun, waiters and cooks developed a rich slang lexicon, in common use until the 1970s. As well as being deliciously humorous, diner slang ensured customers got what they ordered, whether they wanted their eggs **flopped** (fried), **easy over** (briefly cooked then flipped), **busted** (scrambled) or **dropped** (poached). The following menu of slang is just a taster of what the diner had to offer.

BAKERY

B & B	*bread and butter*
PITTSBURGH	*toast*
DOUGH WELL DONE (W/ COW TO COVER)	*toast (with butter)*
WHEAT DOWN	*toasted wheat bread*
WHISKEY DOWN	*toasted rye bread*

WHISKEY	*rye bread*
MAMA ON A RAFT	*marmalade on toast*
JEWISH ROUND	*bagel*
SINKERS AND SUDS	*doughnuts and coffee*
SISSY NUT	*cream cheese on date nut bread*

BREAKFAST GRIDDLE

ETERNAL TWINS	*ham and eggs*
COWBOY WITH SPURS	*western omelette w/ fries*
CLUCK AND GRUNT	*eggs and bacon*
CHICKS ON A RAFT	*eggs on toast*
HAMLETTE	*omelette w/ ham*
BROKEN HENBERRIES	*scrambled eggs*
ADAM & EVE ON A RAFT	*poached eggs on toast*
BLOWOUT PATCHES	*pancakes*
JAYNE MANSFIELD	*tall stack of pancakes*
HAYSTACK	*strawberry pancakes*
MYSTERY IN THE ALLEY	*hash*

BURGERS

C.B.	*cheeseburger*
CHEWED W/ BAD BREATH	*w/ onions*
PLAIN & DRY	*no toppings*
THROUGH THE GARDEN	*w/ lettuce, tomato, onion*

SERVED: Bloody *(very rare)*; Black and blue *(extremely rare)*; Hockey puck *(well done)*

HOT DOGS

BUN PUP	*hot dog*
RIPPER	*deep fried hotdog*
CHICAGO DOG	*w/ steamed bun & relish*

SIDES AND SOME

FOG	*mashed potatoes*
FROG STICKS	*French fries*
STEAMING IDAHO	*baked potato*
LOG ROLL	*link sausages*
WHISTLEBERRIES	*baked beans*
PIG	*bacon*

COW FEED	*salad*
COWCUMBER	*pickle*

Hemorrhage *(ketchup)*, Yellow paint *(mustard)*, Acid *(vinegar)*, Machine oil *(syrup)*, Winter *(whipped cream)*, Rush *(Russian dressing)*, Skid grease *(butter)*, Yum yum *(sugar)*

LUNCH SPECIALS

ABBOTT & COSTELLO	*frank and beans*	FOREIGN ENTANGLEMENTS	*spaghetti*
BARNYARD PILE-UP	*chicken-fried steak w/eggs*	FRIDAY'S CHOICE	*fish dinner*
WET MYSTERY	*beef stew*	HOUNDS ON AN ISLAND	*frank and beans*
BOWL ON FIRE	*chilli*	IRISH TURKEY	*corned beef and cabbage*
ZEPPELINS IN A FOG	*sausages & mashed potatoes*	SHIT ON A SHINGLE	*minced beef w/gravy*
BUTCHER'S REVENGE	*meatloaf*	PUT OUT THE LIGHTS AND CRY	*liver & onions*
FIRST LADY	*spareribs*		
FLAT CAR	*pork chops*		

SANDWICHES

JACK BENNY	*grilled cheese w/ bacon*
BOSSY ON A BOARD	*roast beef*
NOAH BOY ON BREAD	*ham*
CHICKEN IN THE HAY	*egg salad*
FAMILY REUNION	*chicken and egg*

SOUPS

GUESS WATER	*soup of the day*
FRENCHMAN'S DELIGHT	*pea soup*
HOT BALLS	*matzoh ball soup*
SPLASH OF RED NOISE	*tomato soup*
SPLASH OUT OF THE GARDEN	*vegetable soup*

DESSERTS

EVE WITH A LID ON	*apple pie*
MAGOO	*custard pie*
COKE PIE	*coconut pie*
ANT PASTE	*chocolate pudding*
FISH EYES	*tapioca*
SLEIGH RIDE SPECIAL	*vanilla pudding*
NERVOUS PUDDING	*Jello*
CORRUGATED ROOF	*lemon meringue pie*
ICE ON RICE	*rice pudding with ice cream*

ICE CREAM

CHICAGO SUNDAE	*pineapple sundae*
COLD MUD	*chocolate ice cream*
DAGWOOD SPECIAL	*banana split*
GLOB	*plain sundae*
PINK STICK	*strawberry ice cream*
SNOWBALL	*scoop of vanilla ice cream*

SHAKES & FLOATS

WHITE COW	*vanilla milkshake*
IN THE HAY	*strawberry milkshake*
RHINELANDER	*chocolate soda w/ vanilla*

COLD BEVERAGES

FLORIDA TONIC	*orange juice*
BATTERY ACID	*grapefruit juice*
SNOW WHITE	*7-Up*
MOO JUICE	*milk*
BROWN COW	*chocolate milk*
M.D.	*Dr. Pepper*
FORTY-ONE	*lemonade*
FIFTY-FIVE	*root beer*
CITY JUICE	*water*

TEA & COFFEE

MUD	*coffee*
HI-TEST	*strong black coffee*
ALL ARMS AND LEGS	*weak coffee*
BLONDE	*coffee w/ cream*
BLONDE AND SWEET	*coffee w/ cream & sugar*
FROSTY JOE	*iced coffee*
JOE O'MALLEY	*Irish coffee*
SCANDAL SOUP	*tea*
SPOT WITH A TWIST	*tea with lemon*

Tell your soup jockey *(waitress)* if you want your order with legs *(to take away)*.

¶ Were you to have a copy of Webster's *New International Dictionary, Second Edition* – the one published in 1934 – and were you to browse the Ds, you might come across the word ***dord***; defined succinctly, and with no etymological explanation, as 'density'. This may seem unremarkable, but dord is what lexicographers call a ***ghost word*** – a non-word that has inveigled its way into the dictionary because someone, somewhere, has blundered.

¶ In the case of dord, the dictionary's chemistry editor had written an entry slip with two options for the scientific abbreviation of density: 'D or d'. When this was reviewed, the spaces were interpreted as an error and the entry was 'corrected' to dord, which is how it remained until 1947 when the ghost was exorcised from the dictionary.

¶ The term ghost word was coined by the philologist Walter Skeat in 1885. In an address to The Philological Society, Skeat identified over a hundred spectral words haunting different printed texts, including ***desouled***, ***havin***, ***lath***, ***morse***, ***panfray*** and ***sharter***. As he explained, these words didn't exist and were misprints of defouled, harm, lay, nurse, paufrey and charter respectively.

¶ Even Samuel Johnson had ghosts in his 1755 dictionary. ***Adventine***, for instance, was a misreading of adventive (meaning to come from an external source), and was soon copied in other dictionaries. In a curious twist that could only happen to someone whose name was Samuel Johnson, the error resulted in an accidental coinage that can still be found in the *OED*.

¶ Another ghost in Johnson's dictionary was ***foupe***, 'To drive with sudden impetuosity.' Unfortunately, Johnson had misread the source – the word should have been

soupe, a Scots word from which we get swoop. Johnson's foupe remains in the *OED*, but only with the comment, 'Error for soupe.'

¶ Given the rigorous procedures of modern dictionary makers, ghost words are largely historical, but like any good ghost story, people enjoy sharing them. There's ***phantomnation***, for instance, which lexicographers misinterpreted as 'Appearance of a phantom', but which actually referred to a nation of phantoms. That haunted dictionaries for over half a century. Then there's ***abacot***, a misspelling of bycocket – a medieval cap or headdress – that spent over three centuries in the dictionary before the editor of the *OED* exposed it as a spelling mistake and it was escorted out of many lexicons. One might even say that President Trump created one of most famous contemporary ghost words when he tweeted ***covfefe*** late one night in 2017. It was clearly a typo, but the ghost of covfefe still haunts the internet.

¶ But not all mistakes result in a ghost word. The woollen cloth ***tweed*** is either a misinterpretation of tweeld or a misreading of tweel, both Scottish words. The error most likely arose among London cloth merchants, but the result is that the ghost word came to life and now lives among us. A similar mistake, albeit more ancient, gave us syllabus. The original Greek word was ***sittybas***, but some bungling scribe incorrectly copied one of Cicero's letters and rendered it syllabos, from which our English word is derived.

¶ And then there's sneeze. When Chaucer had a cold, he would ***fnese***. But around the fifteenth century, people were confused by a word beginning ***fn*** and started ***neezing***. Neezing led to sneezing while fnesing ceased, another casualty of misspelling.

❡ The proscription against **double negatives** (also known as a **negative concord**) can be attributed to Lindley Murray and his influential manual **English Grammar** (1797). Murray's **Rule XVI** begins: 'Two Negatives, in English, destroy one another, or are equivalent to an Affirmative,' and ends with the pronouncement 'it is better to express an affirmation by a regular affirmative than by two negatives.'

❡ The problem is, Rule XVI was based on the logic of Latin grammar. But in algebraic logic, two negatives added together (-x + -x) make a stronger negative. This makes more sense, given how, historically, double negatives served to **intensify** verbs.

❡ Before being shunned as linguistic delinquents, double negatives enjoyed a long and distinguished history. They appeared in the prologue to Chaucer's *Knight's Tale*: 'He nevere yet no vileynye ne sayde' ('He never yet no vileness spoke'); and Shakespeare used them often, as here in *Richard III*: 'I never was nor never will be false.' They're even in the Bible. In Hebrews 13:5 (translated from the original Greek), God says: 'Never not you will I leave, nor never not you will I forsake.' Which, with the greatest of respect to God, is not wholly unconfusing.

❡ Arguably, the real objection to double negatives wasn't based on logic but snobbery. The grammar books of the eighteenth century were consolidating the rules of **Standard English**; but by this time, double negatives had become the preserve of the uneducated commoner, and there they would remain, a construction to be admonished, for the next 300 years.

❡ Some double negatives were tolerated. The so-called **weak positive** ('He's not unattractive') possessed an acceptably English roundaboutness. Similarly, a **true double negation** ('I wouldn't say no to a drink') is pleasingly indirect. But as for those grubby **emphatic negatives** – they still **ain't not right**.

❡ Except, that is, creatively. Song lyrics in particular demonstrate the arresting power of the double negative, proving how a linguistic no-no can, when used correctly, pack a punch.

57

SEE ALSO: *Pedantry / Word Rage / Zero Plurals*

A GRAMMATICALLY CORRECTED TOP TEN

We don't need an education
PINK FLOYD

It's usual to be loved by someone
TOM JONES

I'm not afraid of ghosts
RAY PARKER JR.

I can't get to sleep
FAITHLESS

I can't get any satisfaction
THE ROLLING STONES

There isn't a mountain high enough
MARVIN GAYE AND
TAMMI TERRELL

There's no sunshine when she's gone
BILL WITHERS

You're a hound dog
ELVIS PRESLEY

Nobody bring me bad news
MABEL KING

It isn't useful to sit and wonder why
BOB DYLAN

¶ According to lexicographer Susie Dent, there are 3,000 synonyms for **drunk**. It's a fantastically large number, but sounds about right. As one of humanity's oldest pastimes, drinking has been as much a source of inspiration as love, which is why it is second only to crime and criminals in *Green's Dictionary of Slang*.

¶ Drunkenness already featured prominently in Old English. As well as **druncan** and **oferdruncen**, there was **druncen-georn** (drink-eager), **drunken-lœwe** (drink-weakened) and **hēafod-swīma** (head-swimming). Middle English provided yet more, including the evocative **cup-shotten**, and the collective noun for a gathering of heavy drinkers, a **drunkship** (also, **pot-parliament**).

¶ By the fifteenth century, the drinker's lexicon was well stocked. Some words indicated a preferred tipple, like **winebibber** or **malt-worm**, while others reflected one's drinking style, from the slow-drinking **merry-drunk** to the guzzling **swill-bowl**.

There was even a word – just one, mind – for people who abstained: **water-drinker**. It's unclear whether it was a compliment.

¶ English is uniquely well equipped for humour and wordplay, which is why it makes such fertile ground for drinking slang. Even in the eighteenth century this was apparent. In 1737, Benjamin Franklin's *The Drinker's Dictionary* documented 228 phrases to describe drunkenness, many of which originated in British drinking holes.

¶ What's striking from Franklin's list, and drinking slang ever since, is the wit and nonsense generated by tavern life. **Got the Indian vapours**, **contending with Pharaoh**, and **kill'd his dog** are utterly bewildering, but so too is the babble of the **rumpot**. As ridiculous are the many inventions that mean nothing, but say everything: **bowz'd**, **cherubimical**, **groat-able**, **globular**, **knapt**, **nimptopsical**, **pungey**… It's a language of its own that could only have been imagined by those **glaiz'd**, **soak'd** and **weary**.

DRUNKONYMS

¶ Comedian Michael McIntyre joked in a routine that any English word can be substituted to mean drunk, particularly if you're posh. **Utterly gazeboed** and **fucking pyjamaed** were his two memorable examples. Neither gazebos nor pyjamas are related to insobriety but, yes, somehow they work.

¶ Linguists investigating the phenomenon of such **drunkonyms** found that while McIntyre was stretching the point, there was a point to stretch. Analysing the

British National Corpus (a 100-million-word sample of written and spoken English), they found the most reliable linguistic construction was:

> *be/get + intensifying premodifier + -ed-form = **very drunk***

¶ For instance: ***I got utterly cashewed, he was completely wall-papered*** or ***they were totally trousered***. Considering the potential for such drunkonyms, Dent's 3,000 synonyms might even be an underestimate.

SEE ALSO: *Mary Jane / Origins of Nonsense / Victorian Slang*

> 'Sometimes too much drink is barely enough.'
> MARK TWAIN

ELIZABETHAN DRUNK
*Foggy Fuddled Overtaken
Mizzled Ripe Soaked*

GEORGIAN DRUNK
*Flustered Groggy Jocular
Lumpy Muzzy Raddled*

VICTORIAN DRUNK
*Muddled Reeling ripe Pixilated
Scammered Squiffed Swizzled*

SCOTTISH DRUNK
*Bleezing Mad wae it Pished
Reekin' Sloshed Steaming*

IRISH DRUNK
*Banjaxed Banjo'd Blutered
Flutered Langered Scuttered*

WELSH DRUNK
*Chillsed Hanging Jarred
Leathered Mangled Spangled*

AUSSIE DRUNK
*Bombed out Buckled Half-cut
Juiced Munted Shit-canned*

HUNGOVER
*Buffy Damaged Fishy
Off Palsied Whupped*

P. G. WODEHOUSE DRUNK
*Boiled Lattered Illuminated
Scrooched Stinko Vooched*

FLAPPER DRUNK
*Juiced Oiled Ossified
Piffled Pie-eyed Splifficated*

HIP HOP DRUNK
*Bent Full Loaded
Posted Tow down Twisted*

GEN XYZ DRUNK
*Beamed Crunk Keyed
Lit Slizzered Tacked*

POLITELY DRUNK
*Befuddled Confused Incapable
In one's cups Lubricated Represhed*

DRUG DRUNK
*2 on Cross-faded Doomed
Faisted Lonnered Tilted*

CANADIAN DRUNK
*Buzzed Hosed Jaked
Plowed Skunked Slambasted*

TEETOTAL
*Bun-puncher Hydropotic On the dry
Pussyfoot Teeto Up the pole*

59

---

83 FOR THE ROAD...

Afflicted • All het up • Amuck • Bagged • Baked • Baptised • Behind the cork • Blackjacked • Bingo'd • Blithered • Boozified • Canned • Cargoed • Carrying a load • Cock-eyed • Comboozelated • Crocked • Dinged out • Discumfuddled • Drinkative • Drunkulent • Elevated • Embalmed • Feshnushkied • Flako • Flummoxed • Full as a boat • Fuzzled • Galvanised • Gingered up • Gin soaked • Goggle-eyed • Grilled • Groggified • Half-looped • Harry Honkers • Hiccius-doccius • Horizontal • Impixlocated • In the altitudes • Jingled • Juiced • Knapped • Lathered • Likkered • Liquefied • Loaded to the barrel • Lushy • Malted • Mizzled • Moony • Muddled • Mugged up • Obfusticated • Oozy • Orry-eyed • Overshot • Pifflicated • Pizzicato • Poggled • Potulent • Pruned • Puggled • Raddled • Reeling • Ripped • Roasted • Rummed • Schlockkered • Scooped • Scrambled • Scronched • Shickered • Schnockered • Souffled • Stozzled • Swozzled • Tipply • Wam-bazzled • Well-sprung • Whipsey • Wiggy • Woofled

E.

EGGCORNS

¶ An **eggcorn** is a word or phrase that has been altered because an element has been misheard or reinterpreted. The resulting error sounds similar and, importantly, *makes sense*: for example, 'growth sprout' instead of 'growth spurt', 'handy-downs' for 'hand-me-downs', or 'windshield factor' for 'windchill factor'.

¶ The word was coined in response to a blog post by linguist Mark Liberman that mentioned a person calling acorns 'eggcorns'. Noting that this kind of linguistic mistake didn't have a name, fellow linguist Geoff Pullum suggested that **eggcorn** itself would be an apt name.

¶ The best eggcorns are a delight. The **Heimlich remover** and **Old-timer's diseases** (for Alzheimer's) might be wrong, but they're also kind of right. Similarly, it seems a shame to waste **extreme court** (for Supreme Court) or **hearbuds** (for earbuds).

¶ Eggcorns often emerge from idioms that use archaic or unfamiliar language. Few people, for instance, know what the **bated** in 'bated breath' means; and it's hardly a surprise that **real troupers** are often overlooked.

¶ Although pedants are happy to educate anyone who **tows** – rather than toes – the line or **chomps**, not champs, at the bit, some eggcorns are an improvement on the 'correct' version. Even the *OED* isn't sure what buck naked means, but its eggcorn, **butt naked**, reveals all.

¶ The online **Eggcorn Database** contains around 650 specimens and is worth a browse. It's **jar-dropping**. In the meantime, the collection below includes some of the most commonly heard eggcorns and should be enough to **wet the appetite**.

A real trooper > a real *trouper*
TROUPER: *a performer in a troupe, one who knows the 'show must go on'.*

Ad homonym > *ad hominem*
AD HOMINEM: *Latin for 'to the man', referring to an argument that criticises the person rather than the position (ad rem).*

Another thing coming* > another *think* coming
THINK: *a thought or idea.*

As dust fell > as *dusk* fell
DUSK: *the last light of the day.*

Baited breath > *bated* breath
BATED: *lowered or restrained.*

Beckon call > *beck* and call
BECK: *a silent signal notifying a command, such as a nod or hand gesture.*

Butt naked > *buck* naked
BUCK: *the 'buck' in question isn't known. It might refer to (1) the smoothness of the buckskin or (2) an offensive term referring to the naked state in which male slaves were sold in America.*

Chomping at the bit > *champing* at the bit
CHAMPING: *vigorous biting or chewing, especially said of horses.*

Damp squid > damp *squib*

SQUID
Cephalopod mollusc with eight arms and two long tentacles.

SQUIB
Small firework that burns with a hissing sound then explodes.

Escape goat > *scape* goat
  SCAPE: *the act of escaping.*

Far-gone conclusion > *foregone* conclusion
  FOREGONE: *an Old English word meaning to precede in time or position.*

Phased by > *fazed* by
  FAZE: *To disturb or agitate (someone).*

Flush out > *flesh* out
  FLESH: *To cover or clothe something; to fill out, as with flesh.*

Free reign > free *rein*
  REIN: *the straps attached to a horse's bridle to guide it.*

Happy as a clown > happy as a *clam*
  CLAM: *a bivalve mollusc adapted for fresh- and salt-water environments, although little is known of their emotional state.*

Hell in a handbag > hell in a *hand basket*
  HAND BASKET: *small hand-held basket.*

Home in on > *hone* in on
  HONE: *to sharpen or refine something, typically a blade or other instrument.*

In one foul swoop > in one *fell* swoop
  FELL: *cruel, fierce or savage.*

Just desserts > just *deserts*
  DESERTS: *that which is deserved.*

Last stitch effort > last *ditch* effort
  LAST DITCH: *figurative last line of defence.*

Mute point > *moot* point
  MOOT: *a debatable issue for discussion, historically in relation to law.*

Nerve-wrecking > nerve-*racking*
  RACKING: *tormenting or torturing.*

Nip it in the butt > nip it in the *bud*
  BUD: *The undeveloped part of a plant.*

Optical delusion > optical *illusion*
  ILLUSION: *a false impression that deceives the eye, or the mind.*

Pass mustard > pass *muster*
  MUSTER: *to assemble soldiers and others for inspection*

Put on a pedal-stool > put on a *pedestal*

PEDAL-STOOL
Non-existent stool with pedals attached for reasons unknown.

PEDESTAL
Structural base on which an object, statue or column is placed.

Rebel rouser > *rabble* rouser
  RABBLE: *an unruly mob.*

Ripe with > *rife* with
  RIFE: *common or widespread.*

Scandally clad > *scantily* clad
  SCANTILY: *in an insufficient quantity.*

Shoe-in > *shoo*-in
  SHOO: *to drive or urge away.*

Slight of hand > *sleight* of hand
  SLEIGHT: *skill or dexterity.*

Spurt of the moment > *spur* of the moment
  SPUR: *spiked device worn on a horserider's heel to urge the horse on; used figuratively to denote speed or haste.*

Takes two to tangle > takes two to *tango*
  TANGO: *a ballroom dance originating in Argentina.*

To the manor born* > to the *manner* born
  MANNER: *customary from birth.*

Towing the line > *toeing* the line
  TOE: *to touch with one's toes.*

Wet your appetite > *whet* your appetite
  WHET: *to sharpen or make ready.*

Wonderlust > *wanderlust*
  WANDERLUST: *a German word meaning a desire to travel.*

61

*Eggcorn is now also accepted usage

ELIZABETHAN COLOURS

❡ The most popular colour in the luxury Farrow & Ball paint range is **Elephant's Breath**, 'an uplifting mid-grey with hints of magenta'. The name has inspired both mirth and parody, as have **Sulking Room Pink**, **Dead Salmon** and **Mouse's Back**. But in the long history of colour names, such creations are relatively modest.

❡ Historically, many colours have been named after their place of origin (**indigo** from India), their pigment source (**vermillion** from the Latin for small worm), or via another language (**khaki** from **khak**, Persian for 'dusty'). And like much of English, many words were imported from Latin (**azure**, **viridian**, **sepia**) and French (**taupe**, **mauve**, **turquoise**). But it was the dye-makers of sixteenth-century England who elevated the evocative language of colour that is seen today.

❡ For Elizabethans, the colour of one's clothes was an indication of wealth. Dull colours, like **puke**, **rat** and **goose-turd**, were worn by lower-class Elizabethans, while those with means could enjoy the deeper tones of **lustie gallant** (light red), **popinjay** (bluish green) and **watchet** (pale greenish blue).

❡ Details of some Elizabethan colours can only be guessed at. It's left to our imaginations what **scratch face**, **ape's laugh** or **kiss-me-darling** looked like. And who knows whether **mortal sin** complimented **resurrection**, but one hopes it did.

❡ Compared to the Elizabethans, Farrow & Ball is almost restrained. That's more than can be said for the colour-naming team at Dulux, who seem to have upped the stakes with ever more memorable creations.

ELIZABETHAN COLOUR NAMES

BEGGAR'S GREY
Dark grey

HORSEFLESH
Dark red

MILK AND WATER
Bluish-white

SAD
A dark tint of any colour

DEAD SPANIARD
Pale greyish tan

JUDAS COLOUR
Sandy reddish yellow

PEASE-PORRIDGE
Yellowish-brown green

SOPPES-IN-WINE
Light red

DEVIL IN THE HEAD
A shade of green

LUSTIE GALLANT
Light red

RAT
Dull grey

GOOSE-TURD
Yellowish-green

HAIR
Bright tan

MAIDEN'S BLUSH
Rose

PUKE
Between russet and black

BASTARD YELLOW
Pale yellow

DULUX COLOUR NAMES

BOWLER HAT

MINT MACAROON

SNAIL TRAIL

LEMON JESTER

MUDDY PUDDLE

TEAL TENSION

LETTERS UNREAD

PURPLE POUT

URBAN OBSESSION

LUNAR FALLS

SAPPHIRE SALUTE

VINTAGE CHANDELIER

SEE ALSO: Racehorse Names

¶ People have used punctuation symbols to 'draw' faces since at least the 1880s, but they have only been used as a means of communication from 1982.

¶ The moment was 19 September, at 11.44 a.m. The Computer Science Department at Carnegie Mellon University had been using bulletin boards to chat and share news. Having seen how easily humourous messages could be misinterpreted, computer scientist Scott Fahlman posted:

> I propose that the following character sequence for joke markers: :-) Read it sideways. Actually, it is probably more economical to mark things that are NOT jokes, given current trends. For this, use :- (

¶ This was the birth of **emoticons** (emotion + icon). They immediately spread – first around CMU, then to other computer labs. When the closed ARPAnet gave way to the open Internet, and when that, in turn, became the World Wide Web, Fahlman's happy and sad faces became part of a new digital lexicon, ever-expanding to express the breadth of human emotions.

¶ While emoticons were taking off on English-speaking networks, **kaomoji** – from Japanese **kao** + **moji** ('face character') – were appearing on the Japanese ASCII Net. With its broader character base, kaomoji could be more varied. There might be two or three angry emoticons, but over twenty kaomoji. Similarly, eyes – a particular focus for kaomoji – could be characterised in numerous ways.

┐┐   ∩ ∩   • •   ∩ ∩   ＾ ＾

π π   ● ●   ♂ ♀   ☉ ☉   ◉ ◉

FIG.1 *Assorted kaomoji eyes*

¶ Emoticons and kaomoji were progenitors to today's **emoji** and have become a defining feature of digital communication. These **pictograms** either bring a commentary track to the written word – 'this is funny', 'this is sad' – or replace words entirely.

¶ While emoticons and kaomoji may look laughably basic, this made them part of a coded language that was an important part of their use, and which has almost vanished with the ascendance of emoji. Like **pager code**, **leetspeak** and **hacker slang**, emoticons and kaomoji were the language of digital insiders. Today, emojis attach to text messages without users even selecting them.

¶ Inevitably, some saw the rise of emoticons and kaomoji as both a cause and effect of the deterioration of language. But as the kids would say, ‾_(ツ)_/‾

SEE ALSO: *Ironic Punctuation / Pager Code*

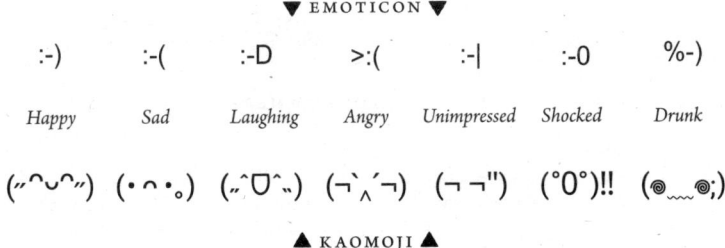

▼ EMOTICON ▼

:-)	:-(	:-D	>:(	:-|	:-0	%-)
Happy	*Sad*	*Laughing*	*Angry*	*Unimpressed*	*Shocked*	*Drunk*

(„∩◡∩„) (•∩•₀) („ˆ∇ˆ„) (¬`ᵥ´¬) (¬ ¬") (°0°)!! (◉﹏◉;)

▲ KAOMOJI ▲

EPONYMOUS EFFECTS

BAADER-MEINHOF EFFECT
(ALSO: FREQUENCY ILLUSION)

On discovering a new word or concept, it is likely to be heard again within twenty-four hours.

Coined by Terry Mullen, a correspondent to the *St. Paul Pioneer Press*, who observed the effect in a friend who had just learned about the Baader-Meinhof gang, then reported hearing about them the following day. Recognising this was a common experience, Mullen suggested the phenomenon be called the *Baader-Meinhof Effect*.

———

BEN FRANKLIN EFFECT

People are inclined to like someone more after doing them a favour.

It may seem counterintuitive, but it's the person doing the favour whose opinion is then changed. Not only can it be flattering to be asked for a favour, but it also builds rapport. The effect is named after Franklin because he described the technique in his autobiography.

———

DIDEROT EFFECT

Acquiring one new thing leads to acquiring more new things.

In his essay 'Regrets on Parting with my Old Dressing Gown' (1769), French philosopher Denis Diderot described how, having received an elegant new dressing gown, he felt compelled to upgrade his wardrobe, replace his artworks, repaint his home, and so on. This consumption spiral was later referred to as the *Diderot Effect* by anthropologist Grant McCracken in 1986.

———

DUNNING-KRUGER EFFECT

The less people know, the more they think they know.

This cognitive bias was identified by social psychologists David Dunning and Justin Kruger in 1999, who described it as 'being ignorant of one's own ignorance'. Not only do such people perform badly, but their ignorance also means they have no idea just how bad they are.

FORER EFFECT
(ALSO: BARNUM EFFECT)

People believe vague personality statements to be highly accurate, even when applicable to everybody.

Identified by psychologist Bertram Forer in 1948, who gave participants identical personality descriptions and saw how they were interpreted as specific to them. The effect explains why people trust horoscopes, fortune-telling and personality tests.

———

HAWTHORNE EFFECT
(ALSO: OBSERVER EFFECT)

People change their behaviour when they know they are being observed.

Named after the Hawthorne Works in Illinois, where research into workplace productivity in the 1920s led to the conclusion that workers were improving productivity because researchers were observing them, not because of the specific changes being tested.

———

IKEA EFFECT

People value items more if they have a hand in making them.

According to researchers at Harvard Business School, products that involve self assembly – like IKEA furniture and meal-kit boxes – are valued by consumers more than ready-made products because of the effort they put in to making it.

———

LAKE WOBEGON EFFECT

People overestimate their abilities.

Coined by physician John Jacob Cannell, who noted that every US state said their elementary school performance was higher than the national average. The effect is named after Lake Wobegon, a fictional town from the US radio show *A Prairie Home Companion*. According to the town's creator, all the residents of Lake Wobegon believe they are 'above average'. This 'above average' feeling is characteristic of the effect, with people believing they are better, smarter and more successful than they really are.

MANDELA EFFECT

A collective false memory.

Coined by paranormal researcher Fiona Broome in 2009 in relation to a widely held false memory that Nelson Mandela had died in prison during the 1980s. Although Broome thought the **Mandela Effect** might be proof of parallel worlds, numerous examples of other large-scale false memories suggest it's not unusual for a lot of people to be wrong about the same thing at the same time.

PELTZMAN EFFECT

More safety measures lead people to increase risky behaviours.

Named after economics professor Sam Peltzman, whose 1975 paper 'The Effects of Automobile Safety Regulation' argued that the benefits of safety measures were offset, sometimes even negated, by people behaving more dangerously as a result.

PYGMALION EFFECT

High expectations achieve better results; low expectations lead to worse results.

Identified by psychologists Jacobson and Rosenthal and named after the Greek myth about the sculptor Pygmalion, who loved one of his creations so much that it came to life. In the Pygmalion Effect, expectations act as a self-fulfilling prophecy.

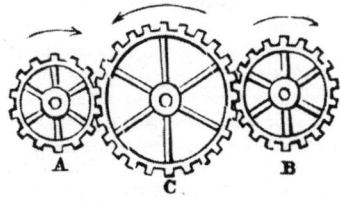

RINGELMANN EFFECT
(ALSO: SOCIAL LOAFING)

When a group becomes larger, its individual members become less productive.

The **Ringelmann Effect**, proposed by French agricultural engineer Maximilien Ringelmann in 1913, describes how, as new members are added to a group, average individual productivity decreases.

STREISAND EFFECT

Efforts to censor or remove information just attracts more attention.

Named after American singer Barbra Streisand, whose legal efforts to suppress a photograph of her Malibu home had the opposite effect of drawing attention to it. The **Streisand Effect** demonstrates the unintended consequences of trying to censor information, as it arouses curiosity and draws attention. Footballer Ryan Giggs found the same when he took out a 'super-injunction' to stop newspapers publishing details of an alleged affair.

VEBLEN EFFECT

The more expensive luxury goods are, the more people want them.

The **Veblen Effect**, identified by American economist Thorstein Veblen in *The Theory of the Leisure Class* (1899), shows how luxury goods become more desirable as their price goes up. Veblen products defy normal laws of supply and demand because their high price makes them a status symbol.

WAITROSE EFFECT

A new Waitrose supermarket increases the value of nearby property.

In 2013, it was reported that opening a new branch of Waitrose – Britain's premium supermarket – could boost local property values by an average of £36,000.

EPONYMS

ALFREDO SAUCE (1929)
Alfredo di Lelio, Italian cook

ASPERGER SYNDROME (1971)
Hans Asperger, Austrian psychologist

BÉCHAMEL SAUCE (1789)
Louis de Béchamel, courtier of Louis XIV

BIRO PEN (1947)
László Bíró, Hungarian inventor

BLOOMERS (1851)
Amelia Bloomer, American newspaper editor

BOWIE-KNIFE (1836)
Jim Bowie, American inventor

BOWDLERISE (1836)
Thomas Bowdler, British editor

BOYCOTT (1880)
Charles Boycott, English land agent

BRAILLE WRITING (1853)
Louis Braille, French inventor

BUNSEN BURNER (1870)
Robert Bunsen, German chemist

CAESAR SALAD (1946)
Caesar Cardini, restaurateur

CHAUVINIST (1877)
Nicolas Chauvin, French soldier

DIESEL FUEL (1894)
Rudolf Diesel, German engineer

DUNCE (1530)
John Duns Scotus, Scottish theologian

FERRIS WHEEL (1892)
George Washington Gale Ferris Jr., engineer

G-SPOT (1982)
Ernst Gräfenberg, German scientist

GALVANISE (1839)
Luigi Galvani, Italian physicist

GERRYMANDERING (1812)
Elbridge Gerry, American politician

GORE-TEX (1972)
Wilbert Gore, American businessman

GUILLOTINE (1793)
Dr Joseph Ignace Guillotin, French doctor

HAMMOND ORGAN (1935)
Laurens Hammond, American inventor

JACUZZI (1966)
Candido Jacuzzi, Italian inventor

LEOTARD (1920)
Jules Léotard, French acrobat

LYNCHING (1835)
Charles Lynch, American politician

MACH NUMBER (1937)
Ernst Mach, Austrian physicist

MACKINTOSH (1835)
Charles Macintosh, Scottish chemist

MAGNOLIA (1748)
Pierre Magnol, French botanist

MARGHERITA PIZZA (1889)
Margherita of Savoy, Italian queen

MASOCHISM (1883)
Leopold von Sacher-Masoch, novelist

MASON JAR (1885)
John L. Mason, American inventor

MAUSOLEUM (ANCIENT GREECE)
Mausolus (d. 353 BC), governor of Caria

MELBA TOAST (1913)
Nellie Melba, Australian opera singer

MESMERISM (1784)
Franz Anton Mesmer, German hypnotist

MILQUETOAST (1932)
Caspar Milquetoast, comic strip character

MOLOTOV COCKTAIL (1940)
Vyacheslav Molotov, Russian politician

MORSE CODE (1849)
Samuel Finley Morse, American inventor

MURPHY'S LAW (1951)
Edward A. Murphy Jr., American engineer

NICOTINE (1817)
Jean Nicot, French diplomat

PANTALOON / PANTS (1592)
Pantalone, Italian theatrical character

PAPARAZZI (1961)
*Paparazzo, a press photographer
in* La Dolce Vita

PAVLOVA (1911)
Anna Pavlova, Russian ballet dancer

PEACH MELBA (1906)
Nellie Melba, Australian opera singer

PILATES (1934)
Joseph Pilates, German physical trainer

PLIMSOLL SHOE (1877)
Samuel Plimsoll, British politician

PONZI SCHEME (1920)
Charles Ponzi, Italian conman

QUISLING (1940)
Vidkun Quisling, Nazi collaborator

RITZY (1919)
César Ritz, Swiss hotel-owner

SADIST (1892)
Marquis de Sade, French writer

SANDWICH (1762)
John Montagu, 4th Earl of Sandwich

SAXOPHONE (1840)
Adolphe Sax, Belgian inventor & musician

SHRAPNEL (1806)
Henry S. Shrapnel, British artillery officer

SIDEBURNS (1876)
Ambrose Burnside, US Civil War general

SILHOUETTE (1798)
Etienne de Silhouette, finance minister

SPOONERISM (1900)
William Spooner, Oxford don

STETSON (c. 1900)
John B. Stetson, American hat-maker

TEDDY BEAR (1906)
Theodore Roosevelt, American president

UZI SUBMACHINE GUN (1959)
Uziel Gal, Israeli firearm designer

VENN DIAGRAM (1918)
John Venn, British mathematician

ZEPPELIN (1900)
Ferdinand von Zeppelin, German general

¶ Every word originates somewhere. It may be borrowed or coined, named after a person, inspired by a place or imitative of a sound. It could have evolved over the long journey from **Proto-Indo European** (a reconstructed ancient language for which no evidence exists), or coined just last year. But for anyone interested in *etymology* – the study of the origin and development of words – there's pleasure in finding out *where*, *why* and *when* words came to be.

¶ Sometimes etymology is a simple business. *Eponyms*, for instance. Words like *dunce* (after John Duns Scotus), *nicotine* (after Jean Nicot) or *diesel* (after Rudolf Diesel) are no riddle. Other words, like *robot*, *poodle* and *porpoise*, are fun to discover, but also well-documented.

¶ Then there are the words of Germanic, French and Latin origin that account for much of the English language. These can require more unravelling, and the further back one goes, the more conjecture there is.

¶ Take *slang*, the informal nonstandard language that fills our world. Everyone knows what slang is, but not where the word comes from. Is it related to the narrow strips of land known as 'slangs', or with the Scots 'slanger', meaning to dawdle, or with the Norwegian 'slengjeord', meaning a mocking word? Neither slang experts nor the *OED* know.

¶ Which brings us to the three words no etymologist wants to write: 'Of unknown origin'. For instance, no-one knows the origin of *dog*. Similarly, *frog*, *hog*, *pig* and *stag*. They certainly look to be related, but beyond that, etymologists are stumped.

¶ What's surprising is how many everyday words are 'of unknown origin'. One might expect the source of *girl* or *ink* or *tantrum* would be known. But such words often have ancient roots, and the longer the history, the murkier the evidence gets.

SEE ALSO: *Eponyms / Misquotations*

WORDS OF UNKNOWN ORIGIN

Bad • Badge • Bamboozle • Barf • Basket • Beach • Beaver • Big • Bird • Blare • Bloke • Blur • Boast • Bob • Boffin • Bore • Boy • Brass • Buffet • Bull • Bully • Bump • Bun • Bung • Bunk • Bunny • Bunting • Butt • Calm • Cane • Case • Clock • Coil • Conniption • Conundrum • Copacetic • Craze • Crease • Cricket • Cub • Curse • Dandruff • Dent • Dig • Dildo • Dock • Dog • Donkey • Dosh • Drug • Dud • Ewe • Fee • Fib • Flabbergast • Flack • Flare • Flaunt • Fleet • Flew • Flue • Fluke • Fob • Forge • Funk • Gab • Gadget • Gaff • Gasket • Gaunt • Gawk • Gaze • Gig • Gimmick • Girl • Gizmo • Gloat • Golf • Gorge • Grail • Grizzle • Grouse • Gun • Haggis • Haze • Hijack • Hockey • Hoodlum • Hug • Humdinger • Hype • Ink • Jade • Jaw • Jitter • Kick • Kid • Lag • Leech • Leer • Log • Love • Marvel • Mug • Nasty • Noodle • Nudge • Pad • Pause • Peat • Perk • Pet • Pink • Plot • Pore • Pound • Prank • Prod • Pry • Punk • Puzzle • Quake • Quandary • Queasy • Queer • Quiz • Race • Ramble • Rat • Rear • Rig • Rogue • Row • Scoundrel • Scout • Shrivel • Shrub • Slang • Snazzy • Sprig • Sprocket • Steer • Stem • Stir • Stooge • Strumpet • Stubborn • Swig • Swill • Tantrum • Tit • Toad • Tug • Twitter • West • Whim • Wick • Yank

¶ Further muddying the waters are the *folk etymologies* people *want* to be true. Like **marmalade**, said to be from *Marie est malade*, the words whispered to a seasick Mary Queen of Scots by her maid, presumably while munching marmalade on toast. Obviously it's hooey – marmalade was borrowed from Portuguese, where it came from the ancient Greek for apple – but because people love a good story, it gets shared, along with hundreds of stories like it.

¶ *Idioms* especially are magnets for folk etymology. And among idioms, *the whole nine yards* has been called 'the holy grail for etymologists' because of the origin stories that swirl around it. Aircraft ammunition belts, bolts of fabric, mine-working, kilt-making, cement-mixing, nuns, saris and American football have all been marshalled as explanations. And although lengths of fabric seem plausible to this author, the idiom remains 'of uncertain origin'.

¶ *Etymology* itself is from Greek *etymon* (original, true) + *logia* (science or study), making it the study of original and true word meanings. But sometimes the truth is that we don't know. Some might regard this as an admission of defeat, but there's also something quite magical about a word whose origins can never be known.

DON'T BELIEVE EVERYTHING YOU HEAR

BRAT is not from British Regiment Attached Traveller • **CABAL** is not from the initials of the plotters seeking to overthrow King Charles II • **COLD AS BRASS MONKEYS** has nothing to do with how cannonballs were stored • **CRAP** is unrelated to Thomas Crapper • **FUCK YOU** is not from *pluck yew* • **GOLF** is not an acronym of *Gentlemen Only, Ladies Forbidden* • **KICK THE BUCKET** is not to do with public executions • **OK** is not from *Old Kinderhook* (or from Scottish *och aye*, Finnish *oikea* or German *Oberst Kammandant*) • **POSH** is not from *Port-Out Starboard-Home* • **RAINING CATS AND DOGS** is not an allusion to the Norse god Odin • **RULE OF THUMB** is not to do with husbands beating wives • **SAVED BY THE BELL** is not to do with being buried alive • **SHIT** is not from *Ship High In Transit* • **SNOB** is not from Latin *sine nobilitate* ('without nobility') • **SOS** does not stand for *Save Our Ships* (or *Send Out Succour*)

❡ Few subjects have so many euphemisms as death. People trip over themselves to avoid the D-word, instead saying someone has **passed**, is **at rest** or, most confusingly, **lost**.

❡ This awkwardness is recent. For much of human history, death was never far away. Disease, war and low life expectancy ensured that. And lest one forgot, art and jewellery inscribed with the Latin **memento mori** ('remember you will die') were reminders of humanity's finitude.

❡ But as lives lengthened, our relationship with death changed, and during the Victorian era death started to become a taboo.

❡ When poet Clara Thompson wrote in 1908: 'We say he is dead; ah, the word is too somber', she reflected a new-found discomfort with the concept. Thankfully, a language of **euphemism** and its gloomy opposite, **dysphemism**, has evolved to help draw death's sting, and even laugh in its face. For at some point, we must all **shake hands with Elvis**.

SEE ALSO: *Vintage Ailments*

RELIGIOUS

Freed from earthly limitations
Gathered to God
Gone to a new life
Joined the choir invisible
Joined the great majority
With the angels
Promoted to glory

JOURNEYING

Crossed over
Departed
Gone away
On the other side
Passed on
Plucked from us
Succumbed

RELIEF

Happy release
Peace at last
Reposing
Resting
Sleeping
Slipped away
Without pain

BLUNT

Bought the farm
Hopped the twig
Popped their clogs
Slipped their cable
Under the hatches

INTERMENT

Counting worms
Heels foremost
Pushing up daisies
Six feet under
Taking a dirt nap

OBSCURE

Cut off
Oofed
Scragged
Turned turtle
Wheels up

BUREAUCRATIC

Combat ineffective
Made the ultimate sacrifice
Non-heart-beating donor
Off the voting list

ENDINGS

Cashed in their chips
That was all they wrote
Pulled his last pint
Stood his last watch

RHYMING

Brown bread
Father Ted
Potted head
Uncle Ned

FIG.1 *An ex-parrot: expired, gone to meet his maker, bereft of life, off the twig, no more and ceased to be.*

❡ Dorothy Parker famously said that her two favourite words were 'cheque' and 'enclosed'. Less well known is that she prefaced that by saying 'cellar-door' was English's most beautiful word.

❡ This might seem a strange choice, but she wasn't the first to suggest it. In a novel thirty years earlier, Cyrus Hooper described the 'sensuous impression' of **cellar-door**; and in 1952, J. R. R. Tolkien said it was 'More beautiful than, say, sky, and far more beautiful than beautiful'.

❡ What Parker, Hooper, Tolkien – and many since – were expressing was the **phonaesthetics** of the word; the quality of its sound, separate from its meaning. Like **serendipity** (often named Britain's 'favourite word'), **chinchilla** and **blossom**, cellar-door is **euphonious**, that is, pleasing to the ear.

❡ Great writers instinctively understand euphony. *'Seasons of mist and mellow fruitfulness'* (John Keats); *'Tomorrow, and tomorrow and tomorrow'* (Shakespeare); *'Butterflies off banks of noon'* (Emily Dickinson): all have a lyrical, euphonious quality. But explaining *why* certain words are so satisfying is harder to pin down.

❡ When linguist David Crystal analysed 114 euphonic words in 1995, he found that:

*Syllables are good, with three or more best, such as **bombinate** and **effervescent**;*

*'L's, 'm's, 's's, 'n's and 'r's were the most common consonant sounds, such as **lassitude, mellifluous, scintilla, nemesis** and **raconteur**;*

*Flowing sounds (so-called **frictionless continuants**) are particularly pleasant, such as **rosemary** and **murmurous**.*

*Words that stress the first syllable are most common, such as **mesmerism** and **nimble**.*

*Short vowels predominate, such as **melody** and **lilt**.*

❡ In all, Crystal identified ten criteria commonly seen in euphonic words, and even proposed some made-up words – **ramelon** and **drematol** – that would fulfil them all.

❡ Although writers don't use a criteria matrix to choose their words, when the *Guardian* asked authors for their favourites, many were naturally euphonic, including: **gloaming** (Sarah Hall), **cochineal** (Tessa Hadley) and **ragabash** (Blake Morrison). A century earlier, Henry James said **summer afternoon** were his two favourite words. Were it only in **Selador**, it would indeed be perfect.

SEE ALSO: *Bee's Knees / Funny Words / Scottish Rain / Word Rage*

71

BEAUTIFUL WORDS

Aurora • Amaranthine • Bloom • Celandine • Chinchilla • Damask • Demure • Diaphanous • Eiderdown • Elision • Elixir • Embrocation • Emollient • Ephemeral • Ethereal • Glamour • Gossamer • Haiku • Humador • Ingenue • Inglenook • Kerfuffle • Limerence • Luminescence • Luminous • Lyrical • Murmuring • Myrrh • Oleander • Palimpsest • Penumbra • Picnic • Sanguine • Sequoia • Shimmer • Sycamore • Tremulous • Truffle • Wherewithal • Woebegone • Zephyr

F.

FANDOM

¶ The first celebrity mania was **Liszto-mania**, coined by nineteenth-century poet Heinrich Heine to describe the wild excitement generated by Hungarian pianist Franz Liszt. Touring Europe in the 1830s, the dashing young Liszt left ladies screaming, swooning and even decanting his leftover tea into scent bottles. In his book *Franz Liszt: The Virtuoso Years*, Alan Walker describes how Liszt's devotees would wear locks of his hair and fight over a dropped handkerchief or glove. One 'infatuated lady' even wore a discarded cigar butt in a diamond-encrusted locket.

¶ Nothing like Lisztomania had been seen before, but he wasn't the only nineteenth-century 'celebrity' to have a named fanbase. Jane Austen had **Janites** – and later, **Austenites** – Charles Dickens had **Dickensites**, Brahms had **Brahmsites** and Sherlock Holmes had **Sherlockians**. These eponymous devotees were more admiring than hysterical, but the enthusiasm of these Victorian superfans has a decidedly modern feel.

¶ Given such passions, the etymology of **fan** is illuminating. It is a shortening of **fanatic**, a sixteenth-century word with some interesting definitions: a mad person, a visionary or, as an adjective, descriptive of someone possessed by a demon. The word was often related to religious fervour and

an excess of enthusiasm bordering on the irrational. The sense of **fan** as an enthusiast or supporter appears in the late-nineteenth century, where it was largely confined to sports, until Hollywood stars were feted with **fan clubs** and **fan mail** in the 1920s.

¶ Stars like Elvis, Sinatra and Shirley Temple all had fans, but **Beatlemania** in 1963 was something more frenzied. With Beatlemania came **Beatlemaniacs**, but this was a journalistic invention not used by the fans themselves, unlike **Deadheads**, the name for Grateful Dead superfans, a term coined by the band and embraced by its fans. Deadheads presaged a new kind of fandom that was more committed than any previous fanbase.

¶ Today's superfan is sometimes known as a **stan** (possibly a portmanteau of **stalker** and **fan**) from the Eminem song 'Stan' (2000). The difference between a fan and a stan is the obsessive, fixated behaviour they bring to their fandom. South Korea's answer to the stan is the **sasaeng**, who can obsess about their K-Pop idols to an unhealthy and sometimes illegal degree. *Sasaeng* have expressed their enthusiasm by stalking, breaking into the house of, and in one case, attempting to kidnap the celebrity they love. Ok Taec-yeon, the rapper in boy band 2PM, even received a marriage proposal from one *sasaeng* written in her menstrual blood.

¶ In Japan, fandom is expressed through **oshi** culture. *Oshi* (literally 'recommendation') is the person or thing you love to love. Your *oshi* might be a pop star, manga character or favourite author, and they might be living, dead or inanimate. **Oshi-katsu** are the activities you pursue

SEE ALSO: *Collective Nouns / Eponymous Effects*

FIG.1 *A different kind of fan*

around your *oshi* (**katsu** is an abbreviation of **katsudo**, meaning 'activity'). A weekend of *oshi-katsu* might involve going to a concert, writing fan mail, shopping for clothes worn by your *oshi*, or meeting up with fellow *oshi* fans. On your *oshi's* birthday, you might even throw a party in an *oshi-katsu* hotel room where, as the Royal Park Canvas in Osaka says, 'You can talk about your feelings for your favourite idol with your fellow fans, and spend your time immersed in the love for your favourite idol.'

¶ Of course, fandom can extend to TV shows and films. **Trekkies**, the die-hard *Star Trek* fans, have been around since the mid 1970s, while **Whovians**, a more recent coinage, are united in their appreciation of *Doctor Who*. Similarly, Harry Potter has **Potterheads**, the US version of the *The Office* has **Dunder-Heads**, and the

cult film *The Big Lebowski* has **Achievers**. And they abide.

¶ Actors have fans too, but only a select few have a named following. Before Timothée Chalamet and his **Chalamaniacs** was Benedict Cumberbatch and his **Cumberbitches**. (Incidentally, 'Cumberbitch' was part of a wider fan meme of Cumberbatch wordplay that included **Buttercup Cumbersnatch**, **Banister Crumblebench**, **Bumblesnuff Crimpysnitch**, and the irresistible **Cadbury Pringle Batch**.) One Cumberbatch fan, Tabitha Carvan, even wrote a book about her experience, *This is Not a Book About Benedict Cumberbatch* (2022). The book's strapline is, 'The joy of loving something – anything – like your life depends on it'. For this is the lure of fandom, and sometimes all it takes is a discarded cigar butt.

73

MUSICIANS AND THEIR FANS

ARIANA GRANDE
Arianators

BEYONCE
The Beyhive

BLACKPINK
Blinks

BROS
Brosettes

BRUCE SPRINGSTEEN
Bruce Tramps

CHRISTINA AGUILERA
Fighters

ELLIE GOULDING
Goulddiggers

KATY PERRY
KatyCats

KENDRICK LAMAR
Kenfolk

DUA LIPA
Loves

DURAN DURAN
Durannies

EMINEM
Stans

GREEN DAY
Idiots

GUNS 'N' ROSES
Gunners

JUSTIN BIEBER
Beliebers

LED ZEPPELIN
Zepheads

LIL WAYNE
Wayniacs

LADY GAGA
Little Monsters

LINKIN PARK
Soldiers

MARIAH CAREY
Lambs

MEGADETH
Droogies

MEGAN THEE STALLION
Hotties

MILEY CYRUS
Smilers

MOTÖRHEAD
Motörheadbangers

NICKI MINAJ
Barbz

NINE INCH NAILS
Pigs

ONE DIRECTION
Directioners

PET SHOP BOYS
Petheads

SLIPKNOT
Maggots

TAKE THAT
Thatters

TAYLOR SWIFT
Swifties

THE KILLERS
Victims

THE WHITE STRIPES
Candy Cane Children

THE WHO
Wholigans

Fart (N.), the emission of wind from the anus, is from the Old English *feortan*, which itself derives from Old High German. The same root is seen in Old Norse, Danish, Old Icelandic and more. Despite this ancient heritage, the word retains a hint of vulgarity and the *OED* notes it is *'generally to be considered unacceptable in formal contexts'*.

To avoid making a faux pas, other options are available. Doctors refer to **flatulence** and **wind**; highbrows might commit an **act of ventosity** or a French **petarade**; and anyone seeking a euphemism could do worse than **bottom burp**, **trouser cough** or, simply, an **escape**. Visitors to Australia and New Zealand might also like to know that while men fart, women **fluff**.

Like most things emanating from the body, farts enjoy a rich lexicon of slang. To fart is to **cut the cheese**, **empty the tank**, **open your lunchbox**, **singe the carpet**, **step on a duck** or **burp the wrong way**; while farts themselves are **air biscuits**, **crowd splitters**, **fog cutters**, **blurters**, **breezers**, **trouser chuffs** and **fragrant fuzzies**. A **razzler** is a loud fart, a **cheeser** is strong-smelling and a **rim slide** will clear any room. But pray you never deliver a **plotcher**.

The etiquette when it comes to farting is to pretend it didn't happen since, as everyone knows, whoever smelt it, dealt it. Alternatively, get on the front foot. In New Zealand one might say, *'an empty house is better than a bad tenant'*, echoing the more British, *'better out than in'*. Neither, however, is much comfort to those in the vicinity.

If this sounds crude, comfort yourself with the rich literary history of farts. Aristophanes, Chaucer, Shakespeare and Virgil all wrote about them. There was the demon in Dante's *Inferno*, who marshalled his hellish horde by making *'a trumpet of his rump'*. And the great Jonathan Swift even wrote a pamphlet, *The Benefit of Farting Explain'd*, extolling the virtues of farting and why women should do more of it.

Farts entertain beyond literature, too. A professional farter is a **flatulist** (or **fartist**). The best known contemporary fartist is Mr Methane, who practices the 'art of controlled anal voicing'. He continues a tradition going back centuries. Roland the Farter was Henry II's court flatulist, and was paid handsomely to perform his annual routine *unum saltum et siffletum et unum bumbulum* ('one jump and whistle and one fart'). The **braigetóir** in medieval Ireland and the **heppiri otoko** (farting men) of the Tokugawa period in Japan performed similar feats of **flatus**.

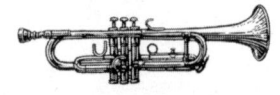

FARTS IN DIFFERENT
LANGUAGES

AFRIKAANS	*poep*
AZERBAIJANI	*zart*
CATALAN	*prut*
DANISH	*fis*
HEBREW	*pook*
INDONESIAN	*tuut*
ITALIAN	*peto*
PERSIAN	*pup*
PORTUGUESE	*pum*
SWEDISH	*prutt*
TAMIL	*karukk*
TURKISH	*zort*

SEE ALSO: *Barry Humphries Glossary / Funny Words*

CATCH-FART (N.)	CLATTERFART (N.)	FART-CATCHER (N.)	SPARROW-FART (N.)
A footservant.	*A chatterbox.*	*A flunkey or flatterer.*	*Very early in the day.*

¶Few problems confound experts in playground jurisprudence more than determining culpability for a fart.

¶When those first sulphurous fumes are detected, an innocent by-stander might be compelled to express their disgust, but doing so can precipitate a well-versed procedure of **fart denial**. Whatever variations exist, the first steps of the dance proceed predictably:

BY-STANDER: *'Eurgh! Who farted?'*
RESPONSE 1: *'He who smelt it, dealt it.'*
RESPONSE 2: *'He who denied it, supplied it.'*
RESPONSE 3: *'He who said the rhyme, did the crime.'*

¶The origin of this tradition is unclear. 'He who smelt it, dealt it' can be seen in a 1976 edition of the *Chicago Tribune*, so it's reasonable to assume it had been around since at least the late sixties, and probably came from American schoolkids. But beyond this, the trail goes cold.

¶Sociologist Trevor J. Blank has studied the folklore around farting – what he calls **fartlore** – and argues that 'He who smelt it' is part of a wider scatological folk wisdom that includes such insights as, 'First comes the poop; then comes the soup', and, 'Why fart and waste it when you can burp and taste it?' While such aphorisms lack scientific authority, they are part of a performative fartlore through which, according to Blank, children navigate the social pressures associated with the flatulence taboo.

¶It is worth noting that fartlore is strongly gendered. Although women fart as least as much as men, flatulence, and the ribaldry associated with it, is a feature of 'manly behaviour', while femininity is held to a different, fart-free standard that doesn't tolerate such latrinalia. This explains why the one who 'dealt it' – or 'blew', 'ripped' or 'biffed' it – is presumed to be 'he'.

EXTENDED FART DENIALS

He who deduced it, produced it.

He who detected it, projected it.

He who knew it, blew it.

He who quipped it, ripped it.

He who excuses himself, accuses himself.

He who observed it, served it.

He who sniffed it, biffed it.

He who articulated it, particulated it.

He who sensed it, dispensed it.

He who said the rap, did the crap.

He who spoke it, broke it.

He who made a frown, laid the brown.

He who made the quip, let it rip.

He who made the call, gassed us all.

He who explained it, ordained it.

He who remarked on it, embarked on it.

He who said it, spread it.

He who sang the song, did the pong.

He who refuted it, tooted it.

He who reported it, exported it.

He who attributed it, distributed it.

He who sensed it, commenced it.

SEE ALSO: Eggcorns / Etymology Mysteries

¶ *Bated*. *Craw*. *Caboodle*. Anyone who isn't a logophile might struggle to define these words, but know they want the *whole caboodle*, that any disappointment *sticks in the craw* and will wait with *bated breath*. They just don't know why.

¶ Linguists call these *fossil words*, because each is a relic of language preserved in idiom. Many of these idioms are so familiar that we don't give them a second thought, but their meaning can be a mystery. We can be *at loggerheads* with someone without ever wondering what a loggerhead is.

¶ More curious still is how fossil words are confined to their set idiomatic forms. The only *riddance* is *good riddance*; the only thing to be *wreaked* is *havoc*; and the only state of *fettle* is *fine* (although in the past one's fettle might be good, bad or splendid). Similarly, fossils like *kith*, *beck*, *knell* and *ado* are incomplete without their partner words, like a *thither* without its *hither*, or a *fro* without its *to*.

¶ Some fossil words are old but their origins are straightforward. *Yore* – as in, *days of* – is an Old English word meaning 'of old'. And the *petard* you're hoisted by is a French word for an explosive charge used to demolish obstacles. (Incidentally, 'petard' is from French *péter*, meaning 'to fart'.)

¶ Other words are more of a riddle. *Shabang* has at least five different meanings dating from 1862, including a rough tavern, a soldier's shelter, a basic dwelling, a hired motor vehicle and a military encampment. Which of those you'd want the whole shabang of is anyone's guess.

FIG.1 *Correct use of a petard*

¶ The *loggerhead* mentioned above could be a thick-headed person, a large iron tool used to melt tar, the chunky wooden butt at the stern of a whale-boat or a heavy-headed turtle. Etymologists have made the case for each – except the turtle – so take your pick.

¶ To complicate matters, some imported words fossilised on contact with English. *Spick and span* combines Old Norse *spann-nyr* (a freshly chopped block of wood) with *spik*, from Dutch *spiksplinternieuw*, meaning a newly built ship. The original seventeenth-century expression was *spick and span new*, reduced to *spick and span* by the eighteenth century. But neither 'spick' nor 'span' ever had a life beyond their double act (although the Old Norse *-nyr* was the origin of the English *new*).

¶ Fossilised words pass unnoticed through language because people don't stop to notice them. But when they do, it's *mind boggling*.

AMOK
run amok

A sixteenth-century import from Indonesia meaning a person in a murderous frenzy.

BATED
bated breath

Subdued or restrained. First documented in Shakespeare's *The Merchant of Venice*.

CABOODLE
the whole caboodle

American nineteenth-century shortening of **kit and boodle**, where boodle was an old slang term for a large sum of money. Incidentally, this makes the alternative phrase **the whole kit and caboodle** tautologous.

CRAW
stick in your craw

A sixteenth-century word for a stomach, either animal or human. (To 'cast your craw' was slang for vomiting.)

DESERTS
just deserts

A thirteenth-century word for that which one deserves.

DINT
by dint of

Originating in Old English, a **dint** was a blow or strike, likely from a weapon. It's where the word 'dent' comes from.

DUDGEON
high dudgeon

A sixteenth-century word meaning indignation or resentment.

FETTLE
in fine fettle

A fifteenth-century word originally meaning to get ready for battle, and later to busy or prepare oneself generally. As Anne Brontë wrote in *Agnes Grey* (1847): 'I'd no heart to sweeping an' fettling, an' washing pots'.

FLOTSAM, JETSAM
flotsam and jetsam

Flotsam: the wreckage of a ship, or remains of its cargo, floating on the water; **Jetsam**: from maritime law, materials thrown from a ship that wash up on shore.

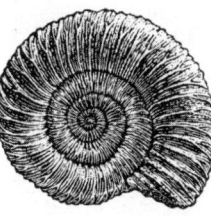

HUE
hue and cry

A fourteenth-century word (from French **hu**) meaning the shouting and noise made by a warring army or pursuing mob.

KITH
kith and kin

An endearing Old English word for one's friends and familiars, as opposed to one's **kin**, or relatives.

LAM
on the lam

Nineteenth-century word for escape or flight.

PALE
beyond the pale

A fourteenth-century word for a wooden fencing stake used to enclose an area. To be 'beyond the pale' was to be outside this space.

SHORT SHRIFT
to give short shrift

The brief moment before execution when a criminal was able to make their confession. (**Shrift** was Old English for the penance following confession.)

ROUGHSHOD
ride roughshod

The seventeenth-century equivalent of snow tyres for horses, in which nails stick out of the horseshoes for grip in slippery conditions. (Incidentally, someone **slipshod** was wearing slippers or loose, falling-apart shoes.)

UMBRAGE
take umbrage

This sixteenth-century word means annoyance or irritation, but comes from a much older French word for **shade** or **shadow**.

¶ **Fuck**'s journey to foul-mouthed prominence began in the sixteenth century. Despite widely repeated claims, it isn't an acronym of **Fornication Under Consent of the King**, nor is it Anglo-Saxon. Instead, the word is likely Germanic, perhaps from German **fochen**, Dutch **fokken** or Swedish **fokka**. Which of these reached the British Isles first isn't known, but a cheeky verse from around 1500 includes the enciphered line *fuccant uuiuys of heli* ('they fuck the wives of Ely'), and is the earliest citation in the *OED*.

¶ From the beginning, **fuck** was taboo. It was rarely seen in print, and when it was, it was in unsavoury circumstances. Shakespeare hints at it with puns and wordplay, and it's found in the letters of Scotland's national poet, Robbie Burns; but even in Francis Grose's *Classical Dictionary of the Vulgar Tongue* (1785), itself a salty work, the word is coyly reduced to **F–k**.

¶ For much of its existence, **fuck** was absent from general dictionaries. The Italian-English dictionary *A World of Wordes* (1598) was the first lexicon to include it, but Samuel Johnson omitted it in 1755, as did Noah Webster in 1806. And while it made the first two editions of the *New and Complete Dictionary* (1755 and 1795), this was the last general dictionary to include the word until 1965.

¶ Since **fuck** was chiefly spoken, it's difficult to track during the nineteenth century. It's found in slang dictionaries, sometimes in court transcripts and frequently in Victorian erotic literature; but between Britain's *Obscene Publications Act* (1857) and America's *Comstock Act* (1873), **fuck** was rarely seen in print.

¶ Everything changed in the twentieth century with a series of firsts that eroded the word's taboo.

> **1922:** *first seen in print in a book (James Joyce's* Ulysses*).*
> **1938:** *first heard in a song (cover of Louis Armstrong's* Ol' Man Moses*);*
> **1956:** *first heard on British TV (Brendan Behan on* Panorama*);*
> **1965:** *first entry in a modern dictionary (*The Penguin Dictionary*);*
> **1967:** *first scripted use in a film (Michael Winner's* I'll Never Forget What's'isname*);*
> **1970:** *first printed (deliberately) in a British newspaper (the* Guardian*).*
> **1981:** *first heard on US TV (*Saturday Night Live*);*
> **1984:** *first appeared in* Newsweek*.*

¶ Each breakthrough saw the word proliferate new uses. By 2010, it had replaced **bloody** as the most commonly spoken swear word in British English. Having only added the word in 1989, the *OED* now has 35 derivations and usages of **fuck**, while *Green's Dictionary of Slang* has 89 entries that include it. Dwarfing both is the online *Urban Dictionary* which has a spectacular 7,734 words and expressions starting **fuck**. (I counted them.)

Etymologists continue to wonder how the people named **Fukkebotere** (c. 1290), **Fuckbeggar** (1287), **Ric Wyndfuck** (1287) and **Fuckebythenavele** (1310) might relate to **fuck**. (**John le Fucker** is mentioned in many histories of the word, but there's no evidence he ever existed.)

The *OED*'s answer is that they probably relate to an earlier sense of **fuck**, meaning 'to strike or beat'. Except **Fuckebythenavele**, who might have done just that.

¶ Ironically, the disapproval that forced *fuck* into the shadows also fuelled its unstoppable rise. It needed that punch to get where it is today.

¶ But *fuck* offers more than shock value. Its grammatical flexibility (as noun, verb, adjective, adverb, interjection and so on) and explosively satisfying mouthfeel, have created what Professor of English Language Magnus Ljung called 'a success story of almost unlikely proportions'. Comedian Lewis Black was more definitive when he declared it English's 'best word ever'.

¶ Today, *fuck* no longer generates hysteria. When the Sex Pistols called Bill Grundy 'a fucking rotter' live on TV in 1976, it was front page news and Grundy's career was over. These days it wouldn't raise an eyebrow.

¶ The word still has power, but its use has changed. As the *Urban Dictionary* demonstrates, it has become the carbon atom of profane language, effortlessly bonding with other words to create new compounds. Now, as *The Thick of It*'s Malcolm Tucker would say, 'Come the fuck in or fuck the fuck off.'

THE MANY FACES OF FUCK

INTENSIFIERS
Abso-fucking-lutely
Fan-fucking-tastic
Un-fucking-believable

PREPOSITIONS
Fuck off
Fuck up
Fuck in
Fuck away
Fuck around
Fuck with

FORMATIONS
Fugly
Fuckola
Fuckster
Futhermucker
F-bomb

SURPRISE
Holy fuck
Fuck a duck

What the fuck
Fuck me sideways
Fuck a doodle do

PLEASURE
Fucking-A
Fucking good
Fuck yes
Fuuuuuuck

DISASTER
Clusterfuck
Fuckup
Goatfuck
Jumble-fuck

DISMISSAL
Fuck you very much
Fuck this shit
Don't give a
[flying] fuck

INSULT
Fucknut

Fuckknuckle
Fuckwit
Fuckstick
Fuckhead
Fuckwad

CONFUSION
Headfuck
Mindfuck
Fuckery
Bugfuck
Fuck knows
Totally fucked

TROUBLEMAKING
Rat fuck
Fuck over
Fuckelry

ACRONYMS
AMF – adios
motherfucker
BFD – big fucking deal

FUBB – fucked up
beyond belief

QUANTITY
Fuck all
Fuckload
Fuck full

PLACES
West Bumblefuck
Bumfuckistan
Bubblefuck

DISMAY
For fuck's sake
What the fuck
Fuck

CONCEPTUAL
Fuck it forward
Fuck shui
Fuckuppable

> It's further testimony to the power of the **F-word** that so many ways have been conjured to *avoid* saying *fuck*, including: **eff, fark, feck, ferk, fiddle, flaming, flip, fooey, fook, fork, freak, frick, fruiting, fuddle duddle, fudge, fug, get to Falkirk, kark, motherfather** and **shut the front door**.

79

¶ Comedians instinctively know how certain words are funny. Willie Clark, the ageing performer in Neil Simon's *The Sunshine Boys*, said it was words with a *'k'* sound: ***Alka Seltzer***, ***chicken***, ***cupcake***, ***cookie***, ***cucumber***, ***car keys*** and ***Cleveland***; all funny. But not ***Maryland***, ***tomatoes*** or ***roast beef***. ***Casey Stengel***; funny. ***Robert Taylor***; not.

¶ Linguists agree that 'k' is a common sound in many humorous words, but it isn't the most common. Psychologists Chris Westbury and Geoff Hollis investigated 'predictors of single-word humour' for their paper 'What Makes Some Words Funny?' (2019), and found a number of other phonological indicators as important, or more, than 'k'. These included:

-oo	*booby, buffoon, goulash*
-le	*jiggle, gobble, nibble*
-y	*fuzzy, nosy, snoozy*
rare sounds	*zither, gargle, schnorrer*
reduplicative	*flim-flam, nik-nak*
double letters	*chatter, bugger, slobber*

¶ Words that combine multiple indicators, like ***canoodle*** or ***skedaddle***, can be doubly effective.

¶ What this doesn't explain, however, is why ***book***, ***clue*** and ***triple*** aren't funny, but ***schnook***, ***moo*** and ***nipple*** are. To understand this, one must look at the unfunny topic of humour analysis, where philosophers since Aristotle have mirthlessly pondered why humans laugh.

¶ For German philosophers Schopenhauer and Kant, humour could be explained by ***incongruity***; a mismatch between expectations and reality. It doesn't sound funny, but this is where absurdity, surprise and uncertain outcomes come into their own.

For Freud, the father of psychoanalysis, humour was a ***release for excessive arousal*** (no surprise there). And in ancient Greece, Plato and Aristotle thought it was about ***superiority***, whereby humour can even have notes of aggression. There are more theories out there, but these are among the most influential.

¶ No theory accounts for all humour, but aspects of each can explain the types of words we laugh at. In Westbury and Hollis's study, most funny words fell into one of five categories: insult words (***doofus***); animal words (***gnu***); body-related words (***pubes***); and good-time words, encompassing food (***gobble***), humour (***chuckle***) and music (***boogie***). Add to these a category for unexpected, unfamiliar or nonsense words (***nurk***), and the various theories of humour are well represented.

¶ The comedy sweet spot is then found when humorous sounds meet humorous semantic categories, as here:

> ***pimple*** *('-le' + body word)*
> ***douche*** *('oo' + insult)*
> ***pickle*** *('k' + 'le' + food)*
> ***poodle*** *('oo' + 'le' + animal)*
> ***fizzy*** *('-y' + drink)*

¶ If this is starting to sound formulaic, that's not entirely an accident. As with other areas of language, AI developers are interested in how authentic human communication can be replicated – and there's nothing more human than humour. A 2019 research paper entitled 'Humour in Word Embeddings' concluded, 'many aspects of humour… may in fact be easier than expected to capture using machine learning', with possible applications in chatbots and AI humour generation. And it won't be a joke when that happens.

SEE ALSO: *Comic Book Sound Effects / Euphonic Words / IKEA Product Naming*

100 FUNNY WORDS

Absquatulate	Crumbly	Guppy	Poppycock
Antics	Darn	Heck	Prank
Backside	Diddle	Honky	Pubes
Bamboozle	Dingle	Hooter	Rascal
Belch	Doodle	Huckster	Romp
Biff	Drivel	Jackanape	Scarry
Blockhead	Ducky	Jackass	Schmuck
Blurt	Fart	Jerk	Schmutz
Booby	Flappy	Jiggle	Scrotum
Bozo	Floozy	Kerfuffle	Shenanigans
Brouhaha	Fluke	Kisser	Skulk
Bucko	Flummox	Knickers	Skunk
Bumfuzzle	Fondue	Kumquat	Smirk
Bunghole	Foolery	Larks	Snicker
Burp	Fornicate	Lollygag	Squiffy
Cattywampus	Frolic	Lummox	Stink
Cavort	Fuckery	Malarkey	Titter
Chitchat	Gabby	Muzzy	Truckle
Chortle	Gazump	Nincompoop	Turdiform
Chuckle	Giggles	Ninny	Unglue
Chump	Goof	Oink	Upchuck
Collywobble	Goombah	Pecker	Waddle
Conniption	Grizzle	Pizzle	Weasel
Cowlicks	Guffaw	Pooch	Whoopee
Crikey	Gullet	Poop	Yack

FIG.1 *Booby*

FIG.2 *Dickcissel*

FIG.3 *Fluffy-backed tit-babbler*

G.

GENDER

¶ In the sensitive debate around gender, one thing everyone can agree on is that language matters. And yet much of the language around gender identity is so recent that many terms are yet to appear in the *OED*.

¶ Before the twentieth century, there were few English words to describe someone who was gender nonconforming, and what words existed were largely derogatory. The oldest English word for someone possessing both masculine and feminine qualities is **androgyne**, which derives from Ancient Greek androgynos (andros meaning man, and gyne, woman). Other historical words – such as **epicene** and **ambosexous** (1600s), and **morphodite** (1700s) – either meant having attributes of both sexes, or of the opposite sex. Similar to historical language around homosexuality, such words were used as insults, and often conflated cross-dressing, effete behaviour and homosexuality, as with terms like **he-she** (1700s) and **invert** (1900s).

¶ A new language around gender expression started to crystallise early in the twentieth century. The German sexologist Dr Magnus Hirschfeld – later dubbed 'The Einstein of Sex' – coined the word *Transvestit* in 1910, from the Latin trans- ('across' or 'on the other side') and vestire ('to clothe'). Hirschfeld, whose Institute of Sexual Research was an early target of Nazi book-burning in the 1930s, also coined *seelischer Transsexualismus* ('psychic transsexualism') in 1923, from which English derived *transsexual* in the 1950s.

¶ *Intersex* was another early coinage, appearing in Xavier Mayne's 1908 book *The Intersexes*. The book itself was about homosexuality, but Mayne – the pen-name of Edward Prime-Stevenson – touched on issues of gender in his description of two 'intersexes' – **Uranian** ('outwardly and inwardly masculine yet not fully a man') and **Uraniad** ('leaning toward the typic feminine yet not fully woman'). Today, intersex has a narrower biological sense, but Mayne's definitions would fit neatly among contemporary gender labels like *demi-guy* or *demi-girl*.

¶ Many words that would come to shape discussions around gender started to appear from the 1970s. The list below of *OED* 'first citations' tells its own linguistic story of how the transgender movement, and the response to it, has evolved over the last four decades.

1956 Transexual	1988 Gender critical
1964 Gender identity	1993 Transphobia
1973 Gender dysphoria	1994 Cisgender
1974 Transgender	1995 Non-binary
1984 Transition	1996 Trans man
1987 Gender-fluid	2008 TERF

¶ Two words in particular have found themselves at the forefront of the debate around gender: *TERF* and *cisgender*.

¶ *TERF*, an abbreviation of Trans-Exclusionary Radical Feminist, describes feminists who don't acknowledge transgender women as women and oppose transgender inclusivity within the women's movement. Viv Smythe, the feminist blogger who coined it in 2008, has said the term was only descriptive, but many who are labelled TERFs have come to regard it as derogatory and dismissive, preferring *gender critical* instead.

¶ *Cisgender*, meaning a gender identity corresponding with one's birth sex, is another polarising word. Coined in 1994 by Dana Defosse, then a research student investigating the health of trans teens. Defosse was looking for a descriptor for non-transgender

SEE ALSO: *Polari*

people that didn't convey the privilege of 'normalcy'. Seeing the Latin prefixes trans- and cis- used in chemistry to describe the arrangement of atoms in molecules, Defosse proposed cisgender as the opposite to transgender. Ironically, while cisgender was created to avoid offense, some people find it offensive to be called *cis*, reflecting what a minefield the language around gender has become.

¶ Early transgender campaigners understood the importance of language, particularly in challenging traditional binaries of sex – i.e. male and female – and sexuality - i.e. straight or gay. This has led to an explosion of new language that is almost without precedent among social justice movements.

¶ One of the most visible aspects of this is gender identity labels, like *agender*, *trans man*, *non-binary* and more. Journalists have written extensively about the 72 genders once offered by Facebook, or the 3000-plus found on websites like genderfandom.com. But many within the trans community see the preoccupation with listing gender labels as a sideshow intended to ridicule. More important is the growing area of *trans linguistics*, the goal of which, according to Lal Zimman, the linguist who coined the term, is 'to find ways to implement linguists' expertise in the empowerment of trans people.'

¶ At the start of the twentieth century, the language didn't exist in English to even describe the transgender experience; it is therefore remarkable how, in less than a century, language has become the battleground on which our understanding of sex and gender is being determined.

THEY / THEM

They, the pronoun of many who identify as non-binary, has twice been Word of the Year; in 2015, chosen by the American Dialect Society, and four years later, by Merriam-Webster.

'They' isn't the only gender-neutral pronoun – *xe* (and its variant, *ze*) was first proposed in 1864, and *hir* in 1920 – but 'they' has the longest history, having been used as a non-gendered singular pronoun since the fourteenth century, where it can be seen in the medieval verse *William and the Werewolf*.

While examples of singular 'they' can be found in Shakespeare, Wordsworth, Chaucer and others, it fell out of fashion as nineteenth-century grammarians prescribed against it, instead teaching that male pronouns be used when someone's gender wasn't known. But as non-binary people adopted 'they' as a pronoun, its broader usefulness has also been rediscovered.

While 'they / them' are the predominant non-binary pronouns, these are joined by an abundance of *neopronouns* – like *ne/nem*, *fae/faer* and *ve/vir*. Like some of the niche gender labels, however, such neopronouns are often of more interest to journalists than they are to many within the trans community, for whom 'they / them' will suffice.

¶ Generations only started to be named in the twentieth century, and only in earnest as **Baby Boomers** began to grow up. The three earlier generations had names, but Boomers were plastered with labels in a way that was different. When the novelist Gertrude Stein called those who fought in World War I the *Lost Generation*, it was a throwaway comment recorded by Ernest Hemingway; in contrast, *Generation Beta* was named intentionally, before its first member was even conceived.

¶ Karl Mannheim's 1928 essay *Das Problem der Generationen* ('The Problem with Generations') introduced the concept of **generational theory**, although Mannheim wasn't interested in what they were called. Later, the birth of youth culture in the 1950s piqued the interest of businesses and ad men who saw young people as a profitable new market. The term **Baby Boomer**, for the first major generational market, was coined in 1963 as the generation started to hit college age, and new sobriquets appeared as the sixties rolled on (see opposite).

¶ The preoccupation with naming generations owes much to William Strauss and Neil Howe, whose 1991 book *Generations: The History of America's Future* named every American generation, starting with the **Puritan Generation** (1584–1614). Strauss and Howe coined **Millennials** for Generation Y, but failed to get **13th Generation** to replace **Generation X**, which had been adopted by Douglas Coupland in 1987. However, the term Generation X is in fact older than Baby Boomer, first appearing in 1952 as another name for the **Silent Generation**.

84

SEE ALSO: *Gender*

LOST GENERATION
1883–1900

GREATEST GENERATION
1901–27
ALSO: G.I. Generation.

SILENT GENERATION
1928–45
ALSO: Traditionalists; Left Out Generation; Generation X.

BABY BOOMERS
1946–64
ALSO: Love Generation; Me Generation; Now Generation; Pepsi Generation; Rock Generation; Protest Generation; Spock Babies; Sputnik Generation; Vietnam Generation; War Babies.

GENERATION X
1965–80
ALSO: MTV Generation; Middle Child Generation; Forgotten Generation; Slacker Generation; Latchkey Generation; Post-Boomers; Baby Busters; New Lost Generation; Thirteenth Generation.

GENERATION Y
1981–96
ALSO: Millennials; Net Generation; Echo Boomers; Generation Me; Generation Next; Snowflake Generation; Burnout Generation; Generation 9/11.

GENERATION Z
1997–2012
ALSO: Gen Tech; post-Millennials; Zoomers; iGeneration; Gen Y-Fi; Meme Generation; Homeland Generation.

GENERATION ALPHA
2013–25
ALSO: Mini Millennials.

GENERATION BETA
2025–39

¶ Always looking ahead, futurologists were quick to pencil in **Generations Gamma** and **Delta**, the children of generations yet to come. The time it takes to move to a new generation is also speeding up. Where the **Greatest Generation** spanned twenty-six years, **Generation Alpha** is scheduled for a mere twelve. But even this is too long for some. The bookends of the Millennial generation are separated by fifteen years; while the oldest could join the US army after 9/11, the youngest was still watching Sesame Street.

¶ To address this anomaly, a new category of **micro-generations** was created. **Xennials** were the first. The word appeared in 2010 to describe the crossover of Gen X and Millennial (in other words, late 1970s–early 1980s). Then came **Zillennials** – also called **Zennials** and **GenZennials** – for the overlap between late-stage Millennials and freshly minted Gen Zs. And now there are **Zalphas**. Not to be left out, some late-stage Baby Boomers prefer to be identified as **Generation Jones**, a word coined in 2009 by social commentator and marketing consultant Jonathan Pontell.

¶ And so it continues. There will be more generations, more micro-generations, and at some point, maybe nano-generations. Regardless of whether these labels are of any use, there will always be journalists, pundits and marketeers ready to invent them.

SNOWFLAKE vs. OK, BOOMER

Generational tension is one of the defining qualities of the dynamic between Young and Old, particularly since the 1960s. Today, this tension is expressed through a war of memes, the most heated being between the cries of *snowflake* and *OK, Boomer!*

Snowflake, the pejorative for Millennials, comes from Chuck Palahniuk's book Fight Club (1996), where he wrote, 'You are not a beautiful and unique snowflake.' **Special snowflake** then appeared in the Urban Dictionary in 2008, defined as, 'A member of that newly-adult, me'er-than-me generation which expects attention and praise just for being themselves – doing anything to deserve it is completely optional.'

'Snowflake' became the put-down wielded against Millennials – often by members of the political right – who are accused of being so fragile that they must be protected with safe-spaces and trigger warnings. The Taiwanese have a similar expression, **strawberry generation**, for those who bruise easily.

'OK, Boomer!' was the Millennial's long overdue comeback to 'snowflake' – but even though it first appeared on Reddit in 2009, it only took off in 2019, where it inspired memes, music videos and plenty of hashtags.

In its narrowest sense, 'OK, Boomer!' is akin to calling someone Grandad, as they struggle to keep up with the modern world. But Gen Zs use it more pointedly as a put-down of the generation they regard not only as entitled and out of touch, but responsible for many of the world's problems.

When MEP Chlöe Swarbrick was heckled during a speech in New Zealand's parliament, her 'OK, Boomer!' retort became famous. It was funny, but it also reflected a sense of frustration. When she wrote about the incident in the *Guardian* newspaper, she called it 'symbolic of the collective exhaustion of multiple generations set to inherit ever-amplifying problems in an ever-diminishing window of time.' And if you don't understand that, well, *OK, Boomer!*

¶ On July 18, 2023 – a Tuesday – American fast food chain Taco John's, noted for its signature Potato Olés, made an historic announcement. Facing a costly legal battle with burrito behemoth Taco Bell, Taco John's ceded its claim to the *Taco Tuesday* trademark, which it had owned since 1989.

¶ Petitioning for the cancellation of the trademark, Taco Bell's lawyers argued that Taco John's had failed to protect the mark and allowed it to become generic. 'Taco Tuesday', they said, was now a ubiquitous term that belonged to everyone, and it was un-American, 'uncool' even, to stop people from pursuing their God-given Taco Tuesday rights.

¶ Taco John's put up a stout defence, arguing that Taco Bell's only priority was to sell more tacos themselves, but it was all for nought. Their Taco Tuesday trademark was lost, a victim of what IP lawyers call *genericide*: the death of a trademark because it has become a generic term.

¶ The Taco John's story has become a cautionary tale among brand managers. The greatest achievement for a brand is to become the category leader everybody knows; but if people forget the name is a brand and it enters language as a generic description, the trademark can be cancelled. *Escalator* (once owned by Otis Elevators); *dumpster* (formerly the property of Dempster Brothers); *trampoline* (trademarked by Griswold-Nissen Trampoline & Tumbling Company); *aspirin* (registered by Bayer in 1899); and now *Taco Tuesday*, are trademarks no more.

¶ While it's fascinating to discover a word that's taken for granted was once – or maybe still is – a trademarked name, it's a big issue for the businesses themselves. Brands like *Jacuzzi®*, *Stetson®*, *Winnebago®*, *Kleenex®*, *Sellotape®*, *Google®*, *Hoover®*, *Band-Aid®*, *Tupperware®*, *Xerox®* (and many more) protect their names both actively and defensively, and make good use of letter-writing lawyers.

¶ Guidance for the Jacuzzi® trademark, for instance, prohibits use of Jacuzzi® as a verb ('Jacuzzi® your troubles away') or in the possessive form ('Jacuzzi®'s spiral action directional jets'). Jacuzzi®, it makes clear, is an adjective that must be used alongside a product name. And on it goes.

¶ Some businesses try public education. A 2003 advertising campaign for Xerox told people, 'When you use "xerox" the way you use "aspirin", we get a headache'. Whether the public listens or cares is another matter, but such are the measures companies take to defend their brands.

¶ Trademarks are a legal mechanism that turns language into property. As such, dictionaries can also find themselves on the front line of the trademark war, as businesses try to manage dictionary entries too. But as any lexicographer will tell you, dictionaries don't make the rules, they just reflect how language is used. And while it is the ultimate compliment for a brand to enter the dictionary, it can take them one step closer to the generic use that can see their trademarks expire.

86

SEE ALSO: *-Cide / IKEA Product Naming*

Ⓡ Ⓡ Ⓡ Ⓡ Ⓡ Ⓡ Ⓡ Ⓡ Ⓡ

DIRECTORY OF UNEXPECTED TRADEMARKS

FOOD

AIRFRYER
Although Philips's US trademark was cancelled in 2022, it is still registered in the UK and EU as a single word, despite 'air fryer' being a generic description.

CHEESEBURGER
Louis Ballast of the Humpty Dumpty Drive-in is reported to have registered a trademark for 'cheeseburger' in 1935. There is no evidence that the trademark was ever defended.

GRANOLA
A registered trademark of United Biscuits in the UK from 1885 to 2007. Granola is still a registered trademark in Australia.

GRANARY BREAD
Owned by UK bakers Hovis since 1936.

POPSICLE
Registered trademark in the US since 1923. Now owned by Unilever subsidiary, Conopco.

TENDERSTEM BROCCOLI
(ALSO, BROCCOLINI)
Both refer to a hybrid vegetable developed by Japan's Sakata Seed Corporation. The first is owned (in the UK) by Sakata UK; the second (again, in the UK) by Mann Packing Co.

HEALTHCARE

HEROIN
A Bayer trademark from 1897–1919. Cancelled by the terms of the Treaty of Versailles.

ADRENALIN
Variant spelling of adrenaline, registered as a 'stimulating preparations for medicinal or surgical purposes' since 1906 by pharmaceutical company Parke, Davis & Co.

TOYS & GAMES

FRISBEE
Trademark held by Wham-O Holdings since 1959. Although 'frisbee' is used generically, rival products are often sold as *flying discs, sport discs* or *flying rings*.

PING-PONG
First registered in UK by Jaques & Son Ltd in 1901. Indian Industries has held the US trademark for Ping-Pong since 1950.

OUIJA BOARDS
The 'talking board' used in seances has been trademarked in the US since 1890, with the name currently owned by Hasbro.

USEFUL THINGS

ALLEN KEY
Although Allen has been a registered trademark since 1910, and remains so today, the hex-head Allen key has long been a generic product.

BUBBLE WRAP
Registered in the USA to the Sealed Air Corporation since 1968, although generic bubble wraps are widely available.

CASHPOINT
Cashpoint, British English for an ATM, has been a trademark of Lloyds Bank since 1986. Although the word has become generic, no other British bank uses it.

KITTY LITTER
Registered in the US by Lowe's Inc in 1961. Removed from the registry in 2000.

MEMORY STICK
Sony has held the trademark for Memory Stick, a compact data storage drive, since 1999, although generic memory sticks are widely sold.

REALTOR
A US trademark of the National Assocation of Realtors since 1950.

ZIP CODE
Registered by the US Postal Service in 1976; removed from the registry in 1997.

¶ God is a linguistic mystery. While Greek and Latin translations of the Bible used **theos** and **deus** respectively, no-one knows where 'god' came from, which is as it should be.

¶ What's known is that the word is Germanic, with related words – what linguists call **cognates** – in Old Icelandic, Old Saxon, Danish, Old Dutch etc. But beyond this, the waters muddy.

¶ *OED* suggests two possible origins, both derived from Sanskrit. One is from *yet*, referring to poured sacrifices (i.e. the recipient of such sacrifices); the other comes from **hūta**, meaning 'to invoke'. *OED* doesn't commit to either, saying the etymology is 'very uncertain'.

¶ Allah, God's name among Muslims, is similarly mysterious. It may be a name that doesn't derive from anything, a borrowing from either the Hebrew or Aramaic words for God (**Eloh** and **Alaha**), or from **al-ilah**, Arabic for 'the One God'. Although the last is considered most likely, it remains contested.

GOD'S NAMES

¶ The focus in this entry is on God's names within the three Abrahamic religions – Judaism, Christianity and Islam – because their histories are so intertwined.

¶ In Exodus, God told Moses His personal name on Mount Sinai: **Ehyeh-Asher-Ehyeh**. This translates as I Am Who I Am, or, I Will Be That Which I Will Be. But for Jews, this is just one of God's seven divine names.

¶ The name most frequently used in the Old Testament is **YHWH** (יהוה), also called the **tetragrammaton** (Greek for 'the word of four letters') or **Shem-ha-Meyuhad** (the Extraordinary Name). Although the English form is written as **Jehovah** or **Yahweh**, the correct pronunciation was only known by the Temple's priests. Even then, the last High Priest allowed to say the Name was Simeon the Righteous, who died before the Second Temple's destruction. Since the priests that followed him weren't worthy to say it, knowledge of how to pronounce the Name was lost and is not attempted by Jews.

¶ The other divine names in the Old Testament are: **Adonai**, **El**, **Elohim**, **Shaddai** and **Zeba'ot**. Scribes who write any of the divine names must not be interrupted once they have started forming the word. If a mistake is made it should be circled rather than crossed out, and the entire page put into a genizah, where worn-out religious scrolls are stored.

¶ Within the Cabala, the ancient tradition of Jewish Mysticism, God has the **Forty-two-lettered Name** – sometimes the **Forty-five-lettered Name** – and an additional 72 names, which come from the text of Exodus 14:19-21. These names, used in the right combination, are said to possess miraculous powers, including the ability to animate a golem, a creature of Jewish folklore formed from mud or clay.

¶ In the Qur'an, God has ninety-nine names, known as **Al Asma ul Husna**. **Allah** is His principal name, but he has ninety-eight others that reflect His divine qualities, like **al-Salam** (The Peace), **al-Latif** (The Subtly Kind), **al-Kabir** (The Great) and **al-Haqq**

(The Truth). It is said that whoever learns these names will enter Paradise.

¶ Within Shia Islam, there are 999 names for God, with Allah making it 1,000. But even this thousand might be an under-estimate. In some Islamic traditions, Allah has 3,000 names: 1,000 are known to Him and His angels; 1,000 are known to the Prophets; 300 each are in the Torah, the Gospel and the Psalms; 99 are in the Qur'an, and one is known only to Him.

¶ Unlike Judaism and Islam, Christianity appears more conservative with its divine nomenclature. The New Testament, prin-cipally written in Koine Greek, refers to **Kyrios** (Lord), **Pater** (Father), and **Theos** (God). Jehovah, derived from the Hebrew YHWH in the Middle Ages, first appears in the *Tyndale Bible* (Exodus 6:3) and is also commonly used. (Incidentally, it is from the abbreviation **Jah** that **Hallelujah** is formed.)

¶ Just how many names God has within the Church depends on who one asks. The website ChristianAnswers.net lists 967 names and titles, from **Abba** (Father) to **Zur** (Rock). Within the Doctrine of the Trinity, these might refer to the Father, the Son or the Holy Spirit.

¶ Where Christianity has excelled is in its many ways to *avoid* saying God's name. Because the Third Commandment prescribes against taking His name in vain, there are dozens of minced oaths to safeguard against this blasphemy. These in turn have numerous variations. Take **Dod**, for instance; this minced oath is listed in *Green's Dictionary of Slang* alongside dod-bimmed, dod-blamed, dod-blasted, dod-busted, dod-fetched, dod-gasted, dod-rotted and dod rabbit.

¶ Among the dozens of ways not to say God's name, are the following:

Ace face	Ding	Gor
Adad	Dod	Gorra
Agad	Dog	Gorry
Big Boss	Gad	Gosh
Bigood	Gar	Guinea
Bob	Gats	Gum
The Boss	Gee	Hannah
Cod	Gloria	Jove
Cor	Gob	Mero
Cow	Godfrey	Old Fellow
Cut	Gog	Ud
Dad	Golly	Your Man Upstairs
Davy	Gom	

FIG.1 *The first day of creation (der erste Schöpfungstag), Die Bibel in Bildern (1860)*

¶ Paul Simon famously promised '50 Ways to Leave Your Lover' in his song, but only made good on five. And frankly, 'don't need to be coy, Roy' was less a method and more of an encouragement.

¶ One humour writer, Michael Leonetti, attempted to plug this gap by sharing the missing forty-five, including 'flee to a cave, Dave' and 'use that canoe, Lou'. But since a number of Leonetti's suggestions didn't rhyme or scan, they can't be regarded as credible relationship advice.

¶ One thing Simon got right, however, was the importance of a good rhyming departure. Even if you're leaving on bad terms, a little versification can ease the pain. In fact, any kind of wordplay to herald your leaving will often be appreciated.

¶ Although the best-known rhyming goodbye, 'see you later, alligator', was first documented in the early 1950s, flappers were making their cutesy goodbyes decades earlier, with their classy 'so long, chum' or 'be seein' you in the funnies'.

¶ Here are forty ways to say goodbye, generously furnished with rhymes and puns. As Haile Selassie was wont to say, **Abyssinia**.

SEE ALSO: Alternatives to Hello / Bee's Knees

Adios, daddy-o.
Arrivederci, pasta churchy.
Bye bye, chicken thigh.
Chop chop, lollypop.
Fly high, butterfly.

Give a hug, ladybug.
Gotta flee, bumblebee.
Gotta go, daddy-o.
Gotta run, honey bun.
Gotta skat, alley cat.
Hasta la vista, little sista.
Hasta mañana, iguana.
Later, tater.
Laters, haters.
Let's go, gecko.
Make like a baby
and head out.
Make like a bad
cheque and bounce.
Make like a
banana and split.
Make like a hockey
player and get the
puck out of here.
Make like a tree and leave.
Make like Santa and
leave my presence.

Miss you, shih tzu.
Out the door, dinosaur.
Peace out, Brussels sprout.
Saloon!
Sayonara, carbonara.
See ya round, like
a doughnut.
See you later, alligator.
(RESPONSES:
Any time, bovine.
In a while, crocodile.
Okie dokie, artichokie.)
See you soon, macaroon.
So long, King Kong.
Stay fresh, cheese bags.
Stay sweet, parakeet.
Take care, polar bear.
Time to bail, blue whale.
Time to trot, ocelot.
Toodle-oo, kangaroo.
Toodles, poodles.

❡ Anyone who has ever heard Chaucer's *Canterbury Tales* being read out loud will know how challenging fourteenth-century English is to the modern ear. The language and grammar are confusing enough, but it's how words are pronounced that is most confounding.

❡ Even for Chaucer, understanding someone from the other end of the country could be difficult. With no concept of **Standard English**, pronunciation and spelling varied widely from region to region. But from around 1400, the sound of English started to change, and more familiar pronunciation began to emerge.

❡ In 1909, Danish linguist Otto Jespersen proposed the concept of the **Great Vowel Shift** to explain this change. In it he showed how long vowels underwent a systematic transformation between 1400 and 1600. Not only did this shape the English we speak today, but it left us with a hangover of inconsistent spelling rules that we can't seem to shake.

❡ When Chaucer was writing, long vowels were pronounced in a way that would sound closer to French, as described here:

WORD	PRONOUNCED
FINE	*feen*
MEAD	*made*
CLEAN	*clan*
MATE	*mart*
SO	*saw*
BOOT	*boat*
NOW	*new*

❡ Jesperson showed how, over two centuries, these long vowel sounds experienced a series of small shifts, as the tongue

became more elevated and the mouth closed. And as one vowel sound changed, so others would too, like a queue of people moving forward in the same line (linguists call this the **chain shift**). In this way, each new vowel sound would remain distinct.

❡ An example of one vowel-sound's journey can be seen below. (The pronunciation guide isn't ideal, but it's difficult without using the **International Phonetic Alphabet**.)

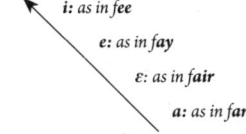

i: as in fee

e: as in fay

ɛ: as in fair

a: as in far

❡ Tracking these changes requires much detective work. Changes in spelling can provide a clue; 'blood', for instance, changed from **blod** (or **bleod**), to **blud** (or **bloud**). Linguists also look at the use of rhymes and puns in poetry and drama to infer how words were pronounced. Particularly helpful are descriptions from writers like Ben Jonson, whose *English Grammar* (1640) described how 'r' was pronounced 'with a trembling about the teeth'.

❡ While the Great Vowel Shift was accepted as fact for a long time, linguists now have their doubts, or at least think it's more complicated than Jespersen first suggested. That something major happened with the pronunciation of English from the 1400s is clear; but the notion of a great, tectonic 'vowel shift' is, while compelling, rather too neat. Maybe, for instance, there were a number of vowel shifts; maybe it went on until the eighteenth century; maybe, even, it is yet to end.

91

SEE ALSO: *Fossilised Words / Inkhorn Controversy*

H.

HACKER JARGON

¶ The first published collection of **computer lingo** was *The Hacker's Dictionary* (1983), which included slang, jargon and in-jokes shared by programmers and engineers in the nascent days of the computer industry.

¶ The dictionary originated at the Stanford AI Lab (SAIL) in 1975, where computer scientist Ralph Finkel saved a collection of humorous techie terms on a shared computer. The file made its way to MIT, where it was discovered by programmer Richard Stallman. It became known as *The Jargon-1 File* and was featured in *CoEvolution Quarterly* (1981). Two years later – and significantly larger – the first edition of *The Hacker's Dictionary* was published.

¶ *The Hacker's Dictionary*, and *The Jargon File* that preceded it, have since become part of computer geek lore. It was a go-to for journalists, and even cited in legal cases (see: SCO-vs-IBM, 2003). Entries like the **one banana problem** (so easy a trained chimp could solve it) and **waving a dead chicken** (a pointless effort required to convince others you've done all you can to help) remain in use. More importantly, the dictionary played an important role in documenting the growing lexicon of the programming community.

SEE ALSO : *Pager Code*

92

AUTOMAGICALLY (ADV.)

Something that appears to 'just happen', for reasons too complex, lengthy or boring to explain.

BAGBITER (N.)

Software or hardware prone to failing.

BIT BUCKET (N.)

Mythic destination for deleted files.

CRUFTY (ADJ.)

Badly made.

FLAME (V.)

To speak at length on a boring or ridiculous subject.

GRITCH (N.)

A complaint.

GUBBISH (N.)

A portmanteau of *garbage* and *rubbish*: 'That's gubbish.'

HANDWAVE (V.)

Brush aside a complex point by diverting listeners onto other matters.

MISFEATURE (N.)

Software feature that screws people over.

PESSIMAL (ADJ.)

Maximally bad.

RUDE (ADJ.)

Badly written, specifically in reference to code.

WALL (INTERJ.)

Shortened from 'hello wall'. Indicates confusion or bafflement; consequently, explanation required.

❡ A *questrist* is one who goes on quests. For centuries, the only questrist found outside a dictionary was in Shakespeare's *The Tempest*, making it a **hapax legomenon**: a word used only once. In fact, Shakespeare coined a number of these singularities. There was the **hodge-pudding** (made from a jumble of ingredients), the **under-fiend** (who lived below the earth), and the fear of evil known as **misdread**. All these words were literal one-offs.

❡ **Hapax legomenon** is Greek for something that has been said once. The term was first applied to a single use of a word in a specific text or body of work, and was most commonly used in relation to the Bible. When it refers to the entire corpus of written English, things get weird.

❡ Like a quantum particle, a *hapax* is affected by its detection. As soon as someone else uses the word, it ceases to be a hapax. The description is only therefore a temporary label. To be strictly accurate, Shakespeare's **hapax legomena** stopped being hapax as soon as scholars started writing about them. Such is the fleeting life of a hapax.

❡ Context and authorship also matter. In this book, **decrustulate**, a word invented five seconds ago, is not a hapax, because its author is not of historical significance. But had Shakespeare coined it, it would be.

❡ One person deemed of historical importance was the poet Anna Seward (d. 1809), the 'swan of Lichfield', whose prolific letter-writing produced a goldmine of hapax for the *OED*. Seward's correspondents must have wondered what the heck she was talking about, given she invented so many words, but lexicographers a century later

entered dozens of her unique creations as hapax in the *OED*'s first edition. These included: **dun** (dark and dusky); **dupism** (in the sense of **duped**); **floret** (a small flower); **illocal** (out of place); **numb-skullism**; **pancheon** (humorous use for paunch); **penphobia** (fear of writing); **squiress** (a female squire).

❡ It would be impossible for any one person to coin such a bounty of hapax today. It would have to be someone of note; and if it was, it would be noticeable, noteful and noted. At which point it would be a hapax no more.

❡ If one is looking for the modern equivalent of the hapax, it would be the **Googlewhack**: a Google search using two words entered without quotation marks that produces only one result. Like hapax, these disappear the moment they are shared with anyone else. While researching this topic, I had a Googlewhack for a search on the subject of hapax. And for a fleeting moment I felt as though the secrets of the universe had been revealed to me.

FIG.1 *A hapax legomenon imagined as a living creature by the author*

SEE ALSO: *Etymology Mysteries*

THE HASH MARK

'How do you feel about using # (pound) for groups. As in #barcamp [msg]?'

¶ This tweet, posted by user Chris Messina on 23 August 2007, marked the invention of the social-media hashtag. The symbol was already being used to tag pictures on photo-sharing sites, but this was the moment it entered Twitter, and from there, social media more broadly. Five years later, the American Dialect Society voted hashtag its Word of the Year. Ben Zimmer, chair of the Society's New Words Committee, said of it, 'This was the year when the hashtag became a ubiquitous phenomenon in online talk'.

¶ The origin of the hash symbol is something of a mystery. Even its first given name is hard to trace. The commonly told story is that it evolved from the abbreviation of the Latin *libra pondo* (a pound by weight), first written as *lb*, then connected with a line, as so: *℔*. But since the hash sign only appeared in the late-nineteenth century, this Roman origin story seems unnecessarily complicated. More plausible, but less exciting, is that it was a symbol that made itself useful to Victorian bookkeepers, who used it to denote number (e.g. #1) and pounds in weight (e.g. 1# of apples). It started appearing around the 1870s, where it pursued a career as a jobbing symbol, used by mathematicians, doctors, proofreaders, even chess players.

¶ Being generally helpful but not exactly essential proved to be the secret of its success. It was just useful enough to be included in the Remington Model Standard No. 2 typewriter in 1890, making it an accepted, if under-used key. Precisely because of this, however, it was one of two symbols chosen by the engineers at Bell Labs for the first Touch-Tone phones in the late 1960s. Not only did this guarantee immortality on telephone keypads, but it bestowed upon it a new name, the ***octothorpe***.

¶ But while the ***hash mark*** – or ***number sign***, ***pound sign***, ***tic-tac-toe***, or call-it-what-you-will – now had visibility, its purpose remained vague. Until Chris Messina's tweet. Two days later, the term ***hashtag*** was coined, and increasing numbers of users started including them in their posts. Even though Twitter itself didn't get behind hashtags until 2009, their usefulness was evident.

¶ So it was that from having no clear job, the hash mark now had the hottest job in the online world: to lubricate the wheels of social media. It was #trending, employed by users, campaigners and corporations to enable conversations, share interests, create communities, promote social issues and sell products. Today, no social movement can exist without its hashtag, from #MeToo to #MAGA.

¶ In a curious twist, and what must be the ultimate accolade for a typographic symbol, hashtags are now spoken as a form of metacommentary, as in 'Hashtag not my problem'. As author Philip Pullman wrote of the symbol, 'A hashtag is like a new form of punctuation'. After a short career as a typographical extra, the hash mark finally triumphed. #blessed

SEE ALSO: *Emoticons and Kaomoji / Ironic Punctuation*

ALGEBRAIC & MEDICAL SIGNS

FIG. 1   FIG. 2   FIG. 3

HERE'S JOHNNY...

¶ John has been one of the most common English names since the thirteenth century. But like Hoover or Xerox, this success led to genericisation, and as early as 1392, **John** (or **Johnny**) came to refer to the **ordinary man**.

¶ Today, **John** has more entries in the *OED* than **Tom**, **Dick** and **Harry** combined. He is both anonymous and ubiquitous; reliable at all times to be the very definition of the thing he's meant to be.

JOHN
A generic man; a toilet; a male servant; an Englishman; a jack in poker; a sex worker's 'client'.

JOHN-A-DREAMS
A day dreamer.

JOHN-A-NODS
Someone who can't stay awake.

JOHN BARLEYCORN
(ALSO: SIR JOHN BARLEYCORN)
Alcohol made from barley.

JOHN BLUNT
(ALSO: JOHN TROTT)
A dull, witless person.

JOHN BULL
The personification of the English nation.

JOHN CHEESE
A foolish, contemptible person.

JOHN CITIZEN
The ordinary man.

JOHN COLLINS
The bourbon equivalent of the Tom Collins cocktail.

JOHN CROW
A turkey vulture.

JOHN DOE
(ALSO: JOHN A NOKES, JOHN A STILES)
A hypothetical, anonymous or unknown person.

JOHN DRINGLE
A dullard.

JOHN DUNN
(ALSO: JOHN HOP, JOHN LAW, JOHNNY DARM)
A police officer.

JOHN HANCOCK
A signature.

JOHN HENRY
(OR THOMAS)
A penis.

JOHN-HOLD-MY-STAFF
A servile attendant.

JOHN INDIFFERENT
An uninterested person.

JOHN LONG
An unreliable messenger.

JOHNNY / JOHNNY BAG
A condom.

JOHNNY APPLESEED
Someone who introduces a new practice or idea to a group.

JOHNNY ARMSTRONG
Something which takes strength or hard work.

JOHNNY-COME-LATELY
(ALSO: JOHNNY NEWCOME)
A recent arrival.

JOHNNY FOREIGNER
Derogatory name for a foreigner.

JOHNNY-ON-THE-SPOT
A reliable person who's ready to act immediately.

JOHNNY RAW
An unsophisticated, untested person.

JOHN-OUT-OF-OFFICE
Someone unemployed.

JOHN Q.
The average person.

JOHN ROSCOE
A handgun.

95

☞ SEE ALSO: *Average Joe*

¶ Among dictionary aficionados, special affection is held for **Hobson-Jobson**, subtitled *A Glossary of Anglo-Indian Colloquial Words and Phrases*, published in 1886. So remarkable is the work that it is one of the few books to have an entry in the *OED*, not to mention over 100 citations.

¶ Most dictionaries hope to be complimented for being 'scholarly' and 'comprehensive'. *Hobson-Jobson* was both, and more. Reviews often called it 'idiosyncratic', 'eclectic', 'maverick' and 'entertaining' – words rarely associated with lexicography. But then this was a most unusual dictionary.

¶ During the nineteenth century, English was absorbing dozens of new words in the course of building its empire; words like *curry*, *toddy*, *pucka*, *typhoon*, *pagoda*, *chin-chin*, *chop chop*, *cutter*, *dinghy*, *loot*, *chintz* and more. *Hobson-Jobson* was interested in this intersection of different languages, but its scope was broader than its subtitle suggested. It included words from Arabic, Burmese, Afghan, Persian, Malay, Chinese and more. But India, or more accurately, British India, was the principal source, accounting for nearly 90 per cent of word senses.

¶ The dictionary was compiled by Arthur Coke Burnell, a former Indian civil servant and an expert in Sanskrit and South Indian languages, and Colonel Henry Yule, formerly of the Bengal Engineers and later vice-president of the Royal Geographical Society. It was fourteen years in the making, although Burnell died before the book's publication, and Yule died shortly after. The 1903 edition, edited by William Crooke – who had spent twenty-three years as an Indian civil servant before taking up the *Hobson-Jobson* mantle – contained 2,467 **headwords** and a further 1,272 **nested entries**, with over 11,500 **citations**.

¶ The unusual title was a stroke of marketing genius. The dictionary explained that 'Hobson-Jobson' was 'A native festal excitement' that had been anglicised by British soldiers from the cry 'Ya Hassan! Ya Hosain!', heard during the Shia festival of Muharram. The title exhibited the interplay of languages that was the focus of the dictionary. But this unusual and engaging title also reflected the informal tone of the dictionary itself, and this explains why *Hobson-Jobson* is still enjoyed today; not only is it an impressive work of scholarship, it's also wonderfully readable, with a discursive, anecdotal style.

¶ *Hobson-Jobson* wasn't the first glossary of Anglo-Indian terms, but unlike earlier efforts that were largely practical, it was more encyclopaedic. People, places, food, religion and culture featured alongside the stuff of colonial administration, like commerce, construction and transport.

¶ As a product of the British Empire, *Hobson-Jobson* is not without issues. There are notes of imperial arrogance, and some entries can feel patronising. Even the title, intriguing though it may be, is arguably problematic. But *Hobson-Jobson* continues to be enjoyed because it holds its own as a work of historical and literary value. It may have been born of the British Empire, but it isn't a candidate to be cancelled. It's far too good for that.

SEE ALSO: *Dictionaries of Interest*

(Edited for length, but quoted verbatim)

AVATAR, Sanskrit Avatdra, an incarnation on earth of a divine Being.

BANG, BHANG, Hindi bhāng, the dried leaves and small stalks of hemp (Cannabis indica), used to cause intoxication, either by smoking, or when eaten mixed up into a sweetmeat. Hashīsh of the Arabs is substantially the same.

BANGED, is also used as a participle, for 'stimulated by bang', e.g. 'banged up to the eyes'.

CASH, A name applied by Europeans to sundry coins of low value in various parts of the Indies. The word in its original form is of extreme antiquity, 'Sanskrit karsha… a weight of silver or gold equal to 1/400 of a Tula'.

CHEESE, This word is well known to be used in modern English slang for 'anything good, first-rate in quality, genuine, pleasant or advantageous'. And the most probable source of the term is Persian and Hindi chīz, 'thing'.

CHOW-CHOW, A common application of the pidgin-English term in China is to mixed preserves […] It is the name given to a book by Viscountess Falkland, whose husband was Governor of Bombay. There it seems to mean 'a medley of trifles'. Chow is, in pidgin, applied to food of any kind.

MUNTRA, mantra, a text of the Vedas; a magic formula.

LOOT, Plunder; Hindi lōt, and that from Sanskrit lotra, 'rob, plunder'.

GHEE, Boiled butter; the universal medium of cookery throughout India, supplying the place of oil in southern Europe, and more.

GHOUL, Arabic ghūl, Persian ghōl. A goblin, or man-devouring demon, especially haunting wildernesses.

PARIAH, The name of a low caste of Hindus in Southern India, constituting one of the most numerous castes, if not the most numerous, in the Tamil country. The word in its present shape means properly 'a drummer'. Tamil parai is the large drum, beaten at certain festivals, and the hereditary beaters of it are called paraiyan.

PUNDIT, Sanskrit pandita, 'a learned man'. Properly a man learned in Sanskrit lore. The Pundit of the Supreme Court was a Hindu law officer, whose duty it was to advise the English judges when needful on questions of Hindu law.

PYJAMMAS [sic], Hindi pāē-jāma, lit. 'leg-clothing'. A pair of loose drawers or trowsers, tied round the waist. Such a garment is used by various persons in India, e.g. by women of various classes, by Sikh men, and by most Mahommedans of both sexes.

SHAMPOO, To knead and press the muscles with the view of relieving fatigue, etc. The word has now long been familiarly used in England […] 'Taking thus their ease, they often call their Barbers, who tenderly gripe and smite their Armes and other parts of their bodies instead of exercise, to stirr the blood'.

THUG, Hindi thag, Sanskrit sthaga, 'a cheat, a swindler.' […] But it has acquired a specific meaning, which cannot be exhibited more precisely or tersely than by Wilson: 'Latterly applied to a robber and assassin of a peculiar class, who sallying forth in a gang … and in the character of wayfarers, either on business or pilgrimage, fall in with other travellers on the road, and having gained their confidence, take a favourable opportunity of strangling them by throwing their handkerchiefs round their necks, and then plundering them and burying their bodies'.

IKEA PRODUCT NAMING

❡ In 2008 a news story broke that the Swedish furniture giant IKEA had been insulting the Danes for years with their choice of product names. It was reported that two Danish researchers had found that while prestige products were named after Swedish towns, Danish towns were associated with inferior items, like doormats and draught excluders. Accusations of **cultural imperialism** appeared under headlines like *Danes' Fury At IKEA Over Product Names*.

❡ There was only one problem with the story: it wasn't true. No Danish researchers had investigated IKEA names, no conspiracy existed, and no Danes were angry about IKEA's product names.

❡ While the Danish doormat story was revealed to be something of a joke, it fed the public's enduring fascination with the language of IKEA. After all, its catalogue has introduced more people to Swedish than any work of Scandinavian literature, and at its peak in 2014, more IKEA catalogues were printed (217 million) than copies of the Bible.

❡ The origin of IKEA's product names goes back to the company's founder, Ingvar Kamprad, who was confused by product numbers and preferred to use names instead. Not only were they easier to remember, but they added emotional value. For people who know little about Sweden, IKEA names are just sounds; hard to read and funny to say. It doesn't matter if people mispronounce **Pjätteryd** or **Sjörapport**, because it's all part of the brand experience, like cheap meatballs and migraine-inducing store design.

❡ The first IKEA catalogue appeared in 1951. (There was a fifteen-page brochure that appeared in 1950, but that doesn't really count.) Back then, naming was a simpler matter because there were just fifty-two product names, most coming from first names or places. Today, with 12,000 products on sale and up to 3,000 new names required every year, product naming has become a mammoth endeavour.

❡ Until the 1980s, names were chosen by just three people, but it now requires a dedicated team to manage the process. Approved names are held in a database ruled by the **IKEA Naming Convention**, established in the late 1970s. What customers might think are random words actually follow a designated **taxonomy**, with specified themes for different product categories. These include:

BOOKSHELVES:
Swedish boys' names, and professions

TEXTILES:
Swedish girls' names

BATHROOM ITEMS:
Swedish bodies of water

KITCHEN:
Abstract nouns

KITCHEN FURNISHING:
Spices, fishes, mushrooms, fruits

CARPETS:
Danish place names

LIGHTING:
Musical terms, units of measurement, seasons, ships and navigation

TOYS:
Animals, birds, adjectives

OUTDOOR FURNITURE:
Scandinavian islands

BOXES, PICTURES, WALL DECORATIONS:
Swedish slang expressions and place names

DESKS AND CHAIRS:
Swedish place names

BEDDING:
Flowers and plants

SEE ALSO: Funny Words / Origins of Nonsense

¶ Additional guidelines cover name length (4–12 letters), appropriateness (no abusive language, registered trademarks or family names) and the use of retired product names (permissible, except for iconic products, like the Klippan sofa or Rebecka chair). And words that use the Swedish letters Å, Ö and Ä are particularly favoured for their Scandinavian aura.

¶ IKEA's naming taxonomy reveals there's method behind the widely perceived madness. But given the relentless stream of new products, the taxonomy has had to become more flexible. If a word sounds nice, has a positive meaning, and can't be trademarked, then it's fair game. Similarly for names that suggest some utility, like the *Variera* ('vary') shelving system, or the *Eneryda* ('everyday') drawer handles.

¶ Thirteen years after the Danish doormat farrago, the Swedish Tourist Board launched a tongue-in-cheek campaign to reclaim Swedish destinations from the IKEA catalogue. Standing on the shores of a serene lake in southern Sweden, the presenter hammers in a sign that reads, 'Welcome to Bolmen – More than an IKEA toilet brush'. IKEA has indeed introduced the world to Sweden, but only by requisitioning the names of its every town, island and lake in the service of its product catalogue. Perhaps the Danes got off lightly after all.

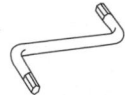

DIMPA
waste sorting bags
(v.) tumble, fall

EKORRE
child's rocking-moose
(n.) squirrel

FNISS
wastepaper basket
(v.) giggle

FÖRNUFT
cutlery
(v.) reason, sense

FRÄCK
bathroom mirror
(n.) cheeky, brazen

GLADSTAD
upholstered bed frame
(n.) happy city

IVRIG
glass tumbler
(adj.) eager

NORNA
chair pad
*Norse goddess of
fate and destiny*

PRUTA
plastic food containers
(v.) haggle, bargain

RABALDER
cable tidy tube
(n.) uproar

RIKTIG
metal curtain hooks
(adj.) correct

RUSIG
children's rocker
(adj.) drunken

RUTER
ironing board
*(n.) diamonds (the
suit in cards)*

SNÅLIS
storage boxes
(adj.) miserly

SYRLIG
round curtain rings
(adj.) ironic

VESSLA
plastic storage crate
(n.) weasel

¶ In 1966, the Catholic Church quietly retired the ***Index Librorum Prohibitorum,*** the list of forbidden books that had determined what Catholics could read for over four centuries.

¶ Supervised by the Sacred Congregation of the Index, the *Index of Forbidden Books* was updated 300 times since it was first ratified in 1546. The final *Index*, issued in 1948, named over 5,000 banned books, including works by some of the greatest thinkers of the Enlightenment.

¶ Up to the fifteenth century, the Catholic Church controlled most books in Europe, because most books in Europe were copied in monasteries. But the arrival of Gutenberg's printing press in 1440, combined with the heretical ideas of the Protestant Reformation, changed everything.

¶ Seeing how the 'wrong' books were threatening the authority of the Catholic Church, a succession of popes sought to prohibit any works they regarded as dangerous. To own, print or sell forbidden books could result in excommunication.

¶ The Church in Rome wasn't alone in attempting to control publishing, but the **Index Librorum Prohibitorum** – ratified by Pope Pius IV after the Council of Trent in 1564 – was a systematic approach to enforce censorship unlike anything seen before.

¶ As well as listing hundreds of unacceptable works, the *Index* codified ten rules governing the Church's approach to censorship. Heretical writings were 'absolutely prohibited', but so too were works that criticised the Catholic Church, that were deemed 'lascivious or obscene' or that dealt with sorcery or magic.

¶ The *Index* was updated every couple of years. Many books were added, but works could also be removed. In 1835, two centuries after his heliocentric beliefs saw him convicted of heresy, the *Index* finally allowed Catholics to read unedited versions of Galileo's work.

¶ Political forces increasingly influenced the decisions of the Sacred Congregation, which explains why many names revered in the history of Western philosophy (see below) were banned in their day. But there were some surprising omissions too, such as Hitler's *Mein Kampf* and Darwin's *Origin of Species*.

¶ Defenders of the *Index* argued that its intentions were noble: 'for the wellbeing of the public', as the preface to the 1940 *Index* put it. But the reality was that the *Index* was becoming harder to justify; worse still, it was seen as a growing embarassment in an age of modernity.

¶ Today, the *Index* is considered a historical document. Bishops may issue a warning – an ***admonitum*** – against corrupting works, but since Vatican II (1962–65), Catholics 'possess a lawful freedom of inquiry and thought'.

SEE ALSO: *God / Minced Oaths / Printers' Marks*

| *Authors banned by the* Index of Forbidden Books | Bacon • Balzac • De Beauvoir • Bentham • Comte • Copernicus • Montaigne • Defoe • Descartes • Dumas • Erasmus • Flaubert • Galileo • Gibbon • Hobbes • Hugo • Hume • Kant • Joyce • Keppler • Locke • Machiavelli • Mill • Milton • Montesquieu • Pascal • Rousseau • De Sade • Sartre • Spinoza • Swift • Voltaire • Zola |

INDEX
Librorū Prohibitor.
BENEDICTI XIV. P.O.M.
jussu editus

Multi eorum, qui fuerant curiosa
sectati, contulerunt Libros, et
combusserunt coram omnibus.
Act. Cap. XIX. V. 19.

FIG.1 *Engraved frontispiece,* Index Librorum Prohibitorum *(1758–63)*

'Many of the people who had been curious to follow brought
the books and burned them in front of everyone.'

¶ Up until the sixteenth century, few foreigners held the English language in high regard. Latin was the language of learning, while English was considered ill-stocked and inelegant.

¶ Over the course of the 1500s, English received an inrush of new words from Latin, Greek, French, Italian and more. The use of foreign imports, and the neologisms they fostered, lay at the heart of the ***inkhorn controversy***, a long-simmering row over what kind of language English should be.

¶ An ***inkhorn*** was a vessel for holding writing ink, often made of horn. But an ***inkhorn term*** (first recorded in the OED in 1543) was an overcomplicated word, often of foreign extraction. Language purists wanting to protect English's Germanic Saxon heritage resisted these linguistic interlopers, while the neologising ***inkhorns*** – not a term they would have used themselves – welcomed them.

¶ Men like Thomas Wilson (d. 1581) and Edmund Spenser (d. 1599) argued hotly against these 'straunge ynkehorne termes', fearful that people would, as Wilson wrote, 'forget altogether their mothers [sic] language.'

Our own tung should be written cleane and pure, unmixt and unmangled with borrowing of other tunges.

JOHN CHEKE, *LETTER TO THOMAS HOBY* (1557)

¶ Others, like philosopher and author Thomas Elyot (d. 1546) and the writer George Pettie (d. 1589) disagreed. Elyot argued that English had no option but to receive new words 'for the necessary augmentation of our language'. For Elyot, Pettie and many others, the ***inkhorn words*** that provoked such ire were needed to enrich English.

It is not unknowen to all men how many woordes we have fetcht from thence within these fewe yeeres, which if they should be all counted inkpot termes, I know not how we should speak any thing without blacking our mouthes with inke…

GEORGE PETTIE, PREFACE TO *THE CIUILE CONUERSATION OF M. STEEUEN GUAZZO* (1581)

¶ Some of the inkhorn terms were indeed a mouthful, like ***anacephalise*** (to recapitulate), ***deruncinate*** (to weed) and ***illecebrous*** (alluring). But many words condemned as inkhorns would go on to become standard English, including ***absurdity, alienate, assassinate, autograph, catastrophe, emphasis, exist, expensive, fact, halo, impersonal, monopoly, pathetic, skeleton, system*** and ***virus***.

¶ By the late-sixteenth century it was becoming clear that the language purists were losing the fight. As well as Latinate newcomers, neologisms were conjured by the addition of prefixes (***counterstroke, disrobe, uncomfortable***), suffixes (***changeful, drizzling, laughable***) or as compounds (***heaven-sent, laughing-stock***).

¶ By the seventeenth century, the inkhorn controversy was all but over. A new kind of English was taking shape, and it was replacing Latin as the language of learning. Purists have railed against foreign words and neologising ever since, but history has shown that it is a battle they're unlikely to win.

SEE ALSO: *The Great Vowel Shift / Word Rage*

102

¶ The ***interrobang*** is the punctuation mark that *almost* made it. Advertising executive Howard Spekter was the mark's inventor. He floated the idea in an editorial for graphic design journal *Type Talks* in 1962, arguing that the world needed a new punctuation mark:

'that combined "interrogation and exclamation". He said what‽ That's how much‽ It's how fast‽ That kind of thing'.

¶ Alongside initial designs, Spekter invited readers to share their thoughts about the look, name and use of such a mark. And the response was emphatic approval.

¶ Readers suggested names including ***exclamaquest***, ***exclarogative***, ***consternation mark*** and more, but Spektor but favoured his original proposal: the ***interrobang***, which combined the Latin for question – *interrogatio* – with the slang for exclamation mark: *bang*.

¶ The innovation was hailed by *Time* magazine and *The Wall Street Journal*. When it was included in the Americana typeface and on the keyboard of the Remington

FIG.1 *Interrobang and early designs by Jack Lipton of Martin K. Speckter Associates*

Rand Model 25 typewriter, it seemed to be breaking through.

¶ Sadly, however, the fortunes of the interrobang were stymied. It wasn't incorporated into typesetting machines, so wasn't used by publishers or printers; and, having the smack of advertising, it wasn't taken seriously among writers. By the early 1970s, the interrobang was on the wane.

¶ Today, the mark is left to be appreciated by graphic designers and typeface connoisseurs. Although it can be found in ***Unicode***, the international standard for encoding different scripts, the interrobang has joined the ranks of other punctuation marks that weren't to be.

103

SEE ALSO: *Ironic Punctuation*

INTONATION POINTS

In his 1966 work *Plumons l'oiseau: divertissement* (*Plucking the Bird: A Diversion*), French author Hervé Bazin suggested some improvements to the French language, including six ***intonation points*** that would convey via symbols what words alone would not.

Bazin's intonation points regularly appear in lists of unusual punctuation, but no-one, including Bazin himself, ever used them. Far from being a frivolity, however, they should be applauded for anticipating the need later fulfilled by ***emoticons*** and ***emojis***.

CONVICTION POINT	AUTHORITY POINT	ACCLAMATION POINT	IRONY POINT	DOUBT POINT	LOVE POINT

FIG.2 *Les points d'intonation* (intonation points)

¶ *Irony* isn't always obvious when it's printed on the page. With no vocal intonation or physical cues to pick up on, readers can overlook it. Some writers have sought to address this problem by proposing punctuation that indicates an irony in progress.

¶ The earliest such mark was Henry Denham's **percontation point**. Denham was a sixteenth-century printmaker who used a reverse question mark to indicate a rhetorical question, a sub-category of irony. Denham's innovation was rather clever, but like the **interrobang**, the challenge of getting printers to adopt it was too great, and the idea withered soon after his death.

¶ Following Denham, a variety of writers devised novel punctuation to indicate the presence not just of irony, but **sarcasm** and **snark**. As the modern keyboard bears witness, however, none made the cut.

¶ The problem with signposting irony is that the effort feels forced. Like explaining a joke, the irony is weakened when it is pointed out. There is also the added confusion of irony marks being used ironically, which then introduces an unhealthy level of meta-irony.

¶ The only successful mark – the winking emoticon – isn't really punctuation, and is limited to personal communications. Perhaps, however, this is the point. *People* need to flag when they're being ironic – or jokey, angry, sad and so on – but a *writer* doesn't. Or shouldn't. And certainly not with the help of a special mark.

SEE ALSO : *Interrobang*

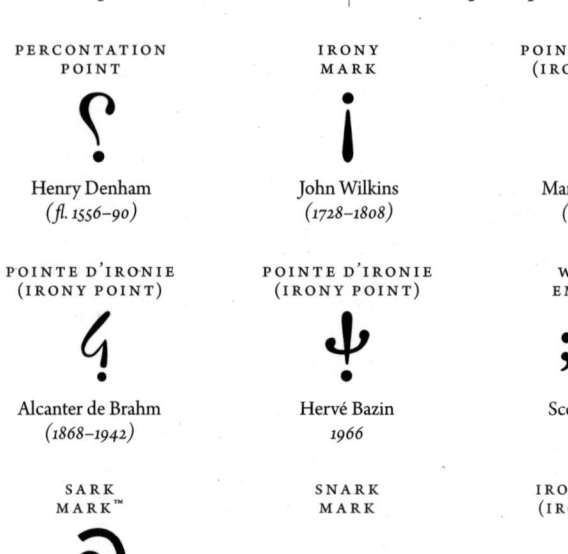

PERCONTATION POINT	IRONY MARK	POINTE D'IRONIE (IRONY POINT)
Henry Denham (*fl. 1556–90*)	John Wilkins (*1728–1808*)	Marcellin Jobard (*1792–1861*)
POINTE D'IRONIE (IRONY POINT)	POINTE D'IRONIE (IRONY POINT)	WINKING EMOTICON
Alcanter de Brahm (*1868–1942*)	Hervé Bazin *1966*	Scott Fahlman *1982*
SARK MARK™	SNARK MARK	IRONIETEKEN (IRONY SIGN)
Douglas Sak *2006*	Choz Cunningham *2006*	Underware *2007*

¶ Almost anything can become collectible; traffic cones, golf balls, even vomit bags all feature in the *Guinness Book of Records*. But not every collector has a word to describe their hobby. There's no special term for Pokémon card collectors, but there is if you collect share certificates, fruit stickers or transport tokens.

¶ The following list of *-ists* and *-philes* is a comprehensive collection of collectors. Many of these date from the eighteenth and nineteenth centuries, and thus reflect the interests of gentlemen and ladies with the requisite money and time. Today, everyone from schoolchildren up are collectors of something, even if the word doesn't always exist to describe it.

ARENOPHILE
sand sample collector

ARCTOPHILE
teddy bear collector

AURELIAN
insect collector

AUTOGRAPHIZER
autograph collector

BIBLIOPHILE
book collector

CARTOPHILIST
cigarette card collector

CHINAMANIAC
china collector

CONCHOLOGIST
shell collector

CRABOLOGIST
crab collector

CURIOSO
collector of curios

DELTIOLOGIST
postcard collector

DISCOPHILE
record colletor

EPHEMERIST
ephemera collector

EXONUMIST
token collector

FOSSILIST
fossil collector

FRUCTOPHILIST
fruit sticker collector

FUSILATELIST
telephone card collector

GALANTHOPHILE
snowdrop collector

HEMIPTERIST
insect collector

LABOLOGIST
beer label collector

LEPIDOPTERIST
butterfly collector

LOTOLOGIST
lottery ticket collector

MEDALIST
medal collector

MIRABILIARY
collector of marvels

NOTAPHILIST
banknote collector

NUMISMATIST
coin collector

OOLOGIST
bird's egg collector

PHILATELIST
stamp collector

PHILLUMENIST
matchbox label collector

PORCELAINIST
porcelain collector

SCRIPOPHILIST
share certificate collector

SUCROLOGIST
sugar packet collector

TEGESTOLOGIST
beer mat collector

TRAINSPOTTER
trivia collector

TROPHY HUNTER
animal trophy collector

TYROSEMIOPHILIST
cheese label collector

VECTURIST
transport token collector

VEXILLOLOGIST
flag collector

VITOLPHILIST
cigar band collector

105

SEE ALSO: *Fandom*

J.

JABBERWOCKY EXPLAINED

¶ Lewis Carroll's **Jabberwocky** is among the most celebrated nonsense poems in English. After Alice reads it in *Through the Looking Glass*, she remarks: 'Somehow it seems to fill my head with ideas—only I don't exactly know what they are!' Many readers would agree.

¶ *Jabberwocky* has been translated into over fifty languages, but any translator faces a daunting task.

¶ Even in English its meaning is something of a riddle.

¶ Carroll offered some explanations, but they're sometimes contradicted by the book's own commentator, Humpty Dumpty.

¶ This glossary is a comprehensive collation of definitions, from Carroll (LC), Humpty Dumpty (HD) and the *OED*.

BANDERSNATCH 'A fleet, furious, fuming, fabulous creature, of dangerous propensities, immune to bribery and too fast to flee from' (*OED*).

BEAMISH sixteenth-century word for shining brightly.

BOROGOVES 'an extinct kind of parrot. They had no wings, beaks turned up, and made their nests under sun-dials; lived on veal' (LC).

BRILLIG 'four o'clock in the afternoon – the time when you begin broiling things for dinner' (HD).

BURBLED Carroll has a first *OED* citation for the sense 'to speak murmurously', although Jane Carlyle used 'burbled' in 1843 to mean to perplex or confuse ('a horribly burbled state').

CALLOOH, CALLAY possibly derivations of Greek kalos (καλός), meaning beautiful.

CHORTLED where chuckle and snort meet.

FRABJOUS a Carroll coinage, suggesting fair or joyous, perhaps with a hint of fabulous too.

FRUMIOUS a blending of furious and fuming.

GALUMPHING a bounding, exultant march, perhaps a blending of gallop and triumphant.

GIMBLE 'to make holes like a giblet' (HD); 'to scratch like a dog' (LC).

GYRE 'to go round and round like a gyroscope' (HD).

JABBERWOCK Carroll explained that wocer was Anglo-Saxon for offspring, and jabber meant excited or voluble discussion, so jabberwock meant 'the result of much excited and voluble discussion'.

JUBJUB described in *The Hunting of the Snark* as a ferocious yet passionate bird, with a shrill scream, an eye for fashion and an honest, unbribable nature. Said to be exquisite to eat.

MANXOME fearsome or monstrous.

MIMSY 'flimsy and miserable' (HD).

MOME 'from home' (HD).

OUTGRABE 'outgribing is something between bellowing and whistling, with a kind of sneeze in the middle' (HD).

RATHS 'a sort of green pig' (HD); or 'grave' (LC).

SLITHY 'lithe and slimy' (HD).

SNICKER-SNACK a snickersnee was a large knife, to which Carroll added some alliterative pop.

TOVE 'something like badgers – they're something like lizards – and they're something like corkscrews' (HD); 'A species of badger. They had smooth white hair, long hind legs, and short horns like a stag; lived chiefly on cheese' (LC).

TULGEY the *OED* suggests thick, dense or dark.

TUMTUM TREE 'tumtum' was a familiar word for the sound of a stringed instrument, but as a tree, no information is available.

UFFISH 'a state of mind when the voice is gruffish, the manner roughish, and the temper huffish' (LC).

VORPAL the *OED* suggests this means keen or deadly.

WABE 'the grass-plot round a sundial' (HD); 'the side of a hill' (LC).

WHIFFLING a sixteenth-century word meaning blowing or blow lightly.

JABBERWOCKY

'Twas **brillig**, and the **slithy toves**
Did **gyre** and **gimble** in the **wabe**:
All **mimsy** were the **borogoves**,
And the **mome raths outgrabe**.

"Beware the **Jabberwock**, my son!
The jaws that bite, the claws that catch!
Beware the **Jubjub** bird, and shun
The **frumious Bandersnatch**!"

He took his **vorpal** sword in hand;
Long time the **manxome** foe he sought—
So rested he by the **Tumtum tree**
And stood awhile in thought.

And, as in **uffish** thought he stood,
The Jabberwock, with eyes of flame,
Came **whiffling** through the **tulgey** wood,
And **burbled** as it came!

One, two! One, two! And through and through
The vorpal blade went **snicker-snack**!
He left it dead, and with its head
He went **galumphing** back.

"And hast thou slain the Jabberwock?
Come to my arms, my **beamish** boy!
O **frabjous** day! **Callooh**! **Callay**!"
He **chortled** in his joy.

'Twas **brillig**, and the **slithy toves**
Did **gyre** and **gimble** in the **wabe**:
All **mimsy** were the **borogoves**,
And the **mome raths outgrabe**.

LEWIS CARROLL, 1871

¶ Samuel Johnson's *A Dictionary of the English Language* was published in 1755. It took him seven years to write; four more than he expected, but thirty-three fewer than it took the forty members of the Académie Française to write theirs, a fact that delighted the Francophobe Johnson.

¶ His wasn't the first English dictionary; that was Cawdrey's *Table Alphabeticall*, published in 1604. In fact, nearly twelve English dictionaries had already been published before Johnson's, but his is acknowledged to be the first modern dictionary. The entries were more exhaustive, the definitions more expansive and, importantly for Johnson, there were over 115,000 quotations used to demonstrate the meaning of words. There was pronunciation and etymology too, but these pale by today's standards.

¶ The dictionary was commissioned by a group of publishers for a fee of £1,575 (around £300,000). This probably seemed a fortune when Johnson started, but it was all gone by the end. A year after publication, Johnson was arrested for a debt of £5 18s (around £1,000) and had to be bailed out by a friend. The same happened again in 1758. His money worries were only eased in 1762 when King George II awarded him a state pension of £300.

¶ The final work, published in two folio volumes, contained some 42,000 entries, although words he regarded as 'low' were omitted. A story recounted in *The Gentleman's Magazine* tells of a lady who thanked Johnson for excluding grubby words, to which he was said to reply, 'I hope I have not daubed my fingers. I find, however that you have been looking for them.'

¶ While Johnson's less rigorous definitions have invited mirth (*stoat*, 'a small stinking animal', and *sock*, 'something put between foot and shoe') and his omissions can seem prudish (neither penis nor vagina appear), many more are admired for their elegance. His definitions of *trance*, 'a state in which the soul is rapt into visions of future or distant things', or *hope*, 'an expectation indulged with pleasure', are literary pearls and they abound. Sometimes his peeves could colour his work (*patron*, 'a wretch who supports with insolence, and is paid with flattery', reflected his bitter experience), but his piercing wit makes it all the more readable.

¶ Johnson was fallible and his *Dictionary* contained errors, omissions and more opinions than modern dictionaries would tolerate. But for over 150 years, his dictionary was *the* dictionary, and today's lexicographers are merely continuing his work.

> *Johnson didn't have a university degree when he started work on his* Dictionary.
>
> *Pirated copies of the* Dictionary *first appeared three years after publication.*
>
> *2,000 copies were printed for the first edition. These were sold for £4 10s each (approximately £750).*
>
> *1,700 of Johnson's definitions appeared in the first OED.*
>
> *America's Noah Webster plagiarised about 7% of Johnson's definitions for his dictionary, and made only minor changes to a further 22%.*

MEMORABLE DEFINITIONS
FROM JOHNSON'S DICTIONARY

AIRLING (N.)
*A young, light,
thoughtless, gay person.*

ANATIFEROUS (ADJ.)
Producing ducks.

BACKFRIEND (N.)
*A friend backwards; that
is, an enemy in secret.*

BELLY-TIMBER (N.)
*Food; materials to
support the belly.*

DULL (ADJ.)
*Not exhilarating; not
delightful: as, to make
dictionaries is dull work.*

EXCISE (N.)
*A hateful tax levied upon
commodities, and adjudged
not by the common
judges of property, but
wretches hired by those
to whom excise is paid.*

EXPLETIVE (N.)
*Something used only to
take up room; something
of which the use is only
to prevent a vacancy.*

FEMALE (N.)
*A she; one of the sex which
brings young; not male.*

TO FORNICATE (N.)
To commit lewdness.

GALERICULATE (ADJ.)
Covered as with a hat.

HATCHET-FACE (N.)
*An ugly face; such, I suppose,
as might be hewn out of
a block by a hatchet.*

HICCUP (V.)
*To sob with a
convulsed stomach.*

HOTCOCKLES (N.)
*A play [game] in which
one covers his eyes, and
guesses who strikes him.*

JIGGUMBOB (N.)
*A trinket; a knick-knack;
a slight contrivance
in machinery.*

JOGGER (N.)
*One who moves
heavily and dully.*

KICKSHAW (N.)
*A dish so changed by
the cookery that it can
scarcely be known.*

LEXICOGRAPHER (N.)
*A writer of dictionaries;
a harmless drudge, that
busies himself in tracing
the original, and detailing
the signification of words.*

LIPLABOR (N.)
*Action of the lips without
concurrence of the mind;
words without sentiments.*

LUNCH (N.)
*As much food as one's
hand can hold.*

MAMMIFORM (ADJ.)
*Having the shape
of paps or dugs.*

MOUTH-FRIEND (N.)
*One who professes friendship
without intending it.*

MUNDUNGUS (N.)
Stinking tobacco.

MUSHROOM (N.)
*An upstart; a wretch
risen from the dunghill; a
director of a company.*

TO NEESE (V.)
*To sneese; to discharge
flatulencies by the nose.*

ORGASM (N.)
Sudden vehemence.

TO PISS (V.)
To make water.

PISSBURNT (ADJ.)
Stained with urine.

POLITICIAN (N.)
*1. One versed in the arts of
government; one skilled in
politicks. 2. A man of artifice;
one of deep contrivance.*

SHAPESMITH (N.)
*One who undertakes to
improve the form of the body.*

STATESWOMAN (N.)
*A woman who meddles
with publick affairs.*

TROLYMDAMES (N.)
*Of this word I know
not the meaning.*

VATICIDE (N.)
A murderer of poets.

WITLING (N.)
*A pretender to wit; a man
of petty smartness.*

TO WORM (V.)
*To deprive a dog of
something, nobody knows
what, under his tongue,
which is said to prevent
him, nobody knows why,
from running mad.*

L.

LANGUAGE HUMOUR

FOR LINGUISTS

I used to think I was the father of structural linguistics, but now I'm not Saussure.

How do you spell descriptivism?
Any way you want.

Flatmate:
You need to do more cleaning around the house.
You:
Can we change the subject?
Flatmate:
OK. More cleaning around the house needs to be done by you.

What is your greatest weakness?
Interpreting semantics of a question but ignoring the pragmatics.
Can you give me an example?
Yes, I could.

What's the difference between a literalist and a kleptomaniac?
A literalist takes things literally.
A kleptomaniac takes things, literally.

Two linguists were walking down the street. Which one was the specialist in contextually indicated deixis and anaphoric reference resolution strategies?
The other one.

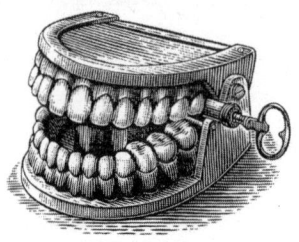

FOR GRAMMAR ENTHUSIASTS

Phil, an ostrich, and an Oxford comma walk into a bar.
They both had a great time.

Three intransitive verbs walk into a bar.
They sit. They drink. They leave.

The Past, Present and Future walk into a bar...
It was tense.

A verb walks into a bar...
Sees a noun and suggests they conjugate.
The noun declines.

Too many people worry about correct grammar.
I couldn't care fewer.

Double negatives are a big No-No.

Never use a preposition to end a sentence with.

Double negatives are positive, but double positives aren't negative.
Yeah, right.

Teacher:
Name two pronouns.
Student:
Who, me?

Knock knock
Who's there?
To.
To who?
No, to whom.

Never date an apostrophe.
They're too possessive.

Capital letters:
The difference between helping your Uncle Jack off a horse, and helping your uncle jack off a horse.

SEE ALSO: *Funny Words*

A priest, a rabbit and a
minister walk into a bar.
The rabbit says, 'I might be a typo'.

A pun, a play on words and a
limerick walk into a bar. No joke.

How many mystery writers does
it take to change a lightbulb?
*Two. One almost screws the bulb in, the
other adds a surprising twist at the end.*

What do you get when you combine
a joke with a rhetorical question?

Not everyone thinks Cleopatra was
beautiful, but that's how Julius Caesar.

Saying 'I'm sorry' is the same
as saying 'I apologise'.
Except at a funeral.

Teacher:
*Write down three letters, but only
pronounce the last one.*
Student:
Why?

Autocorrect is my worst enema.

Dyslexics of the world untie.

Did you hear about the prison library?
It has prose and cons.

What's the first rule of Synonym Club?
*You don't talk about, utter, mention,
discuss or gossip about Synonym Club.*

Don't trust autocorrect.
It'll duck you up.

Someone stole all my dictionaries.
I'm lost for words.

Why did the pregnant woman shout
'Won't! Shan't! Can't! Isn't!'?
She was having contractions.

Whoever put the letter B in the
word 'subtle' deserves a medal.

I made up a new word.
Plagiarism.

Take care making alphabet soup.
It could spell disaster.

A man was severely hurt when a
pile of books fell on him.
He only has his shelf to blame.

Say 'muchos' to Spanish-speakers.
It means a lot to them.

What did the buffalo
say when his son left?
Bison.

111

A FLEA AND A FLY IN A FLUE

A fly and a flea in a flue
Were imprisoned,
so what could they do?
Said the fly, 'Let us flee!'
'Let us fly!' said the flea.
So they flew through
a flaw in the flue.

ANONYMOUS (*but mistakenly
credited to Ogden Nash*)

A SILLY POEM

Said Hamlet to Ophelia,
I'll draw a sketch of thee,
What kind of pencil shall I use?
2B or not 2B?

SPIKE MILLIGAN

¶ When Old English – or *Englisċ*, as it was known – was brought to Britain by the Angles, Saxons and Jutes, it was written in runes. The runic alphabet could vary in size, but the Futhark runes of the Anglo Saxons had 26–33 symbols.

¶ After around a century of runic inscriptions, Old English was shaken up by the arrival of Christian missionaries from 597. Their twenty-three-letter Roman alphabet soon started to displace runes, although it required four new characters to accommodate the sounds of Old English, two of which were runes. These symbols would remain part of the Old English alphabet until the Norman Conquest in 1066, and even then, their retirement was gradual.

112

SEE ALSO: *The Great Vowel Shift*

Æ *æsc* (transliterated: *ash*)

¶ *Ash* is the Romanised form of the runic a symbol. As well as being a letter, the symbol means *ash tree*. Æ made a short *a* sound, as in h*a*t, although this pronunciation has changed in the rare instances when it's still used, as in *encyclopædia* or *dæmon*.

Þ *þorn* (transliterated: *thorn*)

¶ *Thorn* is a runic symbol that made a *th* sound, found in *th*ink and *th*ank. Surviving into the Early Modern English period, thorn was the last rune to be seen in the English alphabet, being increasingly replaced by the digraph *th* from the 1400s.

¶ Confusingly, scribes would often use Þ and Y interchangeably. This is seen as late as 1611 in the *King James Bible*, as in John 15:1, where the text reads: *I am the true vine, and my Father is ye husbandman.*

¶ Today, thorn's fossil remains can be found in quaint English pub names like Ye Olde Cherry Tree, in Ye Olde London Town. What is mistakenly pronounced as '*yee*' is just another form of *Þe*, or *The*.

ȝ *yogh*

¶ *Yogh* – pronounced 'yog' – made two sounds: at the start of a word it made a Y sound (as in *yoke*), and in the middle of words it made the breathier sound now performed by *GH* (as in *night*). After the Norman invasion, *yogh* was increasingly replaced by both Y and GH, such that by the 1400s it was scarcely used.

Ƿ *wynn*

¶ Among the letters missing from the twenty-three letter Roman alphabet was W (see in New Letters); wynn was borrowed from the Futhark runic alphabet to fill this gap and continued to be used until the 1300s.

ð *eth*

¶ *Eth* and *thorn* both made a *th* sound and were often used interchangeably. But unlike its sibling, *eth* was created outside of the runic alphabet and had largely disappeared by 1300.

❡ Following the invasion of French-speaking Normans in 1066, letters associated with Anglo-Saxon English started to be dropped, but new letters arrived.

W *double-U*

❡ Romans had employed U to make a W sound, but Germanic languages in northern Europe needed something more, and since Norman French had itself been influenced by words introduced by Vikings, it did too.

❡ The device used by Christian scribes in the ninth century was two Us (*uu*), which had precedent in Latin within a word like *equus* (horse). With the invention of the printing press in 1444, print-makers created blocks for the double-U device. Type designers started to interpret this with the angular V used by Roman stonemasons to represent a U, first with two Vs adjacent (**VV**) then overlapping (**W**). And thus W came to be.

J *jay*

❡ Like *W*, there was no *J* in the Roman alphabet. Julius Caesar was Iulius Caesar (*yoo-lius*) and Jupiter was Iupiter (*yoo-piter*).

❡ In medieval Europe, *I* functioned both as a vowel and a consonant, where it made a J-sound, as heard in words like *iuge* (judge) and *ielous* (jealous).

❡ Late in the sixteenth century, printers started to use the two letter forms for I – the short **i**, and long-tailed **j** – to distinguish between the consonant and vowel sound. The change was gradual and inconsistent, but *J* was increasingly seen as the consonant form of *I*, although not yet recognised as a letter in its own right.

❡ By the eighteenth century, *J* started to appear in alphabet lists, although its status wasn't assured for another century. Even Samuel Johnson, while acknowledging that the alphabet contained twenty-six letters, didn't include an entry for *J* in his 1755 dictionary. In America, however, Noah Webster removed *J* from *I*'s shadow in his 1806 work, *A Compendious Dictionary Of The English Language*. As other dictionaries followed, *J* became its own letter.

V *vee*

❡ *V*'s story is almost identical to that of *J*, with both entering the alphabet at the same time. *V* also had no place in the Roman alphabet, but was used in medieval Europe as the consonant form of *U*, sometimes written as *U*, sometimes *V*. (Confusingly to us, Roman carvings of the *V* form represent *U*, so that the goddess Vesta, for instance, would have been read as Westa.)

❡ Although Old English already had a *V* sound, represented by *F*, the Normans brought many new V words to the language, for which they used *U*, which became the accepted form by 1400.

❡ It was clearly confusing for *U* and *V* to represent two sounds, and in the seventeenth century the precedent emerged that *U* would be designated the vowel and *V* the consonant. But like *J*, most dictionary writers only gave *V* its own entry in the nineteenth century.

¶ Determining the history of the **limerick** – the witty five-line poem with the sing-song *a-a-b-b-a* rhyme scheme – is no easy matter. Ancient Greece, medieval England, pre-revolutionary France and even Imperial China have all been cited as the origin of the artform, but none convincingly. A strong case is made for County Limerick in Ireland, particularly by the people of County Limerick in Ireland, but the connection between Irish Maigue poets and limericks is not without issue.

¶ The problem is that a lot of verse *looks* limericky. St Thomas Aquinas (d. 1274) wrote five lines in Latin that some call the first limerick. And a 1786 poem by Hester Thrale, a close friend of dictionary-writer Samuel Johnson, also bears a strong resemblance. But the familiar rhyme scheme is seen in different places in different centuries, without a shared sense of the limerick form.

¶ What's certain is that five children's books published between 1820 and 1824 contained 62 unmistakeable limericks, and this was new. Among them, in *Anecdotes and Adventures of Fifteen Gentlemen*, was the verse that inspired the great **limericist** Edward Lear:

> There was a sick man of Tobago
> Liv'd long on rice-gruel and sago;
>   But at last to his bliss,
>   The physician said this –
> 'To a roast leg of mutton you may go.'

¶ Lear, who did much to popularise limericks, never used the word, instead calling his work **nonsense poetry**. The word is first attested in the *OED* in *1879*, and comes from a nineteenth-century game in which a player would recite a humorous verse that ended with everyone singing the refrain 'Won't you come up to Limerick?'

¶ From the 1840s, and assisted by the publication of Edward Lear's *A Book of Nonsense* (1846), the limerick took off. The combination of levity, brevity and wordplay made them uniquely appealing. They could be topical, personal or nonsensical; written on one's own or among friends. And while early limericks were very innocent, they were soon testing saltier waters. The first collection of dirty limericks, featured in *Cythera's Hymnal, or Flakes from the Foreskin*, appeared in 1870 and upends any notion of Victorian prudery, as the example opposite shows.

¶ The heyday of the limerick was 1907–8, when there was a mania for limerick competitions with cash prizes that started in Britain and spread to Australia and America. The craze peaked with a competition offering 'a freehold furnished country house, a horse and trap, and £2 a week guaranteed for life' for the best closing line to a limerick promoting Trallee cigarettes:

> There's a Cigarette commencing with 'T',
> Its full name is Irish, 'Trallee';
>   It's Samuda's, the best,
>   Of fine leaf from the West…

¶ There are still limerick competitions, including the annual **Bring Your Limerick to Limerick** event, but no more houses to be won. Nonetheless, the public's love of limericks is undiminished. And just as limericks attracted the attention of great Victorian writers, so they continue to inspire authors and poets today.

SEE ALSO: *Mary Had a Little Lamb*

LIMERICKS OF NOTE

A CLASSIC EDWARD LEAR

There was an Old Person of Ware,
Who rode on the back of a Bear;
    When they ask'd, 'Does it trot?' –
    He said, 'Certainly not!
He's a Moppsikon, Floppsikon Bear!'

(Edward Lear)

FROM THE FIRST BOOK
OF DIRTY LIMERICKS

A young woman got married at Chester,
Her mother she kisses and she blessed her,
    Says she, 'You're in luck,
    He's a stunning good fuck,
For I've had him myself down in Leicester.'

(Featured in Cythera's Hymnal, *1870)*

FOUR LIMERICKS OF
DUBIOUS LENGTH

There was a young boy from the sticks
Whose limericks stopped at line six.
    They started OK
    But then went astray
When he found himself in a fix
Towards the end.

⌒

There was a young girl from Dundee
Whose limericks stopped at line three.
    I don't know why.

⌒

There was a young boy from Peru
Whose limericks stopped at line two.

⌒

There was was a young man from Verdun.

(unknown)

A LIMERICK ABOUT DEATH

There was an eccentric old boffin
Who said, when he couldn't stop coughin',
    'It isn't the cough
    That carries you off.
It's the coffin they carry you off in!'

(unknown)

A TONGUE-TWISTER LIMERICK

A right-handed fellow named Wright,
In writing 'wrote' always wrote 'right'
    Where he meant to write right,
    If he'd written 'write' right,
Wright would not have wrought rot
    writing 'rite'.

(unknown)

A NON-RHYMING LIMERICK

There was an old man of St Bees,
Who was stung in the arm by a wasp,
    When asked, 'Does it hurt?'
    He replied, 'No, it doesn't,
I'm so glad it wasn't a hornet.

(W. S. Gilbert, 1879)

AND FINALLY, COMPOSED
BY THE AUTHOR'S SON...

There was a young man from Bordeaux,
Whose limericks were very bad,
    Nothing he said rhymed,
    His rhythm was an absolute disaster,
And he always made the last line very
    long with too many syllables.

(Jude Blackburn, 2024)

FIG.1 *A Moppsikon, Floppsikon Bear*

LONG WORDS

¶ Sesquipedalophobia is the fear of long words. It hasn't made it into the *OED* or *Merriam-Webster*, but **sesquipedalian** (from Horace's **sesquipedalia verba**, 'words a foot and a half long') has. Collins also has **hippopotomonstrosesquippedaliophobia** 'under consideration', but this similarly ironic creation is unlikely to appear in a major dictionary either.

¶ The longest words found in general use are around twenty-two letters. These include **counterrevolutionaries**, **reinstitutionalisation** and, with twenty-three letters, **overintellectualisation**. Words longer than these are either scientific, nonsensical or scientific *and* nonsensical.

¶ Scientists have an advantage when it comes to long words because they can string technical terms together. But creating a long word doesn't mean it'll ever be used (see **pneumo-blah-blah** below).

¶ James Joyce was famous for his long words. His novel *Finnegan's Wake* includes nine 100-letter words, with **bababadalgharaghtakamminarronnkonnbronntonnerronntuonnthunntrovarrhounawnskawntoohoohoordenenthurnuk** on the first page. This is the sound of the thunderclap heard at the fall of Adam and Eve and comprises words for thunder from different languages. No major dictionary has yet included it.

SEE ALSO: *Word Records*

10 + 63 LETTERS

Myxococcus llanfairpwllgwyngyllgogerychwyrndrobwllllantysiliogogogochensis

Species of soil-based myxobacteria, currently the longest name in the binomial nomenclature system.

45 LETTERS

Pneumonoultramicroscopicsilicovolcanoconiosis

*A lung disease caused by dust inhalation. Although the longest word in Merriam-Webster, it is a **nonce word** first shared at the National Puzzler's League in 1935 that has never been used scientifically.*

34 LETTERS

Supercalifragilisticexpialidocious

This famous nonsense word is remembered for its appearance in Disney's Mary Poppins *(1964), but an early version of it was invented in 1931.*

30 LETTERS

Pseudopseudohypoparathyroidism

As well as having an impressive 30 letters, this genetic disorder is the only word in the OED to be a 'pseudopseudo'.

29 LETTERS

Floccinaucinihilipilification

*An eighteenth-century word meaning 'the action or habit of estimating as worthless'. Like the twenty-eight-letter **antidisestablishmentarianism** it was invented as a deliberately long word, whose only purpose was to be humorously over-lettered.*

Methylenedioxymethamphetamine

A mood-altering synthetic amphetamine more commonly known as the drug MDMA.

27 LETTERS

Honorificabilitudinitatibus

Appearing in Love's Labours Lost, this is Shakespeare's longest word. It is Latin for 'the state of being able to achieve honors'.

M.

MADE-UP DISEASES

❡ Few writers found it necessary to make up diseases before the twentieth century, presumably because real ones were never far away. Edgar Allen Poe imagined **Red Death** in 1842, with its sharp pains, dizziness and bleeding through the pores; and earlier, in 1826, Mary Shelley described a devastating pandemic, known only as *plague*, that wipes out everyone but her titular *Last Man*. But that was it, until M. P. Shiel concluded the century with **Black Spot**, a man-made plague employed in his distinctly racist novel, *The Yellow Danger*, in 1898.

ANDROMEDA
(*Andromeda Strain*, Michael Crichton)

Alien pathogen that causes
fatal blood clotting.

FLOOD PARASITE
(ALSO: HEPATITIS V, NARVIK,
NECROA VIRUS, RAGE VIRUS,
SOLANUM VIRUS, WILDFIRE VIRUS)

(assorted books, films and games)

Causes people to turn into
flesh-eating zombies.

GRAYSCALE
(*A Song of Fire and Ice*, George R. R. Martin)

Skin disease similar to leprosy that turns
adult patients insane and is ultimately fatal.

SPATTERGROIT
(*Harry Potter*, J. K. Rowling)

Causes an outbreak of purple pustules
that renders patient unable to speak.

PLAGUE OF INSOMNIA
(*One Hundred Years of Solitude*,
Gabriel García Márquez)

Patients feel no tiredness but in
time lose all memories.

WANDERING SICKNESS
(*The Shape of Things to Come*, H. G. Wells)

Bioweapon that causes victims
to enter a zombie-like state.

METHUSELAH SYNDROME
(*Blade Runner*)

Genetic condition that accelerates ageing.

WHITE PLAGUE
(*The White Plague*, Frank Herbert)

Genetically engineered
disease fatal to women.

GROAT'S DISEASE
(*Curb Your Enthusiasm*)

Hyperactivity disorder that leaves sufferers
feeling like they've drunk an excess of coffee.

THRIPSHAW'S DISEASE
(*Monthy Python's Flying Circus*)

A disease that causes people to use the wrong
words, or the right words in the wrong order.

TORSONIC POLARITY
SYNDROME
(*South Park*)

Genetic condition that causes a person
to be born with buttocks on their face.

STAR TREK MED BAY
*Barclay's Protomorphosis syndrome •
Harvester virus • Irumodic syndrome
• Macrovirus • Polywater intoxication
• Rigellian fever • Tarellian virus •
The Phage • Xenopolycythemia*

☞ SEE ALSO: *Medical Conditions that Make Nice Names / Technobabble*

¶ Linguists long assumed that there was no relationship between the sound of a word and its meaning. There's nothing *doggy* about the word 'dog', and no reason why it couldn't refer to a cat; it is merely the linguistic unit, as Swiss semiotician Saussure called it, that has been chosen for **Canis familiaris**. (Onomatopoeia are different because they are intended to imitate sounds.)

¶ But language may not be so arbitrary after all. In 1929, American psychologist Wolfgang Kohler gave people two pictures, one jagged, the other curvy, and asked which was **maluma** and which **takete**, two nonsense words he'd invented. Kohler found that people overwhelmingly identified maluma as curvy and takete as jagged, suggesting an inherent **sound symbolism** (where the sound of a word suggests its meaning), even with words that were meaningless. This effect, first identified in 1924, has important implications for theories about the origins of language.

¶ The **Maluma-Takete Effect** has been tested with different words, in different countries and among different age groups, and the results have been remarkably consistent. **Bouba** and **kiki** were the test words used in a famous 2001 study, and like maluma and takete, bouba was round and kiki sharp. Similarly, the names **Bob** and **Kirk** (among English speakers) and **Benoit** and **Éric** (among French speakers) were identified as round and pointy respectively.

¶ Even toddlers seem to sense the difference. In a 2006 study, children as young as two-and-a-half associated long vowel sounds (in **far** and **moo**) with curviness, and short vowels sounds (in **sit** and **hat**) with pointiness.

¶ Psychologists aren't sure what lies behind the Maluma-Takete (or Bouba-Kiki) Effect. It might be an example of weak **synaesthesia** (the experience of one sensation, such as seeing colours, when another sense is stimulated, for example when listening to music). Or it might be the shape of the mouth when making these sounds. Whatever the explanation, the effect is real and has been verified in over 25 languages. Some, like Mandarin Chinese and Turkish, have a lower response to 'bouba' and 'kiki', but overall, the effect is clear.

¶ The Maluma-Takete Effect might sound like a linguist's party trick, but it chimes with other research findings about universal sound symbolism. In one 1994 study, for instance, English-speakers were given a list of fish and bird names in the Huambisa language (spoken in northern Peru). By merely hearing the words, people could distinguish the avian from the aquatic more often than chance alone would predict. An even larger study in 2016 compared 100 words from over 3,500 languages and found strong associations between different speech sounds, just as maluma and takete drew people to the same pictures. As the origins of language continue to be debated, it's fascinating to see the role maluma and takete, and Bob, Kirk, Benoit and Éric have played in advancing our understanding.

FIG.1 *Shapes used for Maluma and Takete tests*

¶ In 1876, fifty years after Sarah Hale published *Mary Had a Little Lamb*, 70-year-old Mary Sawyer revealed that the rhyme was about her, and the author was not Hale but one John Roulstone. She even sold wool said to be from her famous lamb as a fundraiser for her town's meeting house. Sawyer provided no evidence for her claim, but people wanted to believe it, including industrialist Henry Ford who bought and relocated her old schoolhouse.

¶ Regardless of whether Sawyer's story is true, the rhyme is a classic; cute, whimsical and with a tidy moral message. It's also kept word-fiddlers busy. In *The Dictionary of Wordplay*, Dave Morice claims the rhyme has more wordplay variations than any other literary work in history. If this includes the close to 1,000 parody rewrites, perhaps it is the most re-written literary work. Here are some ingenious bits of wordplay inspired by the rhyme.

LIPOGRAM
(E is the only vowel)

Meg kept the wee sheep,
The sheep's fleece resembled sleet,
Then wherever Meg went
The sheep went there next.

He went where she heeded her texts,
The precedent he neglected;
The pre-teens felt deep cheer
When the sheep entered there.

Paul Hellweg

PALINDROME

Mary bred a Derby ram,
Won some gem o' snow,
Went one romp more, not new
O gods, Mary, rams do go!

Peter Newby / Dave Morice

SPOONERISM
(the first sounds of two words swapped)

Larry lad a middle ham.
Flits niece was sight as woe.
And every there what wary meant,
The gam was lure to show.

He hollowed fur to school done way,
Watch whiz arainst the ghoul.
Skit plaid the ildren chaff and may
Sue lee a scam at tool.

Richard Lederer

PUN

Marry hatter ladle limb.
Itch fleas worse widest snore.
An ever-wear debt Marry win
Door limb worse shorter gore.

Howard Chace

119

SEE ALSO: *Anagrams / Palindromes / Pangrams*

PARODY

Mary had a little lamb,
It always used to tease'er
Her father shot it dead one day
And now it's in the freezer.

Unknown

Mary had a little lamb,
She kept it in the closet,
And every time she let it out,
It had left a small deposit.

Unknown

Mary had a little lamb,
A little steak, a little ham,
A little soda topped with fizz,
Now look how sick Mary is!

Unknown

*There are two eras in the linguistic history of marijuana: **Before the Jazz Age** and **After**.*

BEFORE THE JAZZ AGE

❡ Cannabis has been smoked, drunk and eaten for millennia. In China it was called *ma*, in India there was *bang, majoon, churrus* or *gunja* (from which we get *ganja*), Egypt had *bosa*, Turkey had *malach* and Namibia *dacha*. And *hashish* comes from the Arabic *al-hašiš*.

❡ *Cannabis* is first mentioned by the ancient Greek historian Herodotus in his account of Scythian funeral rites, where *kannabis* was thrown onto red-hot stones and the Scythians would 'howl in their joy at the vapour bath'.

❡ Pre-nineteenth century, all the English-speaking world knew of the drug cannabis was what it saw in foreign lands. Such was the case of merchant Thomas Bowrey, who wrote of the 'soe admirable herb' he found at the Indian port of Machilipatnam in 1673. These written accounts either presented cannabis as something exotic and exciting, or un-Christian and wicked. But in either case, it was definitely *foreign*.

❡ Attitudes started to change after Irish doctor William O'Shaughnessy documented the plant's medicinal qualities in 1842. Cannabis started appearing in Victorian pharmacies in Britain and America, prescribed for menstrual pains, rheumatism, bilious headaches, anxiety, insanity and much else. It could be bought as a generic tincture or a custom preparation, like *Cannabin*, *Bees Laxative Cough Syrup* or *Dr Poppy's Wonder Elixir* (a glass every morning for 'a pleasant feeling that lasts all day').

❡ During this lengthy period of the drug's history, cannabis slang scarcely existed in English.

SEE ALSO: *Drunkenness*

A (VERY INCOMPLETE) MARIJUANA GLOSSARY

CHRONIC *Very strong weed*	**BUDIQUETTE** *Weed smoking etiquette*	**ANGEL WINE** *Weed wine*	**BONG SWAT** *Inhaling from a bong*
CATNIP *Fake weed*	**PEE-WEE** *A thin joint*	**CHALICE** *Pipe for smoking weed*	**CRISPY** *High on weed*
DITCHWEED *Low grade weed*	**DOGWALKER** *A small joint*	**A-BOMB** *Weed and opium*	**MING** *Spliff made from spliff butts*
ELECTRIC PUHA *Homegrown weed*	**BAZOOKA** *A very large joint*	**DONK** *Weed and PCP*	**CHIEFING** *Hogging the weed*
FLY MEXICAN AIRLINES *Weed smoking*	**BLUNT** *A weed-filled cigar*	**FRY DADDY** *Weed and crack*	**CARPET WEED** *OK weed*
CONTACT HIGH *Passive weed smoking*	**DAB** *Potent weed extract*	**EMBALMING FLUID** *Weed and cocaine*	**LID** *Four fingers of weed*
GRASSHOPPER *A weed smoker*	**BOOM TEA** *Weed tea*	**DEUCE** *Two spliffs sold together*	**TROMPIE** *Long conical spliff*

Acapulco Red • Ace • Alfalfa • Amnesia • Asparagus • Astro turf • Aunt Mary • Baby Bhang • Bash • Black Maria • Blue Crush • Bobo bush • Boof • Boogie • Broccoli • Bud • Cabbage • Cheese • Chiba • Chronic • Crud • Dank • Devil's lettuce • Ditchweed • Dizz • Donk • Drag weed • Durban poison • Dynamite • Flower • Funk • Ganja • Geeba • Gong • Gunge • Ha-ha • Hocus • Hot hay • Jive • Ju-ju • Kush • Leaf • Limbo • Loco • Mariquita • Mary and Johnny • Mauie Wowie • Muggle • Nodge • O-boy • Ozone • Piff • Poison • Reefer • Rosa Maria • Sassafras • Scramble grass • Sheeba • Shishkaberry • Shmagma • Sinsemilla • Skank • Skunk • Sweet Lucy • Tea • Wooz • Zaza

AFTER THE JAZZ AGE

❡ From the 1850s, Americans could enjoy cannabis at **hashish houses**, but these secretive places were already shutting down by the 1900s. During the 1920s, however, the jazz scene in New Orleans and Harlem had adopted marijuana as its drug of choice.

❡ The shift in terminology, from cannabis to **marijuana**, is deliberate. Cannabis was respectable(ish), but marijuana, 'the burning weed with its roots in Hell!' as one hysterical anti-drugs film put it, was recreational, and becoming a trigger word for moral panic.

❡ All that's known for certain about the word marijuana is that it comes from Mexican Spanish **mariguana**. That might mean *prisoner*, or derive from the name *Maria Juana*; but in the *OED*, it is 'of uncertain origin'.

❡ Regardless, mariguana, or **Mexican locoweed**, was synonymous with the immigration wave following the Mexican Revolution in 1910. It was therefore not only *foreign* but, worse still, part of a Black American music scene. This set the tone for the drug war that has been fought ever since.

❡ But the Jazz cats weren't talking about marijuana. Or, not only. They were **vipers** and **muggle smokers**… it was *gage, grass, jive, pot, reefer* and **tea**… the *giggle smoke* made them **mellow** and **with the jive**… This slang wasn't just a code necessitated by the drug's illegality; it was a shared language. And it wasn't just talk. The first marijuana song was Lucille Bogan's 'Pot Hound Blues' (1928), then followed 'Reefer Man' (1933), 'Viper's Drag' (1934), 'Weed Smoker's Dream' (1936) and more.

❡ And so the first chapter in the cannabis slang lexicon was written in the Jazz Age. **Beatniks, hippies, hip-hopsters, ravers** and college kids followed, creating more slang for cannabis than any other drug.

❡ Today, *Green's Dictionary of Slang* has over 1,000 cannabis-related entries, and the online *Urban Dictionary* thousands more. And with legalisation, a new chapter for exotic weed strains has been opened, with the likes of **Purple Monkey Balls, Grandpa's Breath, Psycho Crack** and **Alaskan Thunderfuck**.

121

*Within this vast **Cannabisaurus**, the slang term **420** has become enshrined in weed lore, with 20 April (4/20) a hallowed day for pot-smokers, and 4.20 p.m. the time to **spark up**. The story goes that in 1971 a group of pot-smoking friends at San Rafael High School used the code to meet at 4.20 p.m. to hunt for a mythical, untended marijuana crop. After a few fruitless searches, **420** became their shorthand for smoking weed, and so it has remained ever since. **Maria Juana** would have been proud.*

¶ It's interesting to consider that Jesus' **Last Supper** would have been his **Last Tea** if he was from Yorkshire, or his **Last Dinner** if he lived in London. In fact, according to the website *OurDialects.com*, only 3.6% of the British public care for supper at all.

¶ When **dinner** was served in the fourteenth century, it was typically late morning. Some people still call their midday meal dinner; but for most, dinner is the main evening meal. Unless, that is, they have **supper**, although strictly speaking, supper is lighter and later. They could always have dinner *and* supper, but supper would be the final meal, with dinner late afternoon or early evening. Or they could have **tea** instead of dinner; except if it's a late **afternoon tea**, in which case one would probably enjoy a later supper.

¶ If this is hard to follow, then that's because mealtimes have become a confusing business. It was simpler for the Anglo Saxons around AD 1000. They enjoyed **morgen-mete** (morning meat) and maybe **æfen-mete** (evening meat) too, with the **meat** in question simply being food. But with no clocks, and less food to eat, the best time to eat a meal was **mæltime** (meal time).

¶ By the sixteenth century, eating routines were changing. Midday dinner was the main meal of the day, with **luncheon** (or **lunchings**) merely a snack. Samuel Johnson's definition of **lunch** – 'As much food as one's hand can hold' – sounds frivolous, but a **lunch of bacon** was literally what could be grabbed in one's fist.

¶ With urbanisation and industrialisation, the organisation of meals changed further, with the evening meal – call it tea, dinner or supper – becoming the main event. For a lucky few untroubled by factory time, there were new meals to enjoy. As well as **high tea**, there was **low tea**, **thick tea**, **cream tea** and **meat tea**. Even lunch was starting to get some respect, with **lunch-houses** and **lunch-stands** appearing from the 1850s.

¶ As mealtime became more regular, so new celebratory meals were conjured. During the seventeenth and eighteenth centuries, people **feasted**. There was the **oyster feast**, **hog feast**, **swan feast**, **turtle feast** and **dog feast**. (Those last three were, sadly, just as they sound.)

¶ Speaking of feasts, decline any invitation to a **Thyestean banquet**. It sounds tempting but the menu features human flesh.

SEE ALSO: *Diets / Diner Slang*

EATING BETWEEN MEALS

While official meals understandably take the limelight, there is a delicious lexicon for between-meal snacking that reflects a usefulness not always appreciated.

For someone feeling the cold, the Scottish have the **chittery-bite** to stop teeth chattering; for someone feeling pangs of **hanger** there's the **stay-stomach** or **damper**; and anyone embarking on a journey should pack a **bait** or **viaticum** for *en route* snacking.

Kids, always being hungry, must snack. Primary school children have their mid-morning **little lunch**, while mums in Scotland might send the bairns in with a **playpiece** to eat or trade in the playground.

Just the word **snack** is a happy one. Similarly joyous are **nuncheon** (or **unch**), **nacket**, **snackett**, **namkeen** and **prandicle**. They're all words for snack, and the world would be improved if they were used more often.

UNCOMMON MEAL TIMES

7:00 AM
DEW-BIT
A pre-breakfast peck.

9:00 AM
DOCKY
Mid-morning meal or snack.

SECOND BREAKFAST
A light meal taken later in the morning.

MORNING
A light morning snack.

11:00 AM
BRUNCHEON
Meal with elements of breakfast and lunch.

LITTLE LUNCH
Mid-morning snack.

ELEVENER
(ALSO: ELEVENS)
Late morning, pre-luncheon prandicle.

12:00 PM
NUMMIT
(ALSO: NOONING, TIFFIN)
A light midday meal.

PRE-LUNCHEON
A light meal before lunch.

1:00 PM
LUNCHEON
An early afternoon meal.

PERPENDICULAR
A standing lunch.

2:00 PM
UNDERMEAL
(ALSO: MUNCHIN)
A light afternoon meal.

4:00 PM
ANDERSMEAT
(ALSO: AFTERNOONING)
A light afternoon snack.

FOUR-HOURS
(ALSO: FOURSES)
*Refreshment enjoyed
around 4 o'clock.*

5:00 PM
GOUTER
A light afternoon spread.

LIGHT AFTERNOON TEA
Comprising sandwiches, scones and cake.

HIGH TEA
A cooked dish, bread and tea.

7:00 PM
PETIT SOUPER
A small supper shared by a few close friends.

LATE DINNER
*The main evening meal, taken by
adults after the children's dinner.*

9:00 PM
ARRIERE SUPPER
*A late supper ('often served with
devilled bones and prunes', according
to Arthur Conan Doyle).*

11:00 PM
RERE-SUPPER
(ALSO: RERE-BANQUET)
*A large late-night meal following
one's dinner.*

VOIDEE
*Drinks and sweet treats enjoyed before
bed, or before guests depart.*

MEDICAL CONDITIONS THAT MAKE NICE NAMES

❡ Parents-to-be are always on the lookout for new and unusual names. One neglected source of inspiration is *The Cambridge Historical Dictionary of Disease*, a treasure trove of exotic, distinctive and exciting names. If one only focuses on the sound of these words, some intriguing options present themselves.

❡ It's not always clear why one name works while another doesn't, but you know it when you hear it. Nobody wants to be calling for **Conjunctivitis** or **Lumbago** in the playground, but **Frambesia** and **Pinta** are delightful, so long as one doesn't look up the symptoms.

❡ The following list has been prepared for anyone thinking about baby names. The conditions themselves are no laughing matter, but many of the names are nonetheless lovely, and it is unlikely there'll be two **Candidas** in the same class.

●—— GIRLS ——●

Alopecia	Frambesia	Roseola
Anaemia	Orchitis	Rubella
Angina	Oreillons	Sakura
Brucella	Pellagra	Syphilis
Candida	Pica	Tinea
Chancre	Pinta	Varicella
Chlamydia	Pokkuri	Zika

●—— BOYS ——●

Ascites	Favus	Proteus
Blains	Lupus	Quintan
Coyrza	Morphea	Typhus

●—— UNISEX ——●

Beriberi	Parangi	Rocio
Edema	Quinsy	Zara'ath

CHARLES DICKENS OR PATHOLOGY?

This list contains an equal number of names from *The Cambridge Historical Dictionary of Disease* and Charles Dickens' notebook.

Which came from where?
(Answers on page 215)

Rebina	Noma	Melena
Cinchona	Menella	Aramanda
Ethlynida	Seba	Ambrosina
Yersinia	Tetany	Gentilla
Samilias	Rosacea	Marasmus
Variola	Ménière	Sapsea

¶ In a famous Bill Hicks routine, the American comedian told a story about being in his dad's 'talking car' while high on acid. The safety system announced, 'The door is ajar'. 'We pulled over and thought about that for 12 hours', he said.

¶ What Hicks was experiencing, on top of the hallucinations, was what linguists call **metanalysis**. Language relies upon people understanding where words begin and end. We know, for instance, that it's **an umbrella**, not **a numbrella** because the word is familiar. But if the word isn't known and it's phonetically ambiguous, or if you're off your noodle on drugs, mistakes can, and do, happen. Children do it all the time, but they're quickly set right, because that's how kids learn languages. But when enough adults say the same mistake for enough time, it can enter the lexicon alongside, or instead of, the 'correct' form.

¶ It was the linguist Otto Jespersen who coined metanalysis. He was looking at how the singular and plural forms of words have caused confusion, often when they are imported from other languages. Other errors have arisen because of how people hear the indefinite article, **a** or **an**. Here is a selection of **anerrors** and **miss takes** that went from wrong to right.

ADDER
From Middle English **a naddre** (a snake), misread as **an addre**.

APRON
From Middle English **a napron**, misread as **an apron**.

AUGER
From Middle English **a nauger**, misread as **an auger**.

CHORD
From Middle English **accord** (harmony), misread as **a cord**.

HUMBLE PIE
From Middle English **a numble** (deer intestines) misread as **an umble**, to which the **h** was added.

INGOT
From French **lingot**, but misinterpreted as **l'ingot**, from which the **l** was removed.

LONE
From Middle English **al one** (all one), misread as **a lone**.

NEWT
From Middle English **an eute**, misread as **a neute**.

NICKNAME
From Middle English **an eke name** (an additional name), misread as **a neke name**.

NOTCH
From Middle French **oche** (incision mark to keep a record), anglicised to **an oche**, then rebracked to **a notch**.

PEA
From Middle English **pease**, mistakenly interpreted as a plural. (The plural of pease was actually **peasen** or **peason**.)

UMPIRE
From Middle English **a noumpere**, misread as **an oumpere**.

125

☞ SEE ALSO: *Zero Plurals*

SEE ALSO: Barry Humphries Glossary / Fuck

¶ When Robert Arthur was called to London's Hackney Petty Sessions court in 1751, he was accused of 'Six prophane Oaths saying each time **By God**, and cursing Six prophane Curses saying each time **Damn your Blood**'. Each oath and each curse incurred a two shilling fine, with the total penalty equivalent to £300.

¶ Robert Arthur was lucky. The 1694 Act 'for the more effectuall suppressing [of] prophane Cursing and Swearing' allowed for offenders as young as sixteen to be whipped and put into the stocks. And Justices of the Peace who didn't enforce the Act were fined £5 (around £1,500).

¶ Blasphemy laws in America were similarly severe, and a number of states, including Massachusetts, Michigan, Oklahoma, South Carolina and Wyoming, still have them on their books. For example, Section 36 of the Massachusetts General Laws, where someone who 'wilfully blasphemes the holy name of God by denying, cursing or contumeliously reproaching God, his creation, government or final judging of the world' could still be fined, or imprisoned for up to a year.

¶ These laws reflected the prevailing view at the time that profane language both offended God and corrupted society. Historically, **swear words** and **oaths** were solemn declarations made before God; to take them in vain, or use them scornfully, drunkenly or deceitfully, was a sin.

¶ To avoid this evil, and the punishments that followed, people used **minced oaths** to alter or disguise a profanity. The earliest of these – **gog** (c.1400), **gad** (1592) and **dog** (1550) – safeguarded God's name. Over

time, the range of minced oaths grew and their use became more common.

¶ The widespread use of minced oaths owes much to a British parliamentary act issued in 1605 to remove blasphemy from theatres and 'restrain the Abuses of Players'. When playwrights like Shakespeare, Marlowe and Johnson used words like **zounds** ('God's wounds'), **'sblood** ('God's blood') and **Od's my will** ('God's my will') they did so for self-preservation, but it also promoted their use.

¶ As the Minced Oaths Glossary shows, there was a lot to choose from. Most were devised through alliteration or rhyme, and echo the rhythm and emphasis of the word or phrase they're replacing (for example **cor lumme** for 'God love me'). That said, some seem curious. As well as 'God's blood' – a familiar sixteenth-century expression – there were minced oaths for 'God's body' (**gadsbobs**), 'God's flesh' (**odsflesh**), 'God's little body' (**badsbodikins**) and even 'God's eyelids' (**gadslid**).

¶ By the nineteenth century there were new triggers of moral offence. The language around sex, the human body and its effluvia provided a fresh crop of words that required mincing. Thus it was around the late 1800s that **fuck** turned to **fudge** and **shit** became **sugar**.

¶ It might seem that there are no taboos left in the twenty-first century, but as any parent knows, we still depend on minced oaths. It might seem like **horse feathers** but, **shiitake mushrooms**, parents need to set a good example. So **shut the front door** when the kids are around.

MINCED OATHS GLOSSARY

BY GOD!
Begad! Begorrah! By George!
By gum! By Jove! Byngum!

BY JESUS!
Bejabbers! Bejeezes! By Jis!
By jockies! By Joe! Kershewey!

CHRIST!
Christmas! Christopher!
Columbus! Crikey!
Crimast! Criminey! Cripes!
Crimps! Crumbs!

DAMN!
Bang! Blast! Bother!
Jigger! Jim-whizzed!

DAMNATION!
Botheration! Dangnation!
Dingnation! Flaxation!
Tarnation! Thunderation!

DAMNED!
Blowed! Blue Blazes!
Consarned! Contwisted!
Danged! Dasted! Deuced!
Dished! Hanged!

DEVIL!
Darble! Deuce! Dickens!

GOD!
Cor! Cud! Dod! Dog!
Gad! Godfrey! Daniel!
Gor! Od! Ud!

GOD ALMIGHTY!
Gosh all hemlock!
Gosh-almighty!

GOD DAMN!
Dad-burn! Dog-durned!
Dosh-burned! Doggone!
Gallfired! Golblamed!
Gormed! Gosh-hang!
Gosh-dasted! Gosh-diged!

GOD BLIND ME!
Cor blimey! Gorblimey!

DAMN IT!
Confound it! Consarnit!
Dadblame! Dadblast!
Dadgum! Dadsizzle!
Dagnabbit! Dang it! Darn
it! Dash it! Doggone!

GOD'S BODY
Odsbodlikins

GOD'S HOOKS
Gadzooks

GOD'S SAKE!
Goodness' sake!

GOD'S WOUNDS!
Gadswog! Ods swoon!
Od zounds! Zounds!

GOOD GOD!
Great Scott! Good
garden party! Good
gravy! Good grief!

HELL!
Bejabers! Belehack! Billy-o!
Blazes! Heck! Sam Hill!
Thunder! Thunderation!

JESUS!
Jakes! Japers! Jeebus!
Jehu! Jemima! Jeminy-o!
Jericho! Jiminetty! Jingo!

JESUS CHRIST!
Cheese & crust! Gee
whizz! Jeepers creepers!
Jeez Louise! Jeezle-Peezle!
Jiminy Cricket! Judas Priest!
Jumping Jehosephat!

OH GOD!
Egad! Golly! Goodness! Gosh!

SUFFERING SAVIOUR!
Suffering succotash!

HOLY MOLY

Holy Cannelloni! • Holy Catfish! • Holy Cat! • Holy Christmas!
• Holy Cow! • Holy Cripes! • Holy Cuss! • Holy Frost! • Holy
Gee! • Holy Guacamole! • Holy Hailstones! • Holy Mackerel! •
Holy Mackinaw! • Holy Monkey! • Holy Pretzel! • Holy Shit! •
Holy Smoke! • Holy Snakes! • Holy Toads!

MISNOMERS

¶ A **misnomer** is an inaccurate or misleading name. For instance, **peanuts** aren't nuts, **koala bears** aren't bears and the **English horn** is neither English, nor a horn. Most people live quite contentedly neither knowing nor caring about misnomers, but some delight in them, particularly if they can display their knowledge. Not wishing to deny them this pleasure, the following misnomer guide has been assembled. Although, to be accurate, it's more of a list.

ARABIC NUMERALS	*Originated in India*
BATTLE OF BUNKER HILL	*Fought on Breed's Hill*
BAVARIAN CREAM	*Originated in France*
BLACK BOX RECORDER	*Bright orange*
BOMBAY DUCK	*A fish*
BOSTON CREAM PIE	*A cake*
BRAZIL NUT (also: pine nut, gingko nut, macadamia nut)	*A seed, not a nut*
CASHEW NUT (also: coconut, pistachio nut, walnut)	*A drupe, not a nut*
CAT GUT	*Made from sheep gut*
CHINESE CHECKERS	*Originated in Germany*
COLONIAL GOOSE	*Stuffed leg of mutton*
DANISH PASTRY	*Originated in Austria*
DRY CLEANING	*Uses liquid solvents*
ELECTRIC EEL	*Knifefish family*
ENGLISH HORN	*Originated in Silesia, and a woodwind instrument*
FIREFLY	*A beetle*
FRENCH FRIES	*Originated in Belgium*
FRENCH HORN	*Originated in Germany*
FUNNY BONE	*Ulnar nerve*
GLOW WORM	*Insect larvae*
GUINEA PIG	*A rodent*
HERMIT CRAB	*Not a crab*
HORNED TOAD	*A lizard*
HUNDRED YEARS' WAR	*Lasted 116 years*
INCHWORM	*A caterpillar*
JELLYFISH	*Not a fish*
JERUSALEM ARTICHOKE	*From USA, and from sunflower family*
KING CRAB	*Lithodidae*
LIGHT YEAR	*Measures distance*
MONGOLIAN BBQ	*Originated in Taiwan*
MOUNTAIN CHICKEN	*A frog*
PANAMA HAT	*Originated in Ecuador*
PEANUT	*Legume, not nut*
PENNSYLVANIA DUTCH	*From Germany*
RED PANDA	*Ailuridae (closer to racoon and skunk)*
ROCK SALMON	*A species of small shark*
ROCKY MOUNTAIN OYSTERS	*Fried bull testicles*
SLOW WORM	*Lizard, not worm*
STARFISH	*Echinoderm, not a fish*
STRAWBERRY (Also: raspberry, cranberry, blueberry, blackberry)	*Accessory fruit, not a berry*
TASMANIAN TIGER	*A marsupial*
TIN FOIL	*Made of aluminium*
TITMOUSE	*A bird*
VELVET ANT	*A wasp*
WATERMELON	*A berry*
WATER CHESTNUT	*Aquatic vegetable*

128

SEE ALSO: *Pedantry*

¶ Nobody likes making mistakes, but publishers *really* don't like it. It's embarrassing, and can be expensive. It certainly was for Penguin Australia who had to destroy 7,000 copies of *The Pasta Bible* in 2010 because the recipe for tagliatelle with sardines and prosciutto listed 'freshly ground black people' in the ingredients. Not good.

¶ In publishing, mistakes are called **corrigenda** or **errata**. For a long time, such mistakes were common in printing. Shakespeare's First Folio is full of them, and many first editions – from writers like Niccolò Machiavelli, Jane Austen, Oscar Wilde, Charles Dickens and more – feature errata slips. Even the Declaration of Independence has errata, with an **erratum** in the errata itself.

¶ Today, errata cause red faces. When Faber & Faber published *Moortown* by Ted Hughes in 1979, there was a typo in 'Night Arrival of Sea Trout', that required the correction, 'for "rape", read "nape"'. But at least there was good news when the publisher of the *Australian Dictionary of National Biography* corrected one entry with the information: 'for "died in infancy", read "lived to a ripe old age at Orange"'.

¶ More embarrassing than making mistakes is having a reputation for it. Britain's *Guardian* newspaper was so prone to typos that it was nicknamed The Grauniad. It even made mistakes correcting its mistakes, as in 2007 when it misspelled 'misspelled' twice in its *Corrections and Clarifications* column. On the Grauniad's pages, Wim Duisenberg was rendered 'Dim Duisenberg', Miles Davies' *Sketches of Spain* became 'Sketches of Pain' and the Royal Shakespeare Company was praised for its performance of *The Taming of the Screw*. It even misspelt its own Christmas card.

¶ Some mistakes are so bad they're good. Susan Andersen says she's still haunted by the typo on page 293 of her sizzling romance novel, *Baby, I'm Yours*: 'He stiffened for a moment but then she felt his muscles loosen as he shitted on the ground'. And scientists at the Large Hadron Collider in Cern have stopped counting the number of references to their work at the 'Large Hardon Collider'.

¶ Mistakes can slip through for many reasons, but one of the most infuriating must be when an early draft is mistakenly sent to press. It happened with the UK edition of Jonathan Franzen's *Freedom* (2010), and even to the queen of lexicography, Susie Dent, whose publisher recalled early copies of *Word Perfect* (2020) because the wrong text had been printed. (The error happened during the pandemic, so they had an excuse.)

¶ But not all misprints are costly. One of the most valuable *Harry Potter* books sold in auction was a first edition hardback, where the title on the back cover is misspelled *Harry Potter and the Philospher's Stone*. It's not even the only mistake in the book. But thanks to these typos, it sold for £68,812 in 2019.

FIG.1 *The Regretful Printer – art for errata slips created by John DePol.*

SEE ALSO: *Misquotations / Spelling Bee Winners*

❡ There are three types of **misquotation**: the thing that was almost said, the thing that was never said and the thing that may have been said, but not by the person said to have said it. The problem is that determining the truth can be complicated, but sharing a misquotation is easy, as anyone who has spent time on Instagram will know.

❡ Garson O'Toole, better known as the **Quote Investigator**, has spent years researching the origin of quotations and has identified ten ways in which misquotations arise. One of the most common, which he calls **synthesis** and **streamlining**, involves words being paraphrased and re-ordered for quotability.

❡ TV and film lines are particularly susceptible to such abuse. Captain James T. Kirk never said 'Beam me up, Scotty', *Dragnet*'s Jack Webb didn't ask for 'Just the facts, ma'am', and James Cagney didn't say 'You dirty rat' – but they nearly did, and these almost-quotes are now embedded in the public imagination.

❡ Misattributions are arguably more of a problem. People never tire of reading clever things said by famous people – Oscar Wilde, Coco Chanel, Mark Twain, Albert Einstein and the like – particularly on social media. As a result, well-known figures are commonly attached to nuggets of wisdom they never uttered. But correcting these errors is difficult when people don't want them corrected. 'If you're going through Hell, keep going' wasn't said by Winston Churchill, but it's what people

FIG.1 *'Elementary, my dear Watson', said Sherlock Holmes, never*

want *him* to have said, just as they want to believe Marilyn Monroe delivered the sassy line, 'Well-behaved women seldom make history'. It's a lot less exciting that the real author was an academic called Laurel Thatcher Ulrich.

❡ The story of Marie Antoinette's infamous line, 'Let them eat cake' makes the double error of being the wrong quotation attributed to the wrong person. What was said was *Qu'ils mangent de la brioche* ('Let them eat brioche'), and it was recorded by Jean-Jacques Rousseau in 1767. At that time, Antoinette was only twelve years old and yet to visit France. While history doesn't recall which 'great princess' Rousseau was quoting, it wasn't her. Mark Twain probably didn't say 'never let the facts get in the way of a good story.' That makes it an apt motto for those who share dubious quotations. The problem remains, however, that the truth is often a lot less quotable.

SEE ALSO: *Etymology Mysteries / Shakespeare Coinages*

MISREMEMBERED CLASSICS

I have nothing to offer but blood, sweat and tears.

(Winston Churchill)

CORRECT: 'I have nothing to offer but blood, toil, tears and sweat.'

The journey of a thousand miles begins with a single step.

(Lau Tzu)

CORRECT: 'A journey of 400 miles begins beneath one's feet.'

Pride comes before a fall.

(Proverbs 16:18)

CORRECT: 'Pride goes before destruction, a haughty spirit before a fall.'

Water, water, everywhere, / And not a drop to drink.

(*The Rime of the Ancient Mariner*)

CORRECT: 'Water, water, everywhere, / Nor any drop to drink.'

MISQUOTED MOVIES

Mirror, mirror on the wall…

(*Snow White and the Seven Dwarfs*, 1937)

CORRECT: 'Magic mirror on the wall…'

I don't think we're in Kansas anymore.

(*The Wizard of Oz*, 1939)

CORRECT: 'Toto, I guess we're not in Kansas anymore.'

If you build it, they will come.

(*Field of Dreams*, 1989)

CORRECT: 'If you build it, he will come.'

Fasten your seat belts, it's going to be a bumpy ride.

(*All About Eve*, 1950)

CORRECT: 'Fasten your seat belts, it's going to be a bumpy night.'

MISATTRIBUTED TO EINSTEIN

Insanity is doing the same thing over and over again and expecting different results.

(From *Sudden Death* (1983) by Rita Mae Brown)

Everything should be made as simple as possible, but not simpler.

(Source not known, but likely paraphrasing Occam's Razor.)

Education is that which remains, if one has forgotten everything learned in school.

(Source unknown)

If you think intelligence is dangerous, try ignorance.

(No evidence Einstein said it)

MISQUOTED SHAKESPEARE

Bubble, bubble, toil and trouble.

(*Macbeth*, 4.1)

CORRECT: 'Double double, toil and trouble.'

To gild the lily.

– (*King John*, 4.2)

CORRECT: 'To gild refinèd gold, to paint the lily.'

Lead on, Macduff

(*Macbeth*, 5.8)

CORRECT: 'Lay on, Macduff'

Alas, poor Yorick! I knew him well.

(*Hamlet*, 5.1)

CORRECT: 'Alas, poor Yorick. I knew him, Horatio –'

If you've ever misheard a song lyric that your brain then mangled into something quite unlike the original, then you've encountered a *mondegreen*.

Like *eggcorns* (see page 60), mondegreens are a glitch in how we process human speech. But unlike eggcorns, which still make sense, mondegreens are more inclined to nonsense. Of course Michael Stipe isn't singing 'Let's pee in the corner, Let's pee in the spotlight' in 'Losing My Religion'; nor did The Bangles sing 'Just another man, it's Monday' in 'Manic Monday'. Both, however, are mondegreens often heard instead of the correct words.

Song lyrics account for most mondegreens because the brain has to work overtime to decipher what the words are. Not only can vocals be harder to understand, but there's the cacophony of music to contend with too. It's no wonder that the brain sometimes makes things up.

But not all mondegreens come from lyrics, and nor are they always accidental. The Lord's Prayer, for instance, has been thoroughly *mondegreened*, although more deliberately. From 'Our Father, makes art in Heaven, Howard be thy name', to 'Aunt Leda's not into temptation' and 'Deliver us some email'.

America's Pledge of Allegiance has been similarly rendered, with mischievous children ready to 'pledge a lesion to the flag', 'With liver tea and just us four, all.' The same fate has befallen the Australian national anthem, with 'Australians all let us rejoice, for we are young and free' becoming, 'Australians all own ostriches, four minus one is three.'

The technical explanation for mondegreens lies in what linguists call *oronyms*, in which different words sound similar when they're run together, like 'I scream' and 'ice cream', 'nice water' and 'ice water'.

SEE ALSO: *Eggcorns / Metanalysis / Strine*

THE ORIGINAL LADY MONDEGREEN

'Mondegreen' is itself a mondegreen. The word was coined by writer Sylvia Wright in an article titled 'The Death of Lady Mondegreen' for *Harper's Magazine* in 1954. Wright remembered how she was enchanted by a poem her mother would read her from Thomas Percy's *Reliques,* which described the death of Earl Amurray and the Lady Mondegreen. Only later did Wright discover that the poem said something quite different (see below), but by then she fallen in love with the mysterious Lady Mondegreen and decided her version was better. She also shared her delight in the strange imaginings conjured by other mondegreens, writing: 'Nothing like them has ever been seen before, and who knows what lost and lovely things may not come streaming in with them.' Wright's original article is a wonderful read and can be dug up online. It's worth looking for.

ORIGINAL
Ye Highlands and ye Lowlands,
Oh, where hae ye been?
They hae slain the Earl Amurray,
And laid him on the green.

MONDEGREEN
Ye Highlands and ye Lowlands,
Oh, where hae ye been?
They hae slain the Earl Amurray,
And Lady Mondegreen.

¶ The Two Ronnies, those beloved British comedians, based their most famous sketch on oronyms, with Ronnie Barker requesting items from a shopping list rife with wordplay. Asking the shopkeeper for 'fork handles', he's given four candles, and the confusion continues from there.

¶ Letters that sound alike can also confuse the brain. One of the best known mondegreens is from the Jimi Hendrix lyric 'kiss the sky', widely misheard as 'kiss this guy'. It's an understandable mistake when you read it out loud, and if you play the song you'll be able to hear either lyric, depending on what you're listening for.

¶ The brain is a highly sophisticated word processor that doesn't just listen to the sounds, but also makes sense of them in terms of context, expectation and familiarity. A UN representative might be attuned to 'peace talks' while an organic farmer is interested in 'pea stalks'. The brain is adept at divining the correct meaning; but if confused, or mischievous, it's happy to make something up. And that's when mondegreens are born.

¶ Brains have another weakness too: they can be highly suggestible. If you read the Mondegreen Top Ten while listening to the songs, it's difficult *not* to hear these words. And once a mondegreen is attached to one's auditory cortex, it's hard to remove.

¶ When Sylvia Wright first wrote of the mondegreen she warned they could bring with them 'a thousand bright and strange images'. They might arise from pop songs or sacred prayers, be accidental or contrived, but it's hard to resist the delightful nonsense these *earslips* bring. Singer Eddie Money might promise 'two tickets to paradise', but 'two chickens with parrot eyes' are far more interesting.

133

MONDEGREEN TOP TEN

Steak and knife, steak and knife…
(= STAYING ALIVE,
STAYING ALIVE)
'Stayin' Alive' / Bee Gees

Ain't Taco Bell love…
(= TALKING ABOUT)
'Ain't Talkin 'Bout Love' / Van Halen

Hold me closer Tony Danza…
(= TINY DANCER)
'Tiny Dancer' / Elton John

I wanna be a door…
(= ADORED)
'I Wanna Be Adored' / The Stone Roses

Just let me staple the vicar
(= SAY FOR THE RECORD)
'We Are Family' / Sister Sledge

Suitcase Dramamine…
(= OF MEMORIES)
'Time After Time' / Cyndi Lauper

My pony plays the mamba…
(= MARCONI)
'We Built This City' / Starship

Here we are now in containers…
(= ENTERTAIN US)
'Smells Like Teen Spirit' / Nirvana

Oprah got no style!…
(= OPPA GANGNAM)
'Gangnam Style' / Psy

I own a single lettuce…
(= ALL THE SINGLE LADIES)
'Single Ladies' / Beyoncé

¶ **Lillian Virginia Mountweazel** was a fountain-designer-turned-photographer from Bangs, Ohio. She received some acclaim for her portraits of the South Sierra Miwoks, but sadly died in 1973, killed in an explosion while on assignment for *Combustibles Magazine*.

¶ Except, she wasn't. Or to be clear, she *never was*, because Mountweazel was invented by the editors of the *New Oxford American Dictionary* as a **copyright trap** for dictionary plagiarists. And today, the person who never was has become eponymous with dictionary entries that shouldn't be.

¶ Dictionary editors use **mountweazels** (fake dictionary entries) to spot if their work is being copied. Cartographers use a similar trick with non-existent **trap streets** (also, **paper towns**) to catch out lazy map-makers. And encyclopedists and biographers have done the same too. Even Google has set such lures, admitting they used phoney search queries like **mbzrxpg jys** to prove its rivals were stealing its data. (Apparently, they were.)

¶ One legendary mountweazel is **esquiv-alience**, a deliciously complicated word in the *New Oxford American Dictionary* (2001). Asked if their dictionary contained a mountweazel, the editors admitted there was one that started with **E**. Dictionary sleuths identified five possible candidates: **earth loop**; **EGD** (eyeglass display); **electrofish**; **ELSS** (extravehicular life support system); **esquivalience**; and **euro creep**. When the shortlist was sent to *NOAD*'s editor-in-chief, she revealed 'esquivalience' was the bogey; but not before *Webster's New Millennium* had been found using it. They had, in other words, been **mountweazelled**.

134

SEE ALSO: *Dord and Other Ghost Words*

· A MOUND OF
MOUNTWEAZELS

ESQUIVALIENCE (N.)

(1) The wilful avoidance of one's official responsibilities; the shirking of duties,
(2) An unwillingness to work, esp. as part of a group effort,
(3) Lack of interest or motivation.

(New Oxford American Dictionary, 2001)

HINK (V.) / HINKS, HINKING, HINKED

If you hink, you think hopefully and unrealistically about something.

(Collins COBUILD English Language Dictionary, 1987)

JUNGTFAK (N.)

A Persian bird, the male of which had only one wing on the right side, and the female only one wing on the left side.

(Webster's New Twentieth Century Dictionary, 1943)

STEINLAUS (N.), (STONE-LOUSE)

Smallest native rodent from the family *Lapivora* with the subspecies kidney stone-louse, bladder stone-louse, gallstone-louse, cerebral stone-louse, and common stone-louse.

(Pschyrembel Klinisches Wörterbuch, 2001)

ZZXJOANW (N.), MAORI

(1) Drum, (2) Fife, (3) Conclusion.

(Music Lovers' Encyclopedia, 1939)

❡ *Mudball* is a Victorian word for an insult or jibe. Modern English is well stocked with mudballs, but we've heard them all before. That's why it can be a pleasure to rediscover some historical mudballs. This compendium of antique insults spans six centuries. Try introducing them at work or in social gatherings. Not only are they delicious to say, but because they're so unexpected, they won't cause offence. Probably. After all, those *noddypolls* won't know what you're talking about.

AFTERNOON FARMER (1742)
a lazy man

BAGPIPE (1603)
a dull windbag

BEDPRESSER (1598)
a layabout

BEDSWERVER (1616)
an adulterer

BELLY-SLAVE (1562)
a glutton

BLOB-TALE (1670)
a tattle-tale

BRABBLER (1570)
an argumentative person

CAKE FIDDLER (1522)
a sponger

CUMBER-WORLD (1374)
a useless person

DRIVELARD (1530)
a liar

FIZGIG (1529)
a frivolous woman

FLIP-FLAP (1681)
a scatterbrain

FOPDOODLE (1664)
a simpleton

GECK (1530)
a dupe or fool

GETLING (1718)
a brat

GLISTERER (1628)
a showoff

GLOFFER (1440)
a glutton

GROINER (1382)
a complainer

GUPLIN (1802)
a gullible fool

HOOD-PICK (1513)
a skinflint

LICKLADLE (1486)
a freeloader

LOITER-SACK (1594)
a lazy lump

LOSARD (1400)
a ne'er-do-well

LUBBARD (1586)
a lazy oaf

MUCK-SPOUT (1825)
a foulmouth

MUTTON-MONGER (1532)
a lothario

NASH-GAB (1816)
a gossip

NODCOCK (1577)
a fool

PENNY TRUMPETER (1828)
a braggart

QUAKING CUSTARD (1607)
a coward

SKIN PRICKER (1611)
an irritating person

SLOBBER-CHOPS (1670)
a wet kisser

SLOTTERBUG (1440)
a grubby layabout

SLUBBERDEGULLION (1612)
a slob

SMELLFUNGUS (1768)
a complainer

STING-BUM (1698)
a miser

TOAD-EATER (1742)
a sycophant

TRUMPER (1450)
a deceiver

UPCREEPER (1540)
a sycophant

WHIFFLER (1659)
an insignificant person

135

SEE ALSO: *Obsolete Occupations*

N.

NEWSPEAK

¶ *Newspeak*, the constructed language in George Orwell's *Nineteen Eighty-Four*, is unlike any other fictional language. While **Nadsat** from *A Clockwork Orange* and **Quenya** from *Lord of the Rings* are primarily stylistic, Newspeak is of institutional importance to the dystopian world of Oceania, Big Brother and Ingsoc (English Socialism). As the character Syme puts it: 'Newspeak is Ingsoc and Ingsoc is Newspeak.'

¶ For Orwell, Newspeak was the linguistic expression of totalitarian control. It erased words from Standard English (Oldspeak), and pruned meaning from those words remaining, thereby removing the ability to think outside party orthodoxy. In Newspeak, ideas heretical to Ingsoc would be unthinkable because the words to describe them would not exist. As Orwell illustrates in the book's appendix, it would be impossible to translate the Declaration of Independence into Newspeak except to call it **CRIMETHINK**.

¶ Newspeak draws on the theory that language shapes thought, an idea known as **linguistic determinism**. As Orwell wrote in *Politics and the English Language*, 'if thought corrupts language, language can also corrupt thought'.

¶ Although linguistic determinism is widely contested, that hasn't stopped authoritarian regimes from using language just as Orwell described. China and North Korea provide living examples of Newspeak, where information – historical or current – is written to reflect party orthodoxy. In such countries the Thought Police aren't a metaphor, as they are in Western liberal democracies, but very real. Controversy around the Dalai Lama and Tibet, for instance, doesn't exist in China because neither his name, nor that place, can be acknowledged in print.

¶ Western democracies might not face the literal reality of Newspeak, but people are acutely conscious of how language can be, and is, manipulated. When politicians and corporations twist words with **euphemisms** and **counterfactuals**; when lies become **alternative truths**, and truths are rendered **fake news**; when public figures are **cancelled** and **deplatformed**; or when language is altered to reflect changing values, many are quick to call it out as Newspeak… or **doublethink**… or **thoughtcrime**.

¶ Far from fading, the principles of Newspeak seem to have become more resonant than ever in the twenty-first century. **Doubleplusungood**.

ORIGINS OF NEWSPEAK

Orwell's Newspeak took inspiration from different places. Ingsoc ministries like **Miniplenty** and **Miniluv** echoed abbreviations common in Soviet Russia, such as **Comintern** and **Gosplan**. Elsewhere, the contracted language used in Winston Smith's work – like the instruction **bb speech malreported africa rectify** – were imitative of the clipped language of cablegrams. But the vocabulary and grammar of Newspeak was most strongly influenced by **Basic English**, a simplified language created by Charles Ogden that contained just 850 words, and a trimmed, standardised grammar.

NEWSPEAK DICTIONARY

BELLYFEEL
Blind acceptance of an idea.

BLACKWHITE
(a) To accept what one is told, regardless of facts; (b) To unthinkingly say what the party requires.

CRIMESTOP
Instinctively stopping short of thoughtcrime.

CRIMETHINK
Any thought relating to concepts of liberty or equality.

DOUBLEPLUSGOOD
Very good.

DOUBLEPLUSUNGOOD
Very bad.

DOUBLETHINK
Simultaneously believing two mutually contradictory ideas.

DUCKSPEAK
To quack like a duck: 'Applied to an opponent, it is abuse, applied to someone you agree with, it is praise'.

FULLWISE
Fully, completely or totally.

GOODTHINK
(N.) Orthodoxy; (V.) To think in an orthodox way.

GOODSEX
Sexual intercourse intended solely for procreation.

GOODWISE
Well.

INGSOC
The ideology of the Party, 'English Socialism'.

JOYCAMP
Forced-labour camp.

OLDSPEAK
Standard English.

OLDTHINK
Ideas predating Ingsoc, like objectivity and rationalism.

OWNLIFE
Individualism.

PLUSGOOD
Very good.

PLUSUNGOOD
Very bad

PROLEFEED
Worthless entertainment made for the masses.

SEXCRIME
Sexual immorality, including: adultery, homosexuality, oral sex and any unsanctioned intercourse.

TELESCREEN
A combined television and CCTV camera that can never be turned off.

THOUGHTCRIME
Any thought contrary to Party orthodoxy.

THINKPOL
Thought Police; responsible for detecting and managing thoughtcrime.

UNPERSON
An executed person whose existence is no longer acknowledged.

INGSOC MINISTRIES

MINIPLENTY *Ministry of Plenty (economic affairs)*
MINILUV *Ministry of Love (law and order)*
MINIPAX *Ministry of Peace (war)*
MINITRUE *Ministry of Truth (news, entertainment, education and arts)*
RECDEP *Records Department in Minitrue*

ORIGINAL NEWSPEAK

Times 3.12.83 reporting BB dayorder doubleplusungood
refs unperson rewrite fullwise upsub antefiling.

TRANSLATION

The reporting of Big Brother's Order of the Day in the Times of 3 December 1983 is extremely unsatisfactory and makes reference to a non-existent person. Rewrite it in full and submit your draft to higher authority before filing.

SEE ALSO: *Euphemisms for Death*

❡ *Apology* is from Greek *apologia*, meaning a speech in defence of something. This was English's first sense of the word, and only later did it relate to admission and regret of an offense.

❡ Then came the *non-apology*. In the nineteenth century this simply meant the *absence* of an apology, but today more commonly refers to the collection of words that sound like an apology but fall short of being one.

❡ Psychiatrist and apology expert Dr Aaron Lazare has identified four qualities of a true apology: acknowledgement of the offense; an explanation that's not an excuse; a sincere expression of remorse; when possible, the offer to make amends. The non-apology offers none of these. Instead, it is carefully constructed so as to evade, deflect or dilute personal responsibility for wrongdoing.

❡ The non-apology (also: *backhanded apology*, *ifpology*, *fauxpology* and *non-pology*) is often revealed by the words immediately following 'I'm sorry'. Thus, 'I'm sorry *if…*', 'I'm sorry *that…*' and 'I'm sorry *but…*' all give notice that a non-apology is in the post, as does the politicians' favourite, 'I regret that…'.

❡ Non-apologies must be carefully parsed for their real meaning. They may be intended to shift blame, diminish an offence or provide an excuse, particularly if legal, professional or personal consequences are at stake.

❡ The king of non-apologies is '*mistakes were made*', defined in *Safire's Political Dictionary* as 'a passive-evasive way of acknowledging error'. First associated with Richard Nixon's administration, 'mistakes were made' has become the signature denial of the political class.

VARIETIES OF NON-APOLOGY

THE REGRET APOLOGY
I sincerely regret what happened…

THE IF-YOU-NEED-ONE APOLOGY
To anyone who was offended, I apologise…

THE VAGUE APOLOGY
I'm sorry for any anything I did wrong…

THE DISPLACEMENT APOLOGY
I'm sorry you feel I let you down…

YESTERDAY'S APOLOGY
I've said how sorry I am…

THE TELEPATHIC APOLOGY
You know I'm sorry…

THE PREDICTIVE APOLOGY
I guess I owe you an apology…

THE TRANSACTIONAL APOLOGY
I'll apologise if you will…

THE NOT-MINE APOLOGY
I've been asked to apologise…

THE DOWN-PLAY APOLOGY
I was just trying to help…

THE APOLOGY / EXCUSE
I'm sorry, but I was very drunk…

THE MULTIPOLOGY
I'm sorry that I keep upsetting you…

THE VICTIM APOLOGY
I'm sorry for being such a terrible person…

THE CLENCHED-FIST APOLOGY
I'm sorry, OK!

O.

OBSOLETE OCCUPATIONS

❡ The march of time constantly makes jobs obsolete. But while the world has lost film projectionists, telegraph operators and lamp lighters, new professions take their place. The list of obsolete professions can be shocking, amusing and often baffling. But it's no stranger than trying to explain **Decluttering Consultants** or **Pet Psychologists**. In 2021, Facebook Reality Labs advertised for an **Avatar Behaviours Engineering Manager** to 'Own the quality and fidelity of human representation in virtual reality'. Maybe leech gathering isn't so strange after all.

BETWEEN GIRL
(1890S)
A junior maid who helped both cook and housemaid.

BREAKER BOY
(1860S)
A coal worker who removed impurities from coal.

DOG WHIPPER
(1590S)
The official who removed dogs from churches.

DONKEY PUNCHER
(1920S)
The donkey engine operator as used in logging camps.

GLIMMER MAN
(1940S)
An inspector employed by Irish gas companies to detect gas use.

GONG FARMER
(1300S)
The labourer who removed excreta from cesspits and privies.

GROOM OF THE STOOL
(1500S)
A servant of the English monarch who assisted with matters of toilet.

HERB STREWER
(1600S)
Distributed fragrant herbs and flowers around the homes of English monarchs.

HOG CONSTABLE
(1630S)
Appointed to impound stray hogs and prevent any damage they might cause.

KNOCKER-UPPER
(1800S)
Paid to wake people by knocking on their window.

LEECH GATHERER
(1860S)
One who gathers leeches for use in medicine.

LOUSE-FEEDER
(1920S)
Living blood-donors for typhus-infected lice used in the development of vaccines.

MUD CLERK
(1870S)
Employed on a river steamer as the purser's assistant.

SLUGGARD WAKER
(1800S)
The parishioner tasked with waking congregants who fell asleep during a service.

TOSHER
(1800S)
One who scavenged for valuables in sewers and drains.

USEFUL MAN
(1900S)
A junior domestic worker, above hall boy but below footman.

navigation☞ SEE ALSO: *Elizabethan Colours / Vintage Ailments*

ORIGINAL TITLES OF CLASSIC BOOKS

ALL'S WELL THAT ENDS WELL
(WAR AND PEACE)
by Leo Tolstoy

ATTICUS
(TO KILL A MOCKINGBIRD)
by Harper Lee

CATCH-18
(CATCH-22)
by Joseph Heller

DUBLINERS
(ULYSSES)
by James Joyce

FIRST IMPRESSIONS
(PRIDE & PREJUDICE)
by Jane Austen

JOHN THOMAS AND LADY JANE
(LADY CHATTERLEY'S LOVER)
by D. H. Lawrence

PROMETHEUS UNCHAINED
(FRANKENSTEIN)
by Mary Shelley

SISTER MAGGIE
(THE MILL ON THE FLOSS)
by George Eliot

SOMETHING THAT HAPPENED
(OF MICE AND MEN)
by John Steinbeck

STRANGERS FROM WITHIN
(LORD OF THE FLIES)
by William Golding

THE DEAD UN-DEAD
(DRACULA)
by Bram Stoker

THE HOUSE OF FAITH
(BRIDESHEAD REVISITED)
by Evelyn Waugh

THE MAN IN BLACK
(BLEAK HOUSE)
by Charles Dickens

THE LAST MAN IN EUROPE
(NINETEEN EIGHTY-FOUR)
by George Orwell

THE SEA COOK: A STORY FOR BOYS
(TREASURE ISLAND)
by Robert Louis Stevenson

THE SIMPLETONS
(JUDE THE OBSCURE)
by Thomas Hardy

THE STRIKE
(ATLAS SHRUGGED)
by Ayn Rand

TOMORROW IS ANOTHER DAY
(GONE WITH THE WIND)
by Margaret Mitchell

TRIMALCHIO IN WEST EGG
(THE GREAT GATSBY)
by F. Scott Fitzgerald

TWILIGHT
(THE SOUND AND THE FURY)
by William Faulkner

SEE ALSO: *Charles Dickens' Characters*

LEXIPEDIA PEOPLE

WILLIAM MINOR
DICTIONARY RESEARCHER
(1834–1920)

¶Only three people contributed more quotations to *OED* than Dr William Minor. Between his first, in 1883, and last, in 1906, he submitted 62,720 of them. The achievement is doubly astonishing because he did it while incarcerated at the Asylum for Criminal Lunatics in Broadmoor.

¶Minor had served as a surgeon in the American Civil War. It was during this time that he started experiencing paranoid delusions. When he retired from the army in 1871 he moved to London, but unfortunately, his delusions moved with him. On 17 February 1872, he shot and killed a man he thought was an evil spirit. At his trial, there was no doubt of Minor's mental illness and he was sent to Broadmoor on 17 April 1872.

¶Deemed a low-risk prisoner, Minor was allowed personal effects and had two connected cells to put them in. His books were sent from America, and with his officer's pension he bought dozens more. He then paid for floor-to-ceiling bookshelves to turn one cell into a library. He remained haunted by paranoid delusions, but his books and art provided solace.

¶In 1879, the editor of the *OED* appealed to the reading public for help researching the new dictionary. It's unclear how Minor learned of this, but he did, and on 26 June 1883 he sent his first contributions. Nobody at the *OED* knew who Minor was, or connected his Crowthorne address with the nearby asylum, but they were were impressed by the quality and quantity of his work, which arrived week after week. In the first edition of the dictionary, published in 1888, Minor's name appeared in the acknowledgements.

¶The dictionary's editor, the famous Dr James Murray, had corresponded with Minor for years, but only learned of his shocking circumstances in 1890. In January 1891, he visited Broadmoor for the first time, writing later how he found Minor 'a much cultivated and scholarly man, with many artistic tastes.' Indeed he was, but he remained tortured by visions. In 1902, he took to himself with a knife and severed his penis in the hope of stopping them. He survived this gruesome self-mutilation, but the illness continued.

¶Those who met Minor saw he was an extraordinary person. He was generous too. He donated many of his books to the *OED*, and continued to give money to the family of the man he'd murdered. These qualities attracted support from many influential people, including the President of Harvard and British Home Secretary, Winston Churchill. With Murray and others, they petitioned for his release and return to America, which was granted on 16 April 1910. Minor died ten years later in the care of the Retreat for the Elderly Insane in Hertford, Connecticut.

¶ It's often said that **nonsense literature** was a Victorian invention, but that's **bosh**. Long before **jabberwocks** and **jumblies**, seventeenth-century poets were devising nonsense verse that would have delighted nineteenth-century readers.

¶ In *The Origins of English Nonsense*, Noel Malcolm argues that the first work of true nonsense was the *Cabbalistical Verses* of John Hoskyns, written in 1611. It's only twelve lines, but starting as it does on '*waves of brainlesse butter'd fish*' and progressing through the '*equinoctiall pasticrust*', it certainly has the hallmarks of classic nonsense.

¶ But this is Hoskyns's only surviving nonsense poem. His contemporary, John Taylor, the self-styled Water Poet, had over 150 published works, and is acknowledged by many to be the first true nonsense poet. His earliest major work of nonsense, *Sir Gregory Nonsence His Newes from No Place* (1622), is prefaced with a letter addressed *To Nobody*, and begins in characteristic style:

> *Upon a Christmas Even, somewhat nigh*
> *Easter, anon after Whitsuntide, walking*
> *in a Coach from London to Lambeth by*
> *water, I overtooke a Man that met me in the*
> *morning before the Sun set…*

¶ Taylor, a Thames waterman, was proud to be one of the 'Simple Understanders'; not born of the elite, nor educated in Greek and Latin. Fittingly, his 1620 *Jack a Lent* collection was dedicated to the butchers and fishmongers of London. Nevertheless, his work was widely enjoyed, even reaching the Royal Court.

¶ Taylor's crowning achievement, published after his death in 1653, was *The Essence, Quintessence, Insence, Innocence, Lye-sence, & Magnifisence of Nonsence upon Sence: Or, Sence upon Nonsence.* The title page explains that it is:

> *The third Part, the fourth Impression, the*
> *fifth Edition, the sixth Addition, upon*
> *Condition; that (by Tradition) the Reader*
> *may laugh if he list. In Longitude, Latitude,*
> *Crassitude, Magnitude and Amplitude,*
> *lengthened, widened, enlarged, augmented,*
> *encreased, made wider and sider, by the*
> *addition of Letters, Syllables, Words, Lines,*
> *and far fetch'd Sentences.*

¶ With dozens of works published in his lifetime, Taylor's particular brand of nonsense inspired numerous imitators, which is why it's so curious that his name is scarcely known today. His use of invented languages, inverted meanings, strange juxtapositions and surreal humour – all characteristic of the nonsense to come – was hugely inventive in his day. It's impossible to know whether the likes of Lear or Carroll read the Water Poet's work; but if they did, they most certainly would have recognised a kindred spirit.

FIG.1 *John Taylor (1578–1653)*

SIR GREGORY NONSENCE HIS
NEWES FROM NO PLACE

Written on purpose, with much fludy to no end, plentifully flored
with want of wit, learning, Judgement, Rime and Reason, and may
seeme very fitly for the underflanding of Nobody. (etc.)

IT was in June the eight and thirtieth day,
That I imbarked was on Highgate Hill,
After discourteous friendly taking leave:
Of my young Father *Madge* and Mother *John*,
The Wind did ebbe, the tide flou'd North South-east,
We hoist our Sailes of Colloquintida,
And after 13. dayes and 17. nights,
(With certaine Hiroglyphicke houres to boote)
We with tempestuous calmes, and friendly stormes,
Split our maine top-mast, close below the keele.
But I with a dull quick congruity,
Tooke 19. ounces of the Westerne winde,
And with the pith of the pole Artichocke,
Saild by the flaming Coast of Trapezond,
There in a Fort of melting Adamant,
Arm'd in a Crimson Robe, as blacke as Jet,
I saw Alcides with a Spiders thred,
Lead Serberus to the Proponticke Sea,
Then cutting further through the marble Maine,
'Mongst flying Buls, and 4. leg'd Turkicocks,
A dumbe faire spoken, welfac'd aged youth,
Sent to me from the stout Stimphalides,
With tonguelesse silence thus beganne his speech…

EXCERPT FROM THE
INTRODUCTION AND POEM
JOHN TAYLOR (1622)

¶ With its twenty-six letters, the English alphabet can create around forty-four distinct sounds, or **phonemes**. Corresponding to these are the **graphemes**, the letters, or groups of letters, that indicate the sound. Different graphemes can make the same sound – as with *pea*, *see*, and *key* – or one grapheme might make different sounds, like the *o* in *son*, *no*, *on* and *to*.

¶ Most graphemes are two letters, but some have four, like **aigh** (in str*aigh*t), **arre** (in biz*arre*) and **eigh** (in *eigh*t). And then there's **ough**, the grapheme of graphemes, that has become a cautionary tale for anyone learning English. No grapheme has inspired so much bewilderment, or so much poetry, as **ough**, with its nine sounds… maybe eleven. But absolutely no more than twelve.

144

SEE ALSO: *The Great Vowel Shift*

THE OUGH GUIDE

ow	uff
in pl*ough*	in r*ough*
oh	oof
in d*ough*	in w*ough*[3]
oo	up
in thr*ough*	in hicc*ough*
ock	or
in h*ough*[1]	in b*ough*t
och	ow
in l*ough*[2]	in L*ough*ton[4]
off	oot
in c*ough*	in W*ough*ton[4]

(1) part of the leg	(3) dog bark
(2) a lake	(4) English towns

PHONEME RECORDS

Ta'a , a language spoken by around 3,000 people in southern Botswana and eastern Namibia, holds the World Record for **most phonemes**, with 161 distinct sounds. It has 80–130 consonants (linguists can't agree), 28 vowels and three different tones, including **click**, **tsk** and **tut** sounds.

In contrast, **Rotokas**, spoken on Bougainville, an island in Papua New Guinea, holds the record for **fewest phonemes**. Its twelve-letter alphabet can only make eleven distinct sounds (two letters share a sound). Put another way, the English grapheme **ough** has more phonemes than the entire Rotokas alphabet.

THE BARRACLOUGH FOOFAROUGH

We Barracloughs are tough.	*Of Goughs and Houghs—a slough*
We Barracloughs are thorough.	*Of Cloughs and Bloughs. What though*
We've shaken every bough.	*We come down with the cough?*
We've beaten every borough.	*What though we squander dough*
Directories we plough	*And time? It is enough*
Methodically through	*To know there is no -ough*
Are each a very trough	*That rhymes with Barraclough.*

GEORGE STARBUCK

P.

PAGER CODE

¶ Before gifs, emojis, emoticons and text messages, there was *pager code*. Pagers were the preeminent mobile communication technology in the 1980s and 1990s, but many could only receive numeric messages. With necessity the mother of invention, elaborate codes were used for personal messages.

¶ There were three types of pager code. The easiest to read used numbers to represent letters, like Ƅ (G), ☐ (D or O) and ﬔ (M). Some of these messages were read the right way up (e.g. ƅ☐ = GO), while others made sense upside down (e.g. I4 = HI). These messages were readable(ish), but could be long.

¶ More useful, but more mysterious, were the dozens of short codes known to pager users. Some were based on the letter count of individual words (e.g. I (1) love (4) you (3) = I43) while others were more phonetic (e.g. nighty-night = 99). But the majority of short codes were arbitrary. 218, for instance, meant Tired of waiting, I'm leaving; 203 meant Get off the phone and 211 was Pick me up.

¶ Many users would know commonly used codes but experts could relay detailed messages that would be impenetrable to the uninitiated. Today, pager codes are largely forgotten, but they were the precursor of text messaging, and a fascinating chapter in the history of personal communications in the digital age.

8I2II76*88CI5*9863I25
(Translation on page 215)

READ NORMALLY

ƅ☐*4☐I773
Go home

ƅ☐☐☐*843
Good bye

I*8I77*43I23
I am here

I*I77I55*4
I miss you

5☐8*5☐8
Sob sob

ƅ☐☐☐*I7I647
Good night

4I*7☐53I2
Hi loser

READ UPSIDE DOWN

II34*2*☐9
Go to hell

334*334
Hee hee

☐7734
Hello

LETTER COUNT	OTHER SHORT CODES
424	4II
Call me back	*I have a question*
823	9II
Thinking of you	*Emergency / important*
477	420
Best friends forever	*Want to smoke weed?*

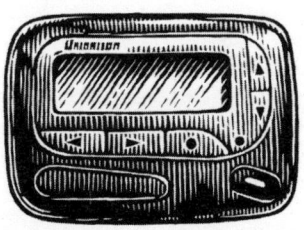

SEE ALSO: *Hacker Jargon*

¶ All words have a past, and sometimes that past is ugly. Fortunately, many words associated with prejudice and bigotry are becoming taboo, but some hide in plain sight, either because their origins have been forgotten or the word has been normalised. But identifying these contentious words can be thorny, and deciding what to do with them is harder still.

¶ Take *cakewalk*, meaning something that's easy, and from which we also get *piece of cake* and *take the cake*. The original cakewalk was a dance performed by enslaved Africans to the amusement of white slave-owners, with the best performance winning a cake. *Except*, the cakewalk was mocking the mannered dances of white people, so in itself was a subversive parody. *Except*, descriptions of cakewalks in the late-nineteenth century were full of hideous caricatures of Black people. *Except*, the cakewalk was also an authentic Black folk form which white people never properly understood. *Except*, it was later a mainstay of minstrel shows with performers in blackface. *Except*... well, so it goes on, with different stories in different contexts.

¶ Words like cakewalk are difficult because they relate to one of the darkest chapters in American history, but the connection is at least known. *Buck naked* is knotty in a different way. It might refer to the smoothness of buckskin, which would only be weird; or it could be a description of enslaved Black men, offensively called *bucks*, being stripped naked for a buyer to inspect. Etymologists don't know. Nor do they agree about *bulldoze*. For a long time, people were sure it came from *bull dose*, an

extreme flogging ('fit for a bull') given to enslaved people. Today, however, the *OED* identifies it as 'of uncertain origin'.

¶ If the examples in this entry seem skewed towards slavery in America, that's because English preserves so many references to the subject. Something sold at auction is *on the block*, a grim allusion to the slaver's auction block. And entrenched in the tech world is the uncomfortable language of *slave servers*, *master servers*, *blacklists* and *webmasters* (although this is starting to change). The expression *n***** in the woodpile* has a nasty habit of reappearing every few years, while the children's counting rhyme, *Eeny, Meeny, Miny, Mo* still featured the same unacceptable word late into the twentieth century. People who can't see the problem with this might consider whether they'd feel equally comfortable with playful idioms about genocide or 9/11.

¶ Native Americans feel a similar sense of anger about the expressions that have either been appropriated from their culture or reflect the history of their mistreatment. Phrases like *Indian giver*, *scalper* and *circle the wagons* all have history, it's just often overlooked.

¶ Opinions differ about whether words with a grim past should be forgotten. Some would have them expunged; others, unhappy about having their language policed, dig in. But perhaps one thing both sides can agree on is the importance of understanding what the history of a word is, and if the skeletons in the closet are real or not.

WORDS WITH RACIST ORIGINS

NO CAN DO (IDIOM)
(ALSO: *LONG TIME NO SEE*)
Both colloquial expressions were coined in the nineteenth century and mock the pidgin English of America's Chinese immigrants.

SOLD DOWN THE RIVER (IDIOM)
Meaning to betray or double-cross someone. This nineteenth-century expression derives from America's slave-owners selling enslaved people they found troublesome to plantations further down the Mississippi.

OFF THE RESERVATION (IDIOM)
Meaning to do something unexpected or that hasn't been approved. This expression appeared in the nineteenth century and is offensive to Native Americans because it makes light of the persecution and violence they experienced.

UPPITY (ADJ.)
Someone **uppity** is haughty and superior. Worse still, they have 'ideas above their station'. The word has a history of being racially loaded, used to describe Black American women who 'don't know their place'. It is therefore considered a coded but well-understood form of racism, particularly in America's South.

COTTON-PICKING (IDIOM)
American slang used as a general expression of disapproval, similar to **damned**. For example, 'Wait a cotton-picking minute' or 'Get your cotton-picking hands off'. An undisguised reference to enslaved Africans picking cotton.

GYP (V.)
Meaning to cheat, defraud or steal. Originated as an eighteenth-century abbreviation of **Gypsy**. The term is offensive because of the association of Gypsies with thievery and criminality.

SLAVING AWAY (V.)
(ALSO: *SLAVE-DRIVER*)
Meaning to work tirelessly, or to drive someone relentlessly. Felt by many to make light of the violence and immorality of the slave trade.

147

THAT DOESN'T MEAN WHAT YOU THINK IT MEANS

CRACK THE WHIP (IDIOM)
This expression, meaning to impose one's authority, isn't a reference to slavery but wagon-drivers snapping their whips to spur on the horses.

HIP HIP HOORAY (INT.)
It is mistakenly said that 'hip hip' comes from the cry **hep-hep**, sounded when Ashkenazi Jews were rounded up in Bavaria's 1819 pogroms. The pogroms happened, but it is not the origin of 'hip hip'.

YELLOW-BELLIED (ADJ.)
Despite the belief that **yellow-bellied** must have racist origins, the association of yellow with cowardice and betrayal goes back to medieval Europe and the character of yellow bile.

CRACKER (N.)
Although **cracker** is itself an offensive term for a poor white Southerner in the US, it has nothing to do with overseers cracking whips on slave plantations.

A **palindrome** is a word, phrase or text that reads the same forwards and backwards. It comes from Greek *palindromos*, meaning 'running back again'. There are around 180 palindromic words in English, from two letters – like **mm** and **aa** – up to James Joyce's 12-letter **tattarrattat**, the World Record-holder for the longest one-word English palindrome. There are even palindromic novels. David Stevens' *Satire: Veritas*, for instance, contains 58,795 letters. It's a hard read, but a good title.

A successful palindromic phrase should exhibit sense and syntax, and feel effortless, even when writing it is anything but. 'Lewd did I live, & evil I did dwel' is a fine example, and one of the oldest palindromes in English, penned by the father of nonsense, John Taylor (see page 142).

One of the most celebrated palindromes was written by Leigh Mercer in 1964; *A man, a plan, a canal: Panama!* Mercer was a prolific collector and writer of palindromes, including such gems as *Niagara, O roar again*, *Pull up if I pull up*, and *Live not on evil*, but 'Panama' was so good that it inspired numerous parodies. For instance: *A man, a plan, a cat, a ham, a yak, a yam, a hat, a canal: Panama!* (Guy Jacobsen). Longer still: *A man, a plan, a canoe, pasta, heros, rajahs, a coloratura, maps, snipe, percale, macaroni, a gag, a banana bag, a tan, a tag, a banana bag again (or a camel), a crepe, pins, Spam, a rut, a Rolo, cash, a jar, sore hats, a peon, a canal: Panama!* (Guy Steele). However both pale when compared to Peter Norvig's 17,826-word 'Panama' palindrome, but that was computer generated and just a long list of words.

Palindromes can sound profound even when they make no sense. Their symmetry, like some linguistic mobius strip, can feel seductive. Scottish poet Alastair Reid wrote with yearning of his hunt for the Great Palindrome that might reveal 'the Final Truth of Things'. Reid never found his linguistic Holy Grail, but he did write some marvellous 'dromes, including this epic: *T. Eliot, top bard, notes putrid tang emanating, is sad. I'd assign it a name – gnat-dirt upset on drab pot toilet*.

The ultimate accolade for palandromists is success at the SymmyS, the Oscars of the palindrome world that has been held since 2013. The date of the SymmyS varies because they take place on palindromic days. In 2024 that was 4/20/2024. Anthony Etherin won the Best Short Palindrome that year with The Struggling Bard: *Too long I go, no gig, no loot*.

Wow.

FIG.1 *Palindrome puzzle in Sam Loyd's* Cyclopedia of 5000 Puzzles, Tricks and Conundrums *(1914)*

PANGRAMS

¶ A **pangram** is a sentence containing every letter of the alphabet, the most famous being **the quick brown fox jumps over the lazy dog**.

¶ At thirty-five letters, it's long; but what it lacks in brevity it makes up for in clarity and poetry. There are many shorter pangrams, including ones with twenty-six letters, but these only squeak in because they use abbreviations.

¶ Pangram itself is from Greek **pan-** (all) and **-gram** (letters). Some call them **holoalphabetic sentences**, but that's a mouthful.

¶ Historically, pangrams were wordplay; but *the quick brown fox*, first seen around 1885, has always been a practical pangram, used in calligraphy, keyboard training, typeface demonstration and more. According to *The Dictionary of Wordplay*, the first 'official' pangram appeared in 1872 and was: **I, quartz pyx, who fling muck beds**.

¶ Less practical, but more humorous, is Riane Konc's reinterpretations of 'the quick brown fox' for the *New Yorker*, including a Tour de Force version, albeit missing D, Y and Z – **The quick brown fox jumps over three generations of interfamilial trauma** – and an Alternate History version (**The lazy dog jumps over the quick brown fox**).

26 LETTERS
Mr Jock, TV quiz PhD, bags few lynx.
New job: fix Mr Gluck's hazy TV, PDQ.

27 LETTERS
Bawds jog, flick quartz, vex nymph.

28 LETTERS
Waltz, bad nymph, for quick jigs vex.
Jived fox nymph grabs quick waltz.

29 LETTERS
Sphinx of black quartz, judge my vow.
Glib jocks quiz nymphs to vex dwarf.

30 LETTERS
How quickly daft jumping zebras vex!

31 LETTERS
The five boxing wizards jump quickly.
Jackdaws love my big sphinx of quartz.

33 LETTERS
Pack my box with five dozen liquor jugs.

34 LETTERS
Go, lazy fat vixen; be shrewd, jump quick.

36 LETTERS
When zombies arrive, quickly fax Judge Pat.

40 LETTERS
Amazingly few discotheques provide jukeboxes.

SEE ALSO: *Unrhymable Words / Word Records*

ISOGRAMS

A perfect pangram shares the qualities of an **isogram**, a word that has no repeated letters. Online sources claim the longest one-word isogram is **subdermatoglyphic**, but it's not in the *OED* or *Merriam-Webster*. Here are three impressive isograms that are.

UNCOPYRIGHTABLES (16 LETTERS)	DERMATOGLYPHICS (15 LETTERS)	AMBIDEXTROUSLY (14 LETTERS)
Things ineligible for copyright.	*The science of skin markings.*	*In an ambidextrous manner.*

ACNESTIS
The part of the back between the shoulder blades which cannot be reached to scratch.

CANTHUS
The corner of the eye where eyelids meet.

DACTYLION
The tip of the middle (third) finger.

FRENULUM
A small ligament that limits the movement of an organ. The **lingual frenulum** *connects the underside of the tongue with the base of the mouth; the* **labial frenulum** *connects the inside lip with the gums.*

GNATHION (ALSO: MENTON)
The lowest point of the chin.

GYNECOMASTIA
The medical term for **man boobs**, *or* **moobs**.

POPLITEAL FOSSA
The shallow depression on the posterior of the knee, also known as the **kneepit**.

GLABELLA (ALSO: MESOPHRYON)
The area on the forehead between the eyebrows.

LUNULA
The white crescent-shaped mark at the bottom of the finger-nail.

NIDDICK
The nape of the neck.

PHILTRUM
The groove between the base of the nose and the edge of the upper lip.

PURLICUE
The fold of skin between thumb and forefinger.

RASCETTA
The skin wrinkles across the wrist at the base of the palm.

SUPRASTERNAL NOTCH (ALSO: JUGULAR NOTCH)
The dip between the neck and the two collarbones (below the Adam's apple).

THENAR EMINENCE
The fleshy part of the hand next to the thumb.

SEE ALSO: *Dictionary of Small Things*

PARTS OF THE BODY NAMED AFTER PEOPLE

More than 175 parts of the body are named after doctors who discovered them, from **Alcock's canal** to the **zonule of Zinn**. To the layman, or certainly to this author, these names sound exotic and unreal. Here then, unsullied by any useful information, are some favourite regions of the human anatomy.

Bartholin's gland • Billroth's cords • Calyx of Held • Organ of Corti • Space of Disse • Hasner's Fold • Loop of Henle • Antrum of Highmore • Pores of Kohn • Crypts of Lieberkühn • Riedel's lobe • Duct of Santorini • Limbus of Viessens • Waldeyer's tonsillar ring • Circle of Willis • Foramen of Winslow

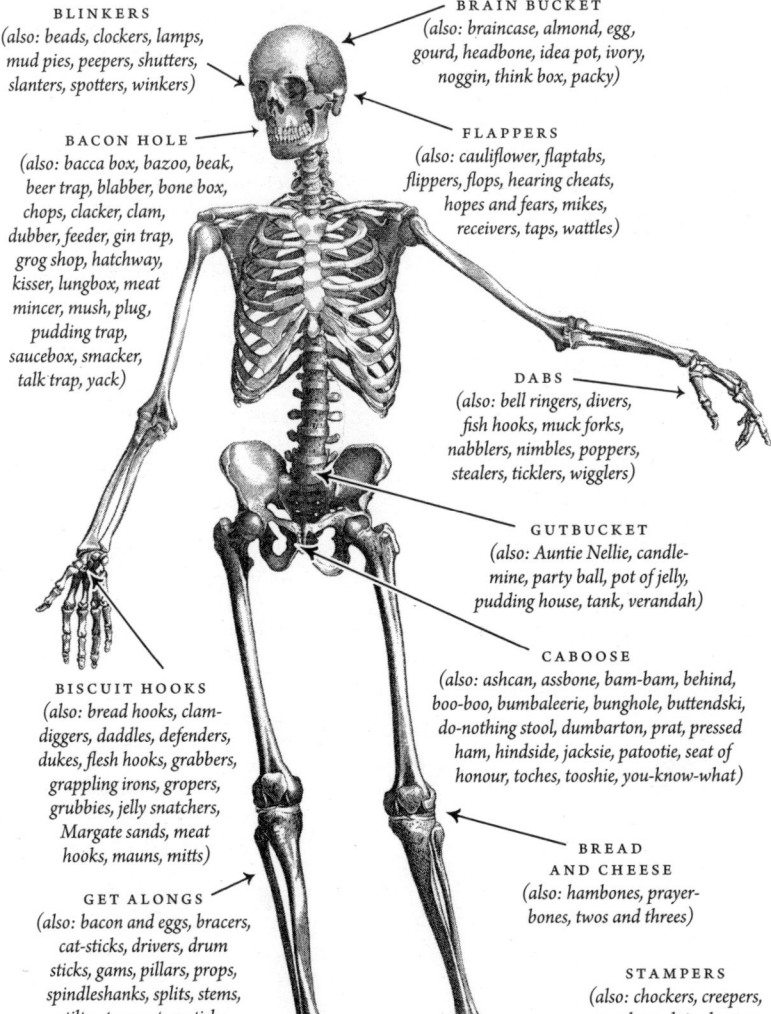

SLANG ANATOMY

BLINKERS
(also: beads, clockers, lamps, mud pies, peepers, shutters, slanters, spotters, winkers)

BRAIN BUCKET
(also: braincase, almond, egg, gourd, headbone, idea pot, ivory, noggin, think box, packy)

BACON HOLE
(also: bacca box, bazoo, beak, beer trap, blabber, bone box, chops, clacker, clam, dubber, feeder, gin trap, grog shop, hatchway, kisser, lungbox, meat mincer, mush, plug, pudding trap, saucebox, smacker, talk trap, yack)

FLAPPERS
(also: cauliflower, flaptabs, flippers, flops, hearing cheats, hopes and fears, mikes, receivers, taps, wattles)

DABS
(also: bell ringers, divers, fish hooks, muck forks, nabblers, nimbles, poppers, stealers, ticklers, wigglers)

GUTBUCKET
(also: Auntie Nellie, candle-mine, party ball, pot of jelly, pudding house, tank, verandah)

CABOOSE
(also: ashcan, assbone, bam-bam, behind, boo-boo, bumbaleerie, bunghole, buttendski, do-nothing stool, dumbarton, prat, pressed ham, hindside, jacksie, patootie, seat of honour, toches, tooshie, you-know-what)

BISCUIT HOOKS
(also: bread hooks, clam-diggers, daddles, defenders, dukes, flesh hooks, grabbers, grappling irons, gropers, grubbies, jelly snatchers, Margate sands, meat hooks, mauns, mitts)

BREAD AND CHEESE
(also: hambones, prayer-bones, twos and threes)

GET ALONGS
(also: bacon and eggs, bracers, cat-sticks, drivers, drum sticks, gams, pillars, props, spindleshanks, splits, stems, stilts, stumps, trapsticks, underpinnings, uprights)

STAMPERS
(also: chockers, creepers, crunchers, daisy-beaters, dew busters, dogs, hocks, kickers, padders, plates, puppies, shufflers, skids)

FIG.1 *A grin (also: ottomy)*

PEDANTRY

¶ So says the *OED*. But the definition in the *Merriam-Webster Collegiate Dictionary* feels closer to common usage: *'a person who annoys other people by correcting small errors and giving too much attention to minor details'*.

¶ Almost as soon as the word appeared in English in the sixteenth century from the French or Italian *pedante*, it was said with a curled lip. Dictionary citations mention the 'learned pedant' as 'domineering', 'lordly' or 'dreaming'. It has never been a compliment.

¶ The modern pedant often introduces themself with a *'Well, actually…'*, or *'I don't mean to be pedantic, but…'*. That their interjection might be correct doesn't diminish the gall such comments can provoke. Grammar pedants in particular are rarely thanked for their input.

Nothing is as peevish and pedantic as men's judgments of one another.

DESIDERIUS ERASMUS (1466–1536)

¶ While some see *extreme pedantry* as nothing short of a virus, psychologists have taken a more clinical approach to understanding why pedants *pedantise* in the first place.

¶ In his 1908 essay 'Character and Anal Eroticism', Sigmund Freud identified what would come to be known as the *anal triad*: the three traits that characterise the *anal-retentive personality*. He called them *orderliness*, *stubbornness* and *miserliness*. Today they're known as the *three Ps*: *pedantry*, *parsimony* and *petulence*.

¶ Freud's theory of *anal eroticism* is now rather dated, but there is an overlap between the *three Ps* and current personality descriptors, like *perfectionism* and *authoritarianism*, as well as *obsessive compulsive disorder* (OCD), all of which can be associated with pedantry. And while the claim that *Grammatical Pedantry Syndrome* was being considered for the manual of mental disorders was a spoof, *Grammar OCD* apparently is not, with one article on the subject warning of the harm it can do to social interactions, work productivity and general mental health.

¶ Research by *PsychTests.com* revealed a less sympathetic side to pedantry. Analysing results from 13,999 respondents to their *Self-Esteem Test*, researchers found 'nitpicking critics' were more likely to have self-esteem issues and incline towards narcissism, leading them to use pedantry 'to fabricate a false sense of superiority'.

¶ And yet… as H. F. Fowler famously argued in *A Dictionary of Modern English Usage*, pedantry is a relative term, wherein 'my pedantry is your scholarship'. Samuel Johnson might have agreed. Although he called pedantry 'the unseasonable ostentation of learning', he saw how the word had become a barb against those who simply Know Their Stuff.

¶ Freud described the pedant as 'a man unable to laugh at himself'; maybe this is the nub of it. People are free to parade their knowledge as they wish; but they shouldn't get upset if they're sometimes teased for it.

SEE ALSO: *Changed Meanings*

❡ Few writers can boast as many pen names as Founding Father Benjamin Franklin, aka **Silence Dogood**, **Alice Addertongue**, **Timothy Turnstone**, **Harry Meanwell**, **Polly Baker**, **Poor Richard** and more. Even Washington Irving's **Diedrich Knickerbocker** and **Geoffrey Crayon** pale by comparison.

❡ Some pseudonyms, like **Edgar Box** (Gore Vidal) provide cover for a well-known name; others, like **George Orwell** or **Lewis Carroll**, eclipse the given name. But most intriguing are the symbolic names, like **C33**, Oscar Wilde's prisoner number at Reading Gaol, or Æ (short for **Æon**) used by Irish writer George Russell.

❡ Incidentally, **nom de plume** ('name of the quill') is a phrase created in America from French. In France it's called a **pseudonyme**.

A LADY	*Jane Austen*
ACTON BELL	*Anne Brontë*
ALCOFRIBAS NASIER	*François Rabelais*
AYN RAND	*Alisa Rosenbaum*
BARBARA VINE	*Ruth Rendell*
BOZ	*Charles Dickens*
BRYNJOLF BJARME	*Henrik Ibsen*
C33	*Oscar Wilde*
C. S. FORESTER	*Cecil Smith*
CLAIRE MORGAN	*Patricia Highsmith*
CLIVE HAMILTON	*C. S. Lewis*
CURRER BELL	*Charlotte Brontë*
DANIEL DEFOE	*Daniel Foe*
DR. SEUSS	*Theodor Seuss Geisel*
E. L. JAMES	*Erika Leonard*
EDGAR BOX	*Gore Vidal*
ELLIS BELL	*Emily Brontë*
EMIL SINCLAIR	*Hermann Hesse*
GEOFFREY CRAYON	*Washington Irving*
GEORGE ELIOT	*Mary Ann Evans*
GEORGE ORWELL	*Eric Arthur Blair*
HERGÉ	*Georges Remi*
ISAAC BICKERSTAFF	*Jonathan Swift*
JAMES HERRIOT	*James Alfred Wight*
JANE SOMERS	*Doris Lessing*
JOHN LANGE	*Michael Crichton*
JOHN LE CARRÉ	*David Cornwell*
JOSEPH CONRAD	*Józef Korzeniowski*
LEMONY SNICKET	*Daniel Handler*
LEWIS CARROLL	*Charles Dodgson*
LEE CHILD	*John Dover Grant*
MAN WITHOUT A SPLEEN	*Anton Chekhov*
MARK TWAIN	*Samuel Clemens*
MARY WESTMACOTT	*Agatha Christie*
MAYA ANGELOU	*Marguerite Johnson*
MOLIÈRE	*Jean Baptiste Poquelin*
MOTHER GOOSE	*Jeannette Walworth*
NEVILLE SHUTE	*Neville Norway*
OGDRED WEARY	*Edward Gorey*
PABLO NERUDA	*Ricardo Basoalto*
PAUL FRENCH	*Isaac Asimov*
RICHARD BACHMAN	*Stephen King*
ROBERT GALBRAITH	*J. K. Rowling*
ROBERT MARKHAM	*Kingsley Amis*
SAKI	*Hector Hugh Munro*
STAN LEE	*Stanley Martin Lieber*
SUE DENIM	*Dav Pilkey*
TIMOTHY SHY	*Wyndham Lewis*
VICTORIA LUCAS	*Sylvia Plath*
VLADIMIR SIRIN	*Vladimir Nabokov*
VOLTAIRE	*François-Marie Arouet*
WILLIAM LEE	*William S. Burroughs*
WOODY ALLEN	*Heywood Allen*

SEE ALSO: *Medical Conditions that Make Nice Names*

¶ *Pig Latin* is a well-known language game popular with children. By following the rules of Pig Latin, words are altered to create a secret code only comprehensible to those familiar with the system. In this it is similar to other secret languages, like *backslang*, *eggy-peggy* and *Double-Dutch*.

¶ The name was inspired by parody languages like *Dog Latin*, *Bog Latin* and *Pig Greek*, the earliest of which appears in the seventeenth century. But while these were meant to sound like classical languages (for example *Nolite te bastardes carborundorum*, the faux-Latin phrase made famous in *The Handmaid's Tale*) the purpose of Pig Latin is to prevent eavesdropping.

¶ Pig Latin is first mentioned at the end of the nineteenth century; by 1919 it was well enough known that Arthur Field could feature it in the song 'Pig Latin Love' ('I-yay ove-lay oo-yay earie-day'). Since then, it has been a mainstay of American popular culture, used by Ginger Rogers, The Three Stooges, the Blues Brothers, Dolly Parton, *The Simpsons*, *Southpark* and many more. With *ix-nay* ('nix') and *am-scray* ('scram') now in *OED* and *Merriam-Webster*, Pig Latin risks becoming the secret language everyone knows.

¶ Other languages have their version of Pig Latin, where syllables are swapped, words reversed and letters inserted to obfuscate meaning. Probably the most famous is French's *Verlan*, a street-language originally associated with criminals; in addition, German has *Löffelsprach*, Portuguese has *Língua do pê*, Spanish has *Jerigonza*, etc.

¶ Anyone still confused by Pig Latin can use one of the many online translation tools. But really, *it-yay is-yay ot-nay at-thay ifficult-day*.

SEE ALSO: *Polari*

154

USING PIG LATIN

Pig Latin is simple to learn, but achieving fluency takes practice. These are the basics.

WORDS STARTING WITH A CONSONANT (OR CONSONANT CLUSTER) SOUND
Put the consonant, or consonant cluster, to the end of the word, and add *-ay*.
e.g. pig = ig-pay, cheese = eese-chay

If a word starts with a vowel that makes a consonant sound, like the *W* in *one*, treat it like a consonant:
e.g. one = un-way

WORDS STARTING WITH A VOWEL SOUND
Add *-hay*, *-yay*, *-nay* or *-way* to the end of the word.
e.g. out = out-hay, apple = apple-yay

COMPOUND WORDS
Translate compound words in their distinct word parts.
e.g. snowball = ow-snay all-bay, hot-dog = ot-hay og-day

CLASSIC BOOK TITLES IN PIG LATIN

Oby-may Ick-day
Ime-cray and-way Unishment-pay

Ave-bray Ew-nay Orld-way
In-yay Old-cay Ood-blay

(Translations provided on page 216)

¶ *Pizza* was invented in Naples at the end of the eighteenth century. Before Neapolitans put *marinara* and *bufala mozzarella* on their round flatbreads, *pizza* was a generic Italian word for anything prepared and flattened, be it a cake, wafer, type of foccacia or even a cheese. The word itself might come from Latin *pinza* (clamp), Medieval Greek *pitta* (cake) or Old High German *bizzo* (morsel), but no one knows for certain.

¶ Although the details of the first *pizzeria* aren't recorded, a letter from 1799 is one of the first mentions of a *pizzaiolo* (one who makes pizza). As more pizzerias opened in the nineteenth century, the *pizzaiolo ambulante* – walking pizza vendor – started to appear across Naples. Being cheap, pizza became a staple of the poorest in Naples; even when they couldn't afford it, *pizza a otto* was bought on credit, repaid eight days later.

¶ Regional interpretations of the Neapolitan dish started appearing across Italy in the 1800s. The Sicilian *sfincione* had a thick, airy base; the *pizza al tegamino* from Piedmont was baked in a pan; the *pizza romana* was thinner and crispier. And then, in 1905, America's first pizzeria opened.

¶ Where Italy is understandably purist about the pizza, America has re-shaped it, often literally. There's Chicago's *deep-dish*, the *Detroit-style* thick-crust, Long Island's *grandma pizza*, Pennsylvania's *Old Forge pizza*, the fusion-inspired *California pizza*, the artery clogging *stuffed crust* and more. And with these interpretations evolved the language of pizza, familiar to many who make, serve or eat them.

AL LIBRETTO ('FOLDED OVER LIKE A BOOK')
A common one-handed pizza-eating style with crust folded over and the slice forming a valley.

AVALANCHE
Toppings sliding off a freshly baked pizza.

CHEESE PULL
The stretchy cheese effect as a slice is lifted from a hot pie.

CHEESE DRAG
When a mouthful of pizza pulls all the cheese off the slice.

CORNICIONE
The edge crust of a pizza (from Italian for moulding).

ISOSCELES SLICE
A perfectly cut slice of pie.

LEOPARD SPOTTING
The spotted char on pizza crust.

MUTZ (ALSO: MOZZ, MOOTZ, MOZZARELL)
Abbreviation for mozzarella.

PARTY CUT (ALSO: TAVERN CUT)
Pizza sliced into rectangular slices.

PIE (ALSO: 'ZA)
Pizza. 'Pomidore pizza' was described as 'tomato pie' as early as 1903.

PIZZA BONES
Uneaten pizza crusts.

PIZZA BURN (ALSO: ROOF BURN, PIZZA PALATE)
The blistering burn to the roof of your mouth from eating a hot pizza too fast.

PIZZA SAVER (ALSO: PIZZA TABLE / STOOL)
The three-legged plastic object used to prevent pizza boxes touching the pizza inside.

ROADIE (ALSO: WALKING SLICE)
A slice of pizza to go.

TIP SAG
A drooping slice arising from overly-loaded or excessively soggy pizzas.

155

SEE ALSO: *Diner Slang / Meal Times*

(Side note: the pizza emoji is also used to say 'I love you', or to suggest a threesome.)

'How bona to vada your dolly old eek!'*

¶ This line from *Round the Horne*, a much-loved British radio comedy show of the late 1960s, was the signature greeting between two popular characters, Julian and Sandy, known for their strange, nonsensical language. But while audiences loved it, the nation's collective marmalade would have been dropped were it known they were using a secret language of gay slang called ***Polari***.

¶ The origin of Polari lies in an older slang language, ***Parlyree***, from Italian ***parlare***, meaning 'to talk', used by sailors, travellers, fairground and circus people, and other seamy itinerant types. Parlyree itself was a hodgepodge of Italian, Yiddish, Irish, back slang, Cockney slang, cant (the language of criminals from the 1500s) and more.

¶ When Parlyree entered the theatre world in the late nineteenth century it was adopted by gay men who, putting their own spin on it, developed Polari. London's gay scene became Polari's natural home, but it also travelled the world with the ***sea queens*** (gay sailors) of the merchant navy and cruise ships.

¶ Homosexuality was criminalised in the UK until 1967. In this hostile environment, Polari allowed gay men to communicate discretely while keeping outsiders out. But the language was also a means of identifying other gay men. A ***bona*** (good) dropped into a sentence could be spotted by someone who was ***so*** (gay), but go unnoticed by anyone else.

¶ Polari's vocabulary is ironic, playful and camp, with notes of caustic humour. It also reflected the reality of life for gay men at the time, with more words for the police than anything else (see opposite).

¶ The decriminalisation of homosexuality hastened the decline of Polari. Not only was the secrecy no longer required, but it was associated with an image of 'mincing old queens' and hidden homosexuality that younger men, fired by the new spirit of gay liberation, wanted to leave behind.

¶ Polari might have vanished were it not for efforts to preserve this important artefact of gay culture. The Sisters of Perpetual Indulgence, an LGBT protest group founded in San Francisco in 1979, adopted ***High Polari*** in many of its 'religious' ceremonies, while the Manchester chapter of the Sisters even translated the *King James Bible* into *The Polari Bible* (2003).

> 1 In the beginning Gloria created the heaven and the earth.
> 2 And the earth was nanti form, and void; and munge was upon the eke of the deep. And the fairy of Gloria trolled upon the eke of the aquas.
> 3 And Gloria cackled, Let there be sparkle: and there was sparkle.

THE POLARI BIBLE,
GENESIS 1:1-3

¶ Having been a source of embarrassment for many years, Polari has found a new lease of life; but instead of being secret it is very much out. As well as a dictionary (*Fantabulosa*, 2004) and history of the language (*Fabulosa*, 2019), there have been novels largely written in Polari. There's even an excellent short film called *Putting on the Dish* (2015) which showcases impressive mastery of the language. It's definitely worth a **vada**.

SEE ALSO: *Gender / Yoda Linguistics*

156

**'How lovely to look at your face.'*

POLARI GUIDE

BONA

BONA	good
BONA CLOBBER	nice clothes
BONA HOUSE	male brothel
BONA LAVS	best wishes
BONA NOCHY	good night
BONA VARDERING	good looking

PHRASES

AND NO FLIES ... HONESTLY!	I'm telling the truth
DON'T BE STRANGE	don't hold back
GARDY LOO	look out!
NANTI POLARI	don't speak
NANTI THAT	leave it alone
SHUT YOUR SCREECH	shut up

FASHION

HAT	capella, mudge
TROUSERS	cats, farting crackers, kaffies, lally-drags, strides, trollies
SUNGLASSES	goolie ogles, fakes, ogle filters
EARRINGS	ear fakes
JEWELLERY	groinage
PERFUME	smellies
SHOES	batts

PEOPLE

A FAT MAN	B-flat omee
A MAN	omee (also: omi, omy, omme)
A WOMAN	dona, zelda
OLD MAN	fungus
YOUNG MAN	filiome, chicken

PARTS OF THE BODY

BREASTS	foofs, jubes
EARS	aunt nells, polari lobes
HANDS	fambles, lills, lappers, martinis
HAIR	ends, riah
LEGS	lallies, lylies, scotches, stimps
MOUTH, FACE	eek, moey, screech
PENIS	bagaga, cavaliers and roundheads
TEETH	delph, matlocks, pots
TESTICLES	cods, quongs
MORE	dish (anus), corybungus (posterior), esong (nose), harris (arse), luppers (fingers), minces (eyes), ogle riahs (eyelashes)

SEX

SEX	arva, do a turn, charver, line grappling
ORAL SEX	gamming, nosh, plate, tip the velvet
ANAL SEX	cleaning the kitchen, rim
ERECTION	colin, fake

GAY MEN

OLDER GAY MAN	auntie, antique HP
RICH GAY MAN	duchess
GAY MAN	margery, molly, nelly, queen
AN EFFEMINATE MAN	palone

THE POLICE

Betty Bracelets, Hilda Handcuffs, Jennifer Justice, Lilly Law, the orderly daughters

COMPLIMENTS

FORTUNI	gorgeous
GILDY	fancy
FABULOSA (ALSO, FANTABULOSA)	wonderful
DOLLY	an attractive woman

VARIOUS

CARSEY	toilet
DINARLY	money
ZHOOSHY	showy
CACKLE	to gossip

¶ **Printers' marks** were used by printers from the fifteenth century onwards to identify and promote their work. Combining the qualities of a **logo**, a **trade mark** and an **illustrated epigram**, these emblems were graphic design before there was graphic design. With their motifs, symbols and typography, they constitute a beautiful chapter in the history of printing.

¶ In 1455, Gutenberg printed just 180 copies of his Bible; in the first decade of the 1500s, two million books were printed in cities across Europe. By 1600 this had risen to 150 million. The continuing fascination with printers' marks lies in how they bear witness to the information revolution fast-spreading across Renaissance Europe.

ICONIC MARKS

¶ The *Mainz Psalter*, printed by Fust and Schöffer in 1457 (the second book ever printed, after Gutenberg's 1455 Bible), was the first to use a printers' mark. The mark, which consisted of two shields featuring the tools of the printer's trade, only appears on one copy of the *Psalter*, so it was possibly stamped at a later date, in which case their 1462 Bible would be the first known use of a printers' mark.

Fust and Schöffer

¶ The famous mark of Aldine Press, founded by Aldus Manutius in Venice in 1494, features a dolphin around an anchor, and the motto *Festina Lente* ('make haste slowly').

Aldine Press

¶ Venice was a centre of European printing and the Aldine Press had a valuable monopoly on Greek works printed in the Republic of Venice. Although the mark was used to ensure authenticity, it was also subject to counterfeit.

¶ In contrast to Aldine's figurative mark is William Caxton's decorative monogram. As well as bringing printing to England, Caxton is famous for his translation of Aesop's *Fables* and the first print edition of *The Canterbury Tales*.

William Caxton

158

¶ Many famous marks were puns on the printer's name. The mark of Mathias Apiarius, whose surname was Latin for bee-keeper, had a bear feasting on a bee-hive. As well as the pun, it symbolised the sweetness of knowledge.

¶ Similarly punnish is the mark of sixteenth-century publisher Christoph Froschauer, whose family name means 'the man from the floodplain full of frogs'. Frogs therefore appear prominently in his printers' mark, and they're pretty large ones.

¶ Other well-known marks are more of a riddle. Over four generations, and in some forty versions, the Venetian Sessa family used the motif of a cat holding a mouse. With no familial or allegorical connections to cats, it was a mysterious choice. Was it an allusion to the old expression that as cats play with mice, so fortune plays with men? Or did the Sessas 'borrow' the symbol from an influential nearby family to drum up business? Either could be true; or, possibly, they just liked cats.

159

Mathias Apiarius *Christoph Froschauer* *Giovanni Battista Sessa*

MOTTOS OF THE ENLIGHTENMENT

¶ Many printers' marks contained mottos, primarily in Latin and Greek. As with the symbols themselves, mottos might be religious or humanist, modest or grandiloquent. If printers' marks were the precursor to today's logos, these were the forerunners of the strapline, the **Just Do It** of the fifteenth century. While some possess a certain fortune-cookie quality, many reflect the intellectual spirit of the age that can still make one tingle.

Ingenium superat vires
Ingenuity surpasses strength

Semper candescet
It will always glow

Cunctando propero
Speed delays

A poco a poco
Little by little

Non solus
Not alone

¶ The University of Barcelona has an online database of over 2,700 printers' marks. One can search for calligraphy, hedgehogs or burning salamanders.

¶ The symbolism seen in these marks, both religious and secular, reflects the intellectual energy of Renaissance thinking and the search for truth and wisdom. As such, the pleasure of these marks is more than aesthetic; they are emblematic of a profound intellectual revolution that is still felt today.

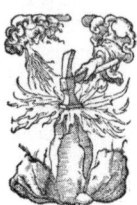

Heinrich Petri

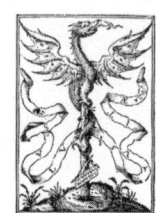

Luis Rodrigues

Aegidius & Jacobus Huguetan

François Frellon

Domenico Ercole

Samuel Crespin

Wolfgang Kopfel

Domenico Ercole

Andrea Brogiotti

Michel Dubois

Piero Pacini da Pescia

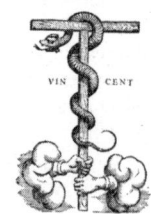

Heredi di Vincenzo Valgrisi

LEXIPEDIA PEOPLE

ANNE FISHER

GRAMMARIAN

(1719–1778)

¶Anne Fisher was the first female English grammarian, and one of the most influential of the eighteenth century. She was a teacher, an author, an entrepreneur and an all-round remarkable woman.

¶Her most famous work, *A New Grammar*, was the fourth-most-published grammar book of the eighteenth century, with over eighteen editions, thirty print runs and numerous pirated copies. She also published at least six other works and was the first woman to write a dictionary, *An Accurate New Spelling Dictionary* (1773). Were this not enough, Fisher co-founded the *Newcastle Chronicle* newspaper, co-ran a printing business and established a girls' school, which she ran for five years. She also had nine children.

¶Born in Cumbria in 1719, Fisher set up a school for young working women when she was only twenty-six. That same year, she published the first edition of her bestselling work, *A New Grammar*. Fisher wasn't interested in the traditional Latin-led grammar, which those outside an elite few, particularly young women, knew little about. Instead she focused on a practical system of native English grammar that was easier to understand. She also introduced a more accessible vernacular. In a preface to a later book, Fisher wrote, 'all the best English school masters in the kingdom consider mine as the quickest and most effectual mode of inculcating the knowledge of the English language'. She wasn't being modest – but given the book's success, she wasn't wrong either.

¶Her books were published under the name A. Fisher to hide that she was a woman, but she was determined that sex should be no barrier to learning. Much of her work reflected her determination to help women, particularly from lower social classes, to improve their lives. She said as much in the preface to *A New Grammar* where she recommended the book to young ladies 'as are desirous of improving themselves'.

¶Fisher likely met her husband, printer Thomas Slack, when publishing her first book. Together they opened a bookshop and printworks in 1763. She was deeply involved in both businesses, not least because the printing office published all her books. A year later, the first edition of the *Newcastle Chronicle* appeared, and again Fisher had an active role.

¶Anne Fisher's success paved the way for future female grammarians, but her own name faded over the centuries. Since she died before her husband, she left no will; and surviving records are few. But from what we have, it's clear that she was not only a force of nature but a woman of compassion, culture and learning. Her name might not be widely known, but it should be.

R.

¶ Racehorse names are a most eccentric feature of a most extraordinary sport. They can sound distinguished (*Godolphin*, *Royal Athlete*), promising (*Zippy Lad*, *Rich Strike*) or like surrealist poetry (*The Canary Lived*, *Whykickamoocow*). And then there are names like *Domestic Dispute*, *Vicar In Trouble* and *Salmonella*.

¶ In the UK, racehorse names are administered through Weatherbys, whose Register of Horse Names contains 250,000 names, with 15,000 added each year. Combine the detailed rules for naming (see below) with the unique character of the owners and the results can be very strange. (Speaking of, *Very Strange* came first at Penn National in 1977.)

¶ Every owner approaches naming differently. Queen Elizabeth II was said to name all her racehorses personally, with *Doublet*, *Highclere* and *Doutelle* being typical of her sophisticated approach. Unlike James Carr-Boyle, 5th Earl of Glasgow (d. 1869), who only named horses that won races. Since he didn't have many of these, his hapless stable was home to *Give-Him-A-Name*, *He-Has-A-Name*, and *He-Isn't-Worth-A-Name*. A century later, owner Stan Powell put 'stan' into every name (e.g. *The Culstan* and *The Jeanstan*); Colonel Bradley (who wasn't a colonel) chose names starting with B; and Lady Beaverbrook's stable only used seven-letter names. In the late 1980s, owner Steven Astaire had a thing for naming horses after Groucho Marx characters, so his stable included *Rufus T. Firefly*, *J. Cheever Loophole* and *Hugo Z. Hackenbush*.

¶ A tried-and-trusted approach to naming draws on the horse's parentage. For instance, the name of the legendary *Red Rum* comes from the last three letters of his dam, Mared, and sire, Quorum. More playfully, there was *Eat Cake*, sired by Legend of France with the mare Guillotina; and the union of Shy Groom and Dance Alone produced the winner *Celibate*. Such ingenious combinations possess the logic of a cryptic crossword and never fail to delight.

SEE ALSO: *Elizabethan Colours*

RACEHORSE NAMING RULES

The British Horseracing Authority administers the registration of racehorse names in the UK. It has detailed guidelines forbidding names that:

Contain more than eighteen characters;

Contain more than seven syllables;

Start with a sign other than a letter;

Start or end with a number;

Are made up entirely of initials, or include figures, hyphens, full-stops, commas, signs, exclamation marks and other punctuation marks;

Are considered offensive, be they suggestive, vulgar, obscene or insulting;

Are offensive to religious, political or ethnic groups;

Are named after a well-known person without their permission.

¶ Although traditionalists disapprove, many owners enjoy a good joke, particularly of the punning variety. **Mr Pointment**, **Usain Colt** and **Irish You Well** deserve special mention. Some names promise victory, like **Leading By A Length**, who rarely did; others, like **Really Slow**, were just the opposite. Deliberately bad names, like **Glue**, **I'llRuinYou** and **Last**, are hard to fathom, but all have raced. **Last** even came first, unlike **Come First** who never did.

¶ Some owners simply want to make mischief. Names like **Racehorse**, **The Winner Is** and **Cunning Stunt** keep commentators on their toes. Others trip them up. There were the tongue twisters, like **Flat Fleet Feet** and **Sayedaty Sadaty** – and unpronouncibles, like **Uimhiraceathair** and **Sumomomomomomomomo**.

¶ One name that wasn't confusing was **Arrrrr**, who won at Saratoga in 2008. The owner must surely have been delighted to hear the commentator go 'full pirate' as Arrrrr crossed the finish line (you can watch it on YouTube).

¶ And then there are the rude names which some owners love trying to sneak through. But while horses called **Noble Locks**, **Peony's Envy** and **Sofa Can Fast** have all reached the turf, the registrars are clamping down on such shenanigans. Hundreds of names are rejected each year, which is why you'll never see **Hugh Gorgy** or **Arfur Foulkesaycke** at the 2.20 at Aintree.

INGENIOUS NAMES

WARNING (1985)
Known Fact (sire) / Slightly Dangerous (dam)

HARASSMENT CASE (1991)
Badger Land (sire) / Cherry Tart (dam)

BACHELORS PAD (1994)
Pursuit of Love (sire) / Note Book (dam)

MAREOFLOT (1999)
Moscow Society (sire) / Mrs Pegasus (dam)

GEESPOT (1999)
Pursuit of Love (sire) / My Discovery (dam)

SERVICE (2000)
College Chapel (sire) / Centre Court (dam)

EMBEZZLEMENT (2003)
Cat Thief (sire) / The Administrator (dam)

OVERDRAWN (2013)
Charitable Man (sire) / Bank Teller (dam)

TERRIBLE NAMES

VENTIQUATTROFOGLI (1990)
ESTATE AGENT (1993)
BEEF OR SALMON (1996)
THE SLUG (2004)
BEER BELLY (2010)
TACKLETOMMYWOOWOO (2020)
FUTURE CUTLET (2021)
UNEXPECTED ISSUES (2022)

ALSO RAN

WHY 'O' WHY (1970)
SINCE WHEN (1996)
WHERE NEXT (2013)
WOTSIZNAME (2015)

¶ *Reduplicative words*, also called **repetition compounds**, are the show-offs of the language world, proudly flaunting their **glairy-flairy** charms. Samuel Johnson thus hated them, dismissing them as corrupt and barbarous. (His definition of **twittle-twattle** is typical of his opinion: 'A ludicrous reduplication of twattle... A vile word.')

¶ But what Johnson deplored then, and what linguists might sniff at now, is precisely why reduplicatives bring such pleasure. Words like **hocus-pocus** (1624), **hanky-panky** (1841) and **hurry-scurry** (1732) aren't merely expressive, they're playful. They also echo a child's first year of language development, when up to 50 per cent of their vocabulary comprises words like **mama**, **nana** and **pee-pee**. So when people enjoy the lilt of **walkie-talkie** or **herky-jerky**, they are, perhaps, unconsciously returning to the first sounds of the nursery.

¶ There are around 2,000 reduplicative words in English. One of the oldest, **weilawei**, an Old English lament, dates to the ninth century. And the first usage of **tee-hee** (the sound of laughter) is found in Chaucer's *Knight's Tale* in 1386. But it was the Elizabethans who developed our appreciation of reduplicatives. Words like **helter-skelter**, **roly-poly** and **willy-nilly** all date from this period, and both Shakespeare and Marlowe made good use of them.

¶ Reduplicative words are formed by altering vowels for an alliterative effect (**ding-dong**), changing consonants for a rhyming effect (**hurly-burly**), or using full reduplication for an emphatic effect (**girly-**

girly). What's fascinating is how these words group around clearly discernible themes, including:

SOUNDS: *click-clack, rumble-bumble*

MOVEMENT: *hurry-scurry, zigzag*

CONFUSION: *hanchum-scranchum, hubbub*

NONSENSE: *gibble-gabble, flubdub*

SIZE: *itsy-bitsy, teeny-tiny*

DECEPTION: *shim-sham, hush-hush*

ANXIETY: *jumpy-wumpies, mubble-fubbles*

¶ The power of these words is that they scarcely need defining; these are words you feel. And if some make you laugh, well, **super-duper**.

¶ A curious new area of study is **contrastive focus reduplication**, where something is contrasted with its prototypical self. As in, **Do you want a drink, or a DRINK-drink?** or **Do you like her, or LIKE-like her?** The seminal work on this is *The Salad-Salad Paper* (2004), which is worth a read, even a READ-read.

SEE ALSO: *Euphonic Words / Origins of Nonsense*

THE DICTIONARY SCHMICTIONARY

ARGIE-BARGIE: *a heated argument*

BIBBERY-BOBBERY: *a squabble*

BLISH-BLASH: *nonsense*

CLITTERY-CLUTTERY: *weather inclined to be stormy*

CRINGLE-CRANGLE: *a zigzag*

CRINKLE-CRANKLE: *a wrinkle*

CRINKUM-CRANKUM: *adultery*

CUDDLE-MUDDLE: *a secret confabulation*

DINGLE-DANGLE: *to tremble*

ECKLE-FECKLE: *cheerful*

FANCY-SCHMANCY: *pretentiously fancy*

FID-FAD: *a pleasant but trifling person*

FINGLE-FANGLE: *a whimsical trifle*

FLIM-FLAM: *a confidence trick, or a lie*

FUDDY-DUDDY: *an old fogy*

GLAIRY-FAIRY: *ostentatious or gaudy*

HANDY-DANDY: *particularly useful or handy*

HANKY-PANKY: *surreptitious sexual behaviour*

HARUM-SCARUM: *reckless and wild*

HEEBIE-JEEBIES: *a disconcerting feeling*

HIPPERTIE-SKIPPERTIE: *a skipping kind of run*

HIRDUM-DURDUM: *topsy-turvy*

HOCKERTY-COCKERTY: *to ride on another's shoulders*

HOITY-TOITY: *snobbish or superior*

HOOTCHY-KOOTCHY: *a type of erotic dance*

HUBBLE-BUBBLE: *a pipe, similar to a hookah*

HUFF-SNUFF: *an aggressive, intimidating person*

HUFFLE-SCUFFLE: *a noisy quarrel*

HURKLE-DURKLE: *lounge lazily in bed*

JIGGERY-POKERY: *deceitful behaviour*

KIBTY-COBTY: *lingering or loitering*

LOCO-FOCO: *a self-igniting cigar*

MIFF-MAFF: *nonsense*

NICK-NACKATORY: *a museum or shop for curiosities*

NIDDLE-NADDLE: *nodding*

NIFF-NAFF: *a trifle*

NIFFLE-NAFFLE: *to work without making progress*

NING-NANG: *a worthless thoroughbred horse*

NIPPERTY-TIPPERTY: *an unstable person*

PELL-MELL: *confused or disorderly haste*

PIBBLE-PABBLE: *empty, childish talk*

PONGY-BONGY: *a kind of snuff*

QUAVERY-MAVERY: *hesitating or indecisive*

RANTUM-SCANTUM: *reckless behaviour*

RAZZLE-DAZZLE: *an ostentatious show*

RICKY-TICK: *old-fashioned jazz style*

RIFF-RAFF: *the mob or rabble*

RIM-RAM: *a disorderly state*

ROYSTER-DOYSTER: *one who roysters*

SCRIBBLE-SCRABBLE: *inane writing*

SHILLY-SHALLY: *to be indecisive*

SKIMBLE-SKAMBLE: *confused or nonsensical*

SLIBBER-SLABBER: *carelessness*

SMICK-SMACK: *a kiss*

SUPER-DUPER: *marvellous*

TICKSY-WICKSY: *a baby*

TINKLE-TANKLE: *an icicle*

TORY-RORY: *wild*

TOZY-MOZY: *tipsy*

WHIFF-WHAFF: *a trifling word or action*

WHIM-WHAM: *a trifling object*

WHITTER-WHATTER: *whispering*

WIM-WOM: *circuitous*

WISKY-FRISKY: *very frisky*

YIFF-YAFF: *a small person who talks too much*

SHAKESPEARE SCHMAKESPEARE

'Endeavour thy selfe to sleepe, and leave thy vaine bibble babble.'
Twelfth Night

'When the Hurley-burley's done, When the Battaile's lost, and wonne.'
Macbeth

'We have done but greenly In hugger mugger to inter him.'
Hamlet

¶ *If it doesn't fit, you must acquit* is among the most memorable lines in legal history. Had O. J.'s defence instead said, 'If the gloves are too tight, you must find him innocent', the jury might have reached a different conclusion; but as it was, the rhyme dismissed the crime.

¶ Although poetry is no guarantor of truth, linguists have found that rhyming statements can promote *cognitive bias*. In what is called the *rhyme as reason effect*, people appear more inclined to believe statements that rhyme.

¶ Marketeers have long exploited this neural loophole. From *I like Ike* – Dwight D. Eisenhower's campaign slogan – to the Pringles promise, *Once you pop, you can't stop*, advertisers use rhyming straplines because they get under the skin. Why else do we all know what fruit keeps the doctor away?

¶ The mechanics are simple. As well as aesthetic appeal, rhyme improves the fluency of statements which, in turn, makes them more memorable, and therefore more familiar. These qualities bring a stubborn authority to rhyming aphorisms. Perhaps that £5 *was* yours, but it's hard to contest the ancient precedent of *finders keepers*, particularly when combined with the watertight *you snooze, you lose* defence.

¶ *Rhyme as reason* is one of the rhetorician's tools of the trade. Well-crafted alliterations and textural metaphors can have a similar cognitive effect. But there's something about a rhyme, with its cadence and brevity, that lends what one researcher called 'a perceived truth advantage'. One might resent being manipulated in such a childish way, but *tough titty said the kitty*… the rhyme has spoken.

166

COLLECTED RHYMING WISDOM

Beer after whiskey, mighty risky; whiskey on beer, have no fear.

Buy when it snows, sell when it goes.

Candy is dandy, but liquor is quicker.

Don't do the crime if you can't do the time.

Drive for show, putt for dough.

Fake it till you make it.

Finders keepers, losers weepers.

He that mischief hatches, mischief catches.

He who smelt it, dealt it. (He who said the rhyme, did the crime.)

If it bleeds, it leads.

If it's yellow let if mellow, if it's brown flush it down.

Last hired, first fired.

Loose lips sink ships.

Might is right.

Money talks, bullshit walks.

Name it, claim it.

No money, no honey.

No pain, no gain.

Publish or perish.

Risk it for the biscuit.

Sisters before misters.

Snitches get stitches.

They hate us 'cause they ain't us.

Too much bed makes a dull head.

When in doubt, do nowt.

SATAN

¶ Given his status as the **Prince of Evil** and **Father of Lies**, Satan's role in the Old Testament is modest.

¶ His name is from a Hebrew word meaning **adversary** or **accuser**, and he appears in the Old Testament as God's agent, tasked with putting men to the test. His name is mentioned only fifteen times in the Old Testament.

¶ But then things changed. In the New Testament, and later in the Qur'an, Satan is a fallen angel: a tempter, a liar and a corruptor of men. By the time of the Book of Revelation, Satan, the Devil, the **great dragon** and the **old serpent** had become one, gathering new names and titles that reflected his temporal power. These are some of his names.

ABADDON
(ALSO: APOLLYON)

Mentioned in Revelation as the 'angel of the bottomless pit'. Considered by some another name for Satan.

ANGRA MAINYU
(ALSO: AHRIMAN)

The apotheosis of evil in Zoroastrianism and a key influence in Jewish and Christian concepts of Satan.

ANTICHRIST

As Christians believe Christ to be the son of God, so the antichrist is the son of Satan. Nonetheless, the two names are often used synonymously.

IBLIS
(ALSO: ASH-SHAYTAN, AZAZEL)

Islam's Satan. His evil originated when he refused to bow down to Adam, who he considered his inferior. Also called **Aduw Allāh** *(Enemy of God).*

BEELZEBUB
(ALSO: BA'AL ZABUL, LORD OF THE FLIES, LORD OF DUNG)

Named in the New Testament as the **Prince of the Devils**, *Beelzebub was a common name for Satan from the fifteenth century.*

BELIAL

A fallen angel in Milton's Paradise Lost; later, another of Satan's names.

THE DEVIL

While devil does not appear in the Old Testament, it occurs 57 times in the New Testament. The word comes from Greek **diaballein** *(to slander or attack).*

FATHER OF LIES

Another of Satan's monikers, from: 'For he is a liar, and the father of it' (John 8:44).

LUCIFER
(ALSO: HEYLEL, DAY STAR, MORNING STAR)

Named in Isaiah as the rebel archangel who fell from heaven. From Latin for **light-bringing**.

PRINCE OF DARKNESS
(ALSO: PRINCE OF HELL, PRINCE OF THE AIR, PRINCE OF THIS WORLD, BLACK PRINCE)

Assorted princeley titles for Satan, featured in works by Milton, Defoe, Scott and so on.

SEE ALSO: Minced Oaths / God

ALSO KNOWN AS...

OLD BENDY	OLD HARRY	OLD MR GRIM	OLD SCRATCH
OLD CLUBFOOT	OLD HENRY	OLD NED	OLD SHAVER
OLD GOOSEBERRY	OLD HORNIE	OLD NICK	OLD SIMMIE
OLD HAIRY TOE	OLD JOE	OLD ROGER	

¶ The **Sator Square** is an acrostic word square dating to the Roman period. It is a palindromic, cryptographic puzzle comprising five Latin words that can be read vertically or horizontally, forwards or backwards. The five words are: **SATOR** (*sower*), **AREPO** (unknown, probably a name), **TENET** (*to hold*), **OPERA** (*work* or *care*) and **ROTAS** (*wheels*). Although numerous translations have been put forward, one that is widely accepted goes: *The sower, Arepo, works the wheels with care.*

¶ The earliest known carving of the Sator Square (or the **Rotas-Sator Square** when re-oriented) was discovered in Pompeii, dated AD 62. It was later adopted by early Christians and started appearing in writings, carvings and amulets across the Christian world.

168

¶ The Sator Square has been described as the oldest unsolved word puzzle in the world, but this doesn't do justice to the religious and cultural significance of this curious acrostic. Known also as the **Magic Square** (or **Templar Magic Square**) its origin is a mystery, variously ascribed to early Christians, Jewish mystics, Greek Gnostics, Italian pagans and more. The most mundane explanation, but maybe the most plausible, is that it is simply a Roman word puzzle immortalised in ancient graffiti. While this may be true, there's no denying that the Sator Square was adopted by medieval Christians, who interpreted Christ as the sower.

¶ From the early Middle Ages, the Sator Square was held to have mystical powers.

```
S A T O R
A R E P O
T E N E T
O P E R A
R O T A S
```

It was incorporated into cures for vertigo, rabies, toothache and insanity. In Germany, discs inscribed with the Sator Square were thrown into fires to extinguish them. Duke Ernest Auguste of Saxe-Weimar even issued an edict in 1743 requiring all towns to be adequately stocked with fire-fighting Sator discs.

¶ Academics have wrestled over the meaning of the Sator Square for centuries, testing different translations, shuffling letters and reading the square in alternating directions. A discovery in the 1920s that the letters could be rearranged to form PATERNOSTER (Lord's Prayer) in the form of a cross generated much excitement, but this was negated after the find in Pompeii.

¶ Curiously, the origin of the Sator Square may be less interesting than the mystery and mythology it later inspired. It is, as British historian Donald Atkinson wrote, in the 'mysterious region where religion, superstition and magic meet'.

❡ Scotland is to insults what France is to cuisine. It's not just the breadth and ingenuity, but the delivery. *Arsepiece knobdobber, fart lozenge, fannybaws*; insults like these combine wit and bite with a poetic punch.

❡ Scots are particularly well-stocked when it comes to calling out idiots and arseholes. They're a *rocket*, a *roaster*, a *melt*, a *walloper*, a *dafty*, a *tube*, a *spoon*, a *nugget*, a *fud* and more. And if you meet a *grade-A weapon*, beware! The beauty of these insults is that any innocuous noun can be weaponised with the right adjective – ya *specky hotdog*, ya *utter dropkick*, etc.

❡ Like many cultures, Scottish insults make use of parents. *Yer Da sells Avon* (your dad sells cosmetics) was a popular zinger, but dated now. *Yer Ma's yer Da* (your mum's your dad) is old too, but timeless. Special mention should also be made of *Bobby Davro sniffs yer Maw's knickers* and *Yer Da sits in the middle seat of the works van*. It's hard to find the right comeback for these.

❡ Some of the finest Scottish insults are compounds, like *chanty rassler, bugger lugs* and *bawjaws*. They're delicious, even if it's not always clear what they mean. But then you could always look them up, *ya bampot*.

A FACE LIKE A MELTED WELLY
Looking miserable

AWA AN BILE YER HEID
'Away and boil your head', i.e. get lost!

AWA AN TAKE YER FACE
FOR A SHITE
Leave now

CHEW MAH BANGER
Eat my dick

FACE LIKE A SKELPT ERSE
'Face like a slapped arse', i.e. ugly

LAVVY HEID
*'Toilet head', i.e. someone
who spouts nonsense*

LIKE A DUG LICKING
PISH AFF A NETTLE
'Like a dog licking piss off a nettle', i.e. ugly

PURE WEE RADGE
A crazy, violently excited nutter

YER TALKING MINCE
You're talking rubbish

YER BUMS OOT THE WINDAE
*'Your bum's out the window', i.e. you're talking
rubbish (although nobody's sure why!)*

YER MAW'S GIT BALLS N
YER DA' LOVES IT
A uniquely Scottish 'yo Mamma' insult

TONGUE MY FART-BOX
Lick my arse

169

SEE ALSO: *Barry Humphries Glossary / Fuck*

YER A BAWBAG

Bawbag is the great Scottish insult, entering the *OED* in 1999 – the same time as fanny baws, but fifteen years after scrote.

The word is merely the Scottish pronunciation of ball-bag (scrotum), slang that's been around since the late nineteenth-century. But 'bawbag' graduated from Scottish play-grounds in the 1970s to become a national treasure, alongside haggis, tartan and whisky. When Cyclone Friedhelm hit in 2011, it was widely referred to as Hurricane Bawbag; and when President Trump visited his Turnberry golf course in 2016, he was given an unprecedented introduction to the word by placard-waving protesters.

¶ Scotland has a lot of weather, and a large lexicon to describe it. **Dreich**, which describes a cheerless bleak day, is said to be the nation's favourite word, but when there's the **doondrap** that gives you a **baffin** (drenching) or the **driffle** that leaves you **bedrizzled**, one is spoilt for choice.

¶ Here are over 120 Scottish terms for rain, all found in the online *Dictionaries of the Scots Language*. Even on their own the words are expressive, but there's a nuance to each that is hard to convey in such limited space. The thick drizzle of **smuick**, for instance, is unlike the passing **skub**, or the thin fall of **pewlin** rain. At the wetter end of the spectrum, **groff** rain falls in large drops, **slabbering** rain splashes heavily, and definitely stay indoors when it's about to **plump**, because it'll sheet down.

¶ The beauty of these words lies in how naturally they evoke a sound, a feeling and an image. But they need to be spoken to

SEE ALSO: *Beaufort Scale*

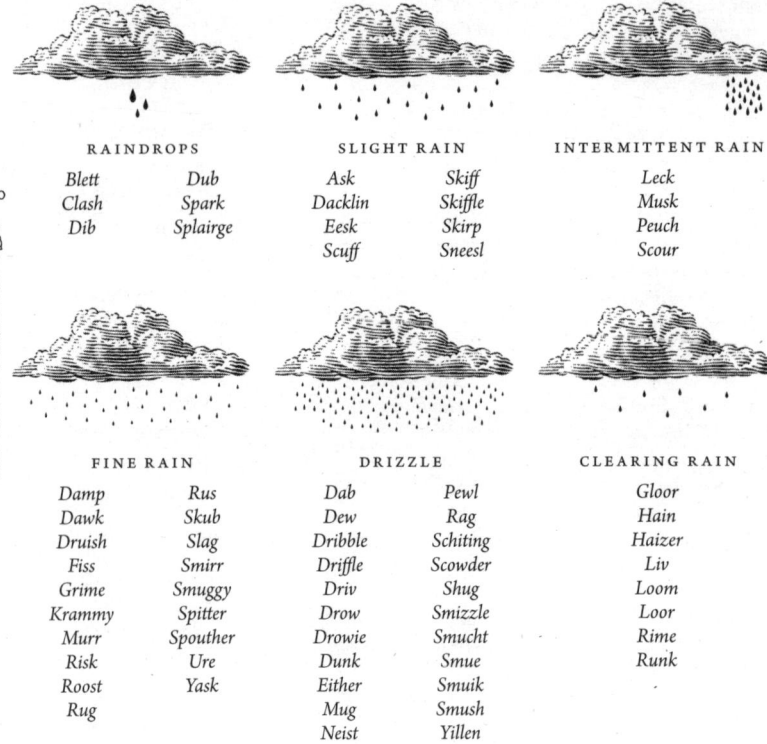

RAINDROPS

Blett	Dub
Clash	Spark
Dib	Splairge

SLIGHT RAIN

Ask	Skiff
Dacklin	Skiffle
Eesk	Skirp
Scuff	Sneesl

INTERMITTENT RAIN

Leck
Musk
Peuch
Scour

FINE RAIN

Damp	Rus
Dawk	Skub
Druish	Slag
Fiss	Smirr
Grime	Smuggy
Krammy	Spitter
Murr	Spouther
Risk	Ure
Roost	Yask
Rug	

DRIZZLE

Dab	Pewl
Dew	Rag
Dribble	Schiting
Driffle	Scowder
Driv	Shug
Drow	Smizzle
Drowie	Smucht
Dunk	Smue
Either	Smuik
Mug	Smush
Neist	Yillen

CLEARING RAIN

Gloor
Hain
Haizer
Liv
Loom
Loor
Rime
Runk

reveal themselves. A **peuchling o' rain** sounds, and is, light and fitful. A **scudder**, that driving rain, has a sharp edge of discomfort, while **smirr** sounds as thin and gentle as the fine drizzle it is.

¶ And then there are the rainbows. The **skafer**, seen through mist; the **stuthe**, a trace of rainbow that hovers over the sea; the **gollan**, spotted through the clouds; and the imperfect **naipken** that presages bad weather. It's as if J. R. R. Tolkien were a meteorologist.

¶ Although most of Scotland has no more rain than the British average, it knows how to appreciate it, from the **flobby** clouds, heavy with rain, to the **clash** and **slob** of fat raindrops hitting puddles. There's even a word, optimistic one might think, for the prolonged *absence* of rain. It's **dortie**, they say, meaning loathe to rain. But it's not an expression that's heard often.

RAIN AND SNOW

Sleek

RAIN AND SLEET

Snift

STORMY RAIN

Blatter	*Bleatery*
Fern-storm	*Gouster*

WIND AND RAIN

Daggastö	*Flaw*
Scudder	*Spleiter*

TORRENTIAL RAIN

Lavish	*Plash*
Leash	*Slatch*
Owse	*String*

HEAVY RAIN

Blash	*Ondag*
Creep	*Onfa*
Ding	*Plump*
Doon-come	*Slabber*
Doondrap	*Slunge*
Gandiegow	*Stepe*
Groff	*Trash o'weet*
Lay	*Uar*
Oncome	*Uplowsin*

DOWNPOUR

Blaud	*Peg*
Brave	*Pelsh*
Clash	*Pish*
Dish	*Pish-oot*
Goselet	*Plunge*
Lash	*Plunk*
Lum	*Rash*
Nebert	*Sab*
Outpour	*Slock*
Peeggirin	*Sump*

SCOTTISH RAIN

Gets in yer neb, lugs,
unner thi oxters tae.
Oan yer heid, in yer een
til ye're drookit, ken?

An it's aye cauld
an gaes sidie-ways.
Whit, warm rain?
Nae here (mebbe
in Spain).

Woke up this mornin,
crawled oot o bed,
keeked oot thi
windae pane
Aw naw! Rainin again!

TOM BRYAN

¶ William Shakespeare contributed 1,500 words to the English language. Or 1,700. Or maybe 2,500. Opinions on the internet vary, but such inflated claims are characteristic of the **Shakespeare Myth**, in which it is imagined one sixteenth-century playwright almost invented modern English. One dictionary that shall remain nameless even claims that Shakespeare 'introduced some six hundred new words to the English language in *Hamlet* alone', which is impressively ludicrous.

¶ George Bernard Shaw had a word for this tendency: **bardolatry**. Although the *OED* defines bardolatry as 'worship of the "Bard of Avon"', Shaw was actually describing the combination of ignorance and adulation that swirls around him. The overblown claims about the words he created, not to mention his unrivalled vocabulary – said to be twice that of his contemporaries, or four times that of a typical undergraduate, or sixty times that of the *Sun* newspaper – are the result of centuries of fanciful bardolatry.

¶ One of the most widely shared paeans to Shakespearean coinages was written by Bernard Levin. Called *Quoting Shakespeare*, it begins, 'If you cannot understand my argument, and declare "It's Greek to me", you are quoting Shakespeare.' Levin then weaves together sixty-two well-known idioms that are all, he says, 'quoting Shakespeare':

> …*if you wish I was* **dead as a door-nail**, *if you think I am an* **eyesore, a laughing stock, the devil incarnate**, *a* **stony-hearted villain, bloody-minded** *or a* **blinking idiot**, *then* – **by Jove! O Lord! Tut tut! For goodness' sake! What the dickens! But me no buts!** – *it is all one to me, for you are quoting Shakespeare.*

¶ It's a delightful piece of writing, and a great compilation of Shakespearean *bon mots*. The only problem is that forty-two of the phrases (68 per cent) are found in earlier sources and a number weren't even used by Shakespeare, including 'but me no buts' (coined in 1709).

¶ At time of writing, Shakespeare is quoted 32,508 times in the *OED*, making him the dictionary's most referenced individual source (the most quoted overall is *The Times*). Of these, 2,273 are first quotations. But what they're not, or not necessarily, is **coinages**.

¶ Samuel Johnson, father of the modern dictionary, deserves some of the blame here. He trawled the Shakespeare corpus for his 1755 dictionary and used around 17,500 quotations, which were later absorbed into the *OED*. In many cases, neither Johnson nor later *OED* editors looked beyond Shakespeare for earlier uses, so the Bard became the *de facto* 'first use' for thousands of words.

FIG.1 *Portrait of William Shakespeare by Martin Droeshout from the First Folio*

¶ The impression of Shakespeare as some word-coining machine has been promoted by what some refer to as the **Shakespeare Industry**. Like the Shakespeare Birthplace Trust, whose teaching resources credit the Bard with conjuring **alligator, apostrophe, assassination, bandit, birthplace, eyeball** and **zany**. He coined none of these. Nor did he 'invent' **aerial, critical, dislocate, eventful, frugal, gloom, lonely, pious** or **suspicious**, as claimed by educators No Sweat Shakespeare.

¶ Without evidence to the contrary, these fantastic claims have gone unchecked. But in 2025, groundbreaking research by Jonathan Culpeper, Jonathan Hope and Sam Hollands reviewed Shakespeare's language more scientifically. By comparing everything he wrote with a huge corpus of historical texts, and the resources of the *OED*, Culpeper *et al* arrived at a list of around 558 words first seen in Shakespeare (or rather, first seen in English, since 20 of these are loan words from other languages).

¶ Among these 558 words are many novel creations, like **slug-a-bed, hodge-pudding, toad-spotted, sheep-biting** and **hedge-born**. They're intriguing contributions, but no 'alligator' or 'apostrophe'. In fact, eighty-nine words are what linguists call **nonce words** (created for one specific use) or **hapax legomenon** (words that don't appear anywhere else). So while Shakespeare may well have coined **wonder-wounded** and **irregulous**, they didn't catch on.

¶ Many more words in Culpeper's list are either new senses of existing words – such as a noun used as a verb – or words modified with a prefix or suffix (known as **affixation**). In fact, 281 words (over 50 per cent) were created with affixes, of which a quarter were prefixed with **un-**, like **unbefit, unfix, unhelpful, untended** and more. When people talk about how many words Shakespeare created, his prolific use of **un-** may not be what they have in mind.

¶ Shakespeare himself might have found the preoccupation with his coinages to be **unmeritable** (*Richard III*), even **claybrained** (*Henry IV, Part 1*). Many of his contemporaries, like Marlowe, Webster and Jonson, coined plenty of words themselves, often using affixes or compounds. But Shakespeare's coinages have been ridiculously, and unecessarily, inflated. 173

¶ None of this should detract from Shakespeare's genius. Even the 'modest' tally of 558 words is 558 more than this author will ever add to the dictionary. But more important than the words he created is what he did with them. There's no need to invent mythical achievements when the real brilliance is there to see.

WORDS SHAKESPEARE MAYBE POSSIBLY *DID* COIN

Airless • Bacon-fed • Beast-eating • Blood-drinking • Blue-veined • Clay-brained • Comfort-killing • Double-damn • Droplet • Dwindle • Ear-piercing • Fashion-monger • Far-off • Fat-witted • Fiery • Flap-eared • Footfall • Glass-faced • Heart-struck • Ill-starred • Misquote • Remorseless • Rose-cheeked • Self-abuse • Short-lived • Silver-voiced • Soundless • Subcontract • Tickle-brain • Unhelpful • Unhospitable • Unintelligent • Unvarnished • Wasp-tongued • Well-educated

¶It is **unpossible** to exaggerate how the world's longest-running TV show, *The Simpsons*, has **embiggened*** the English language since it **beginulated** on the **picto-cube** in 1989. Despite criticism that it was **dumbening** viewers with **craptacular numbskullery**, it knew the secret of **successmanship**; and coining new words was part of it.

¶In the world of *The Simpsons*, stupidity is the mother of linguistic invention, as characters struggle to get the right **dealie** out of their **word holes**. Like Ralph Wiggum, whose **arm pants** (sleeves), **coffee peanuts** (coffee beans) and **cooking machines** (ovens) are the tip of a not very clever iceberg. Homer likewise, with **nuleules** at work and other **sophistimicated doowhackeys**. And from other **senseless dunderpates** have sprung **yellow fatty-beans** (bananas), **saxamaphone** (saxophone), **Italian-American sauce bread** (pizza), **uppity box** (elevator) and **reversifying glass** (mirror). They're all **cromulent*** (acceptable) words. Even Mr Burns's archaic vocabulary makes a kind of sense, whether he's searching for the **velocitator** or **deceleratrix** (accelerator or brakes) in his **Mobilomobile** (car), or snacking on **pretzeled bread** in the **bathiola** (bath).

¶There are smart people in Springfield too – the kind who frequent the **Learnatorium** and **Knowledgeum**. Professor Frink, for instance, Springfield's best known **scientician**, invented the **debigulator** and **rebigulator** to shrink people, and then return them to normal size. (He also discovered the radioactive substance **Frinkium nitrate**.) And the town's doctors

– Hibbert and Riviera – can diagnose rare conditions like **Bonus Eruptus**, **Crayola Oblongata** and **Hurricane Vomiting**.

¶Homer himself invented the tomato-to-bacco cross breed, **tomacco**; the beer with a candy float, **Skittlebrau**; and the jock-strap-mounted **Butt-ski**. And while his **anyhoo***, **d'oh***, **meh*** and **yoink*** weren't coined by the show's writers – they just made them famous – **Jebus** (instead of Jesus), **unblowuppable** and **tracted** (the opposite of *distracted*) were.

¶Springfield's most irritating **neighborino**, Ned Flanders, has his own language, with its **okily-dokilies**, **howdily-doodillies** and **de-diddly-lighteds**. Just **askaroonie**. Irritating in a different way is young Bart, with his own linguistic contribution, including **Dorkus Malorkus**, **dweebazoid**, **crap-factory** (stomach) and **suck shack** (school). The writers even coined a word for people who **introubulate** others by behaving like Bart: **Bartesque**.

¶Some of the show's most inspired creations are portmanteaux, like **avoision**, **crisitunity** and the timeless **traumedy**, where trauma and comedy meet. Something delicious eaten in a holy place is **sacrilicious**, probably **snacktacular** too. And have you ever played that game with the brick? You know the one... **volleybrick**.

¶Many *Simpsons'* coinages have entered the real world, where any **capdabbler** or **Johnny Lunchpail** can use them. Some, like **cheese-eating surrender monkey** (the French) have become iconic. And while there'll always be **don'ters** who disapprove, the show goes on. **Smell ya later**.

(*now in the dictionary)

¶ In 1925, America's first **National Spelling Bee** winner earned $500 for successfully spelling **gladiolus**. Nearly a century later, the 96th Scripps National Spelling Bee (Scripps became the sponsor in 1941) saw a starting field of 11 million students compete to win $50,000. With such fierce competition, top spellers now rely on spelling tutors and expensive software to get an edge. Because to earn great *éclat*, one must spell it first.

WINNING WORDS FROM THE SCRIPS NATIONAL SPELLING BEE

1925	Gladiolus	1960	Eudaemonic	1992	Lyceum
1926	Cerise	1961	Smaragdine	1993	Kamikaze
1927	Abrogate	1962	Esquamulose	1994	Antediluvian
1928	Knack	1963	Equipage	1995	Xanthosis
1929	Luxuriance	1964	Sycophant	1996	Vivisepulture
1930	Albumen	1965	Eczema	1997	Euonym
1931	Foulard	1966	Ratoon	1998	Chiaroscurist
1932	Invulnerable	1967	Chihuahua	1999	Logorrhea
1933	Torsion	1968	Abalone	2000	Demarche
1934	Brethren	1969	Interlocutory	2001	Succedaneum
1935	Intelligible	1970	Croissant	2002	Prospicience
1936	Eczema	1971	Shalloon	2003	Pococurante
1937	Promiscuous	1972	Macerate	2004	Autochthonous
1938	Sanitarium	1973	Vouchsafe	2005	Appoggiatura
1939	Canonical	1974	Hydrophyte	2006	Ursprache
1940	Therapy	1975	Incisor	2007	Serrefine
1941	Initials	1976	Narcolepsy	2008	Guerdon
1942	Sacrilegious	1977	Cambist	2009	Laodicean
1946	Semaphore	1978	Deification	2010	Stromuhr
1947	Chlorophyll	1979	Maculature	2011	Cymotrichous
1948	Psychiatry	1980	Elucubrate	2012	Guetapens
1949	Onerous	1981	Sarcophagus	2013	Knaidel
1950	Meticulosity	1982	Psoriasis	2014	Stichomythia
1951	Insouciant	1983	Purim	2015	Scherenschnitte
1952	Vignette	1984	Luge	2016	Feldenkrais
1953	Soubrette	1985	Milieu	2017	Marocain
1954	Transept	1986	Odontalgia	2018	Koinonia
1955	Crustaceology	1987	Staphylococci	2019	Auslaut
1956	Condominium	1988	Elegiacal	2021	Murraya
1957	Schappe	1989	Spoliator	2022	Moorhen
1958	Syllepsis	1990	Fibranne	2023	Psammophile
1959	Catamaran	1991	Antipyretic	2024	Abseil

175

SEE ALSO: *Pedantry*

A **bee** is an informal social gathering convened for a specific activity. As well as **spelling bees** there are **quilting bees**, **apple bees** and **raising bees**; and in the past, notes *Merriam-Webster* darkly, there was evidence of **hanging bees** and **lynching bees**. Curiously, the etymology of **bee** in all these senses is unknown.

In April 1967, the *Melbourne Herald* announced the opening of the Wydinia kindergarten in Colac, on Australia's south-eastern tip. The name, the article explained, emerged from all the advice offered during construction: 'Why dinya built it of brick?', 'Why dinya build it in the east?', 'Why dinya do this?', 'Why dinya do that?'. So **Wydinia** it was.

The Wydinia story is an example of ***strine***, the phonetic expression of Australian English that parodies how the broad Australian accent can make vowels and consonants stretch, morph and disappear. The word – itself strine for Australian – was the humourous creation of Afferbeck Lauder (say it out loud), aka Alastair Morrison, who first documented it in the *Sydney Morning Herald* in 1964.

According to Morrison, strine was inspired by the story of an author autographing books in a Sydney bookshop. She signed one to 'Emma Chisit', the name given by the lady who had handed the book to her. On giving it back, the lady was irritated. She hadn't said her name was 'Emma Chisit', but asked 'How much is it?' (Incidentally, the story was true, and the author in question was Charles Dickens's granddaughter.)

Strine is both humorous and ingenious. It can also be a challenge for anyone unfamiliar with thick Australian brogue to disentangle. Fortunately, Afferbeck Lauder, the self-proclaimed 'Professor of Strine Studies at the University of Sinny', wrote two invaluable works on the subject – *Let Stalk Strine* (1965) and *Nose Tone Unturned* (1967) – as well as the strine classic *With Air Chew*, shared in full, and with translation, opposite.

GLOSSARY OF STRINE

AORTA	*I ought to*
ASSPRAD	*house proud*
BAKED NECKS	*bacon and eggs*
DENT-SHOE WORRY	*don't you worry*
EBB TIDE	*appetite*
EGG JELLY	*actually*
EGG NISHING	*air conditioning*
EMENY	*how many?*
FURRY TILES	*fairy tales*
GARBLER MINCE	*couple of minutes*
GESS VONNER	*guest of honour*
GLORIA STY	*glorious day*
GUNGA DIN	*can't get in*
LAZE AND GEM	*ladies and gentlemen*
LONDGER RAY	*lingerie*
MARE CHECK	*magic*
ORPHEUS ROCKER	*off his rocker*
SAG RAPES	*sour grapes*
SANDER'S LAPE	*sound asleep*
SEMMITCH	*sandwich*
SOUP-MARKED	*supermarket*
SPIN-EAR MITCH	*spitting image*
TAN CANCEL	*town council*
TEA NATURE	*teenager*
TERROR SOUSE	*terraced house*
TO GORF	*took off*
TRINE	*train*
WATER BAT	*what about?*
WEZZME	*where is my*
X	*eggs*
YEGGOWAN	*are you going?*

WITH AIR CHEW

With air chew, with air chew,
Iker nardly liver there chew,
An I dream a badger kisser snite and die.
Phoney wicked beer loan,
Jars-chewer mere nonnair roan,
An weed dreamer batter mooner pinner sky.

With air chew, with air chew,
Hair mike-owner liver there chew?
Wile yerrony immy dream sigh maulwye scrine.
Anna strewer seffner barf,
Yuma snow-eye Nietzsche laugh,
Cars with air chew immy arm sit snow-eye Strine.

AFFERBECK LAUDER

 TRANSLATION

WITHOUT YOU

Without you, without you,
I can hardly live without you,
And I dream about your kisses night and day.
If only we could be alone,
Just you and me here on our own,
And we'd dream about the moon up in the sky.

Without you, without you,
How am I going to live without you?
While you are only in my dreams I'm always crying.
And it's as true as heaven above,
You must know I need your love,
Because without you in my arms it's no use trying.

T.

TECHNOBABBLE

¶ In a very forgettable scene from a very forgettable *Star Trek* episode, Starfleet engineer Reginald Barclay explained how he set up 'a frequency harmonic between the deflector and the shield grid using the warp field generator as a power flow anti-attenuator'. It was classic *Star Trek*, in that the science was complete gibberish – or, more accurately, ***technobabble***.

¶ It's a given that the *Star Trek* universe couldn't function without technobabble, where ***inverted tachyon beams***, ***Heisenberg compensators*** and ***dilithium crystals*** are essential. But while *Star Trek* does technobabble more and better than anyone else, this meaningless science-sounding jargon is a familiar feature across the sci-fi genre. Doctor Who has escaped many sticky situations by ***reversing the polarity of the neutron flow***, and were it not for the ***flux capacitor*** in *Back to the Future*, or the ***plasma beam tuning cavity*** in *Ghostbusters*, both time travel and ghost-catching respectively would be a lot harder.

¶ Sci-fi has always needed its own language to describe futuristic concepts that are either unknown or unachievable. ***Technobabble*** (also: ***science speak*** and ***space talk***) is a sub-category of the lexicon that acts as a sciency plot-sealant.

¶ Science jargon has existed for as long as there were scientists to spout it, but sci-fi technobabble took off with the pulp magazines in the 1930s and 1940s. Writers like Edward E. Smith – 'The Father of the Space Opera' – Edmond Hamilton and John Campbell, whose bylines appeared in *Weird Stories*, *Amazing Stories*, *Astounding Stories* (and so on) coined literally hundreds of technobabble miracles, including: ***thionite***, ***neutronium***, ***pressor***

beam, ***sub-ether***, ***force beam***, ***gravitonic***, ***positronic***, ***uchronic***, ***transdimensional***, ***astrogational***, ***hyperspatial*** and the time-stopping ***stasis field***. This was the Golden Age of technobabble.

¶ *Star Trek* writer Garret Wang was said to use two decks of cards to conjure his technobabble: one for prefixes (***bio***, ***chrono***, ***iso***), the other for adjectives (***kinetic***, ***metric***, ***phasic***); combined, they provided instant futuristic results. But with modern audiences no longer impressed by ***para-plasmic phase disruptors***, technical consultants now provide a semblance of authentic science. Fortunately, since quantum physics and the multiverse barely make sense to the scientists themselves, there's a rich new seam of ***almost-science*** capable of powering sci-fi writers to the furthest corners of the universe.

THE SCIENCE OF *STAR TREK*

...*scan the quantum fissure using a subspace differential pulse*...

...*place the neural output pods in contact with the tricorder scanner heads*...

...*a multi-phasic temporal convergence in the space-time continuum*...

...*chronoton-infused hypospray casing*...

...*if the dekyon emission is modulated correctly, it will set up resonances in my positronic subprocessors*...

...*the gravimetric field displacement manifold*...

...*the warp coils are in multiphase-lock*...

and so on.

SEE ALSO: *Hacker Jargon* / *Pager Code*

¶ The world's longest-running engineering in-joke is the **turbo-encabulator**, a fictional machine built on cutting-edge **technobabble**.

¶ In December 1944, the *Students' Quarterly Journal* of the Institution of Electrical Engineers unveiled the turbo-encabulator, a machine mounted on a base-plate of **prefabulated amulite** which could not only operate **nofer trunnions** but also reduce **side-fumbling** via its **ambifacient lunar waneshaft**. It was, of course, all nonsense.

¶ Over the years, the turbo-encabulator has featured in *Time* magazine, General Electric product manuals and a series of convincing promotional films made by engineers at GMC, Rockwell Automation, Chrysler and others. (All can be found online and are worth watching.)

¶ New versions of the machine have appeared over the last eighty years,

like the **retro-encabulator, hyper-encabulator** and **magneto-turbo-encabulator**, each incorporating a range of technobabble features, like **hydrocoptic marzelvanes, reciprocating dingle arms** and those all-important **anhydrous nangling pins**.

¶ Eighty years after its 'invention', the turbo-encabulator shows no sign of being retired. Its 'inventor', J. H. Quick, would surely be gratified to see how his machine remains the world-leader in technobabble generation.

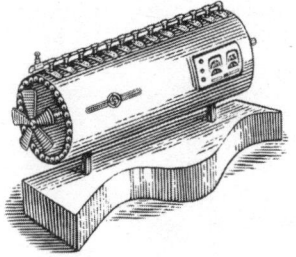

FIG.1 *Turbo-encabulator,*
GE Handbook *(1962)*

179

SEE ALSO: Breasts

TESTICLES

Apples	Chicken tenders	Goolies	Nadgers	Stones
Balls	Chuckles	Gooseberries	Nards	Sweetmeats
Bangers	Clockweights	Itchy and scratchy	Norbs	Swingers
Bannocks	Cobblers		Nuts	Teabags
Bawbags	Cojones	Jibblies	Pebbles	Testes
Beanbags	Danglers	Junk	Plums	Twins
Bollocks	Doo-dahs	Klackers	Potatoes	Yarbles
Boys	Family jewels	Knackers	Rocks	
Brovaries	Fun bags	Love spuds	Sprouts	
Cherries	Giggle berries	Marbles	Spuds	
	Gonads	Meat clackers		

¶ The first **thingummy** was **what-d'ye-call-'em**, which the *Oxford English Doodad* dates to 1473. People have been coming up with names for things they can't remember the names for ever since.

¶ **Thingummies** and **doodads** are a sub-category of **placeholder words** and are indispensable when one can't remember the name of a person, place or thing. Judging by the length of this list, that's apparently quite often.

Bizzo	Frammis	So-and-so	What-not
Boondoggle	Gilguy	Thingamadodger	What's-her-face
Callit	Gilhooley	Thingamadoodle	Whatsisname
Dingbat	Gizmo	Thingamadudgeon	Whatsit
Dingus	Hickey	Thingamajig	Whiblin
Doodad	Jiggumbob	Thingamananny	Whifflow
Doodah	Kajody	Thingummy	Whodjamaflip
Doofer	Oobyjiver	Thingy	Who knows what
Doohickey	Oojah	Tiddlypush	Whosis
Doowhistle	Oojamaflip	Whangoodle	Whosit
Doowillie	Oojiboo	What-d'ye-call-'em	Wingdoodle

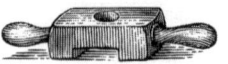

FIG.1 *Handheld thingum*

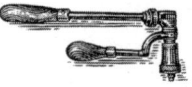

FIG.2 *Mechanical whatsit*

FIG.3 *Digital doodad*

THE TV REMOTE CONTROL

The first TV remote control was the **Lazy-Bones**, a wired device made by the Zenith Radio Corporation in 1950. Then came the **Blab-off** (which muted the TV), the **Flashmatic** (now wireless) and the **Stealth Command**. Today, people have invented more names for the TV remote than maybe any other household item. Here are some favourites shared by British viewers.

Blaster • Bleeper • Blipper • Blodger • Bopper • Click Clack • Clicker • Diddler • Diddly-Do • Dinger • Dip Dap • Ditter • Do-Flicker • Donker • Doodlestick • Doot-Doot • Flicker • Flickybox • Flipper • Hoofer Doofer • Jigger • Jobber • Oobrie Doobi • Oofa Doofa • Plinker • Plonker • Pointything • Presser • Ronnie Remote • Stick • Switcher • Telly Commander • Tellything • Turny-Over Machine • TV Gun • Widger • Zapper

¶ Peter Piper, of pickled-pepper-picking fame, apparently existed. He was a French horticulturalist called Pierre Poivre (pepper) who introduced cloves and nutmeg to Mauritius in the eighteenth century. The claim can't be proven, but it's a nice story which you can choose to believe if you wish.

¶ True or not, Monsieur Poivre certainly wasn't alive to see his eponymous tongue-twister first published in *Peter Piper's Practical Principles of Plain and Perfect Pronunciation* in 1813. Like tongue-twisters ever since, the *Practical Principals* were part-fun, part-purposeful: **to Prevent the Pernicious Prevalence of Perverse Pronunciation**. Today, the *Anthology of British Tongue-Twisters* is similarly used by actors, presenters and voice coaches for vocal exercises and elocution practice.

¶ Why tongue-twisters twist tongues isn't straightforward. It seems self-evident that the physical movements required to produce distinct but similar **phonemes** – the smallest linguistic units of sound – might get confused, particularly when they're rapidly alternating (**red lorry, yellow lorry**); but why is it hard to read a tongue twister *silently*?

¶ Researchers looking at electrical activity in the brain found an overlap based on where sounds were formed. Front-of-tongue sounds, like **sss** and **shh** for instance, are processed by the same part of the brain, regardless of whether they're said or read. Sign language has similar neural overlaps, which is why **finger fumblers**, such as 'good blood, bad blood', can be particularly hard.

¶ Ultimately, it's not the tongue that's being twisted, but the brain; so bear this in mind when you next give a **cop top** to the **top cop**.

KILLER TONGUE-TWISTERS

Pad kid poured curd pulled cod.

Clean clams crammed in clean cans.

The sixth sheik's sixth sheep's sick.

Fresh fried fish, fish fresh fried, fried fish fresh, fish fried fresh.

The seething sea ceaseth and thus the seething sea sufficeth us.

Unique New York.

Many an anemone sees an enemy anemone.

Chop shops stock chops.

Whoever slits the sheets is a good sheet slitter.

I saw Susie sitting in a shoe shine shop.

Where she shines, she sits, and where she sits, she shines.

181

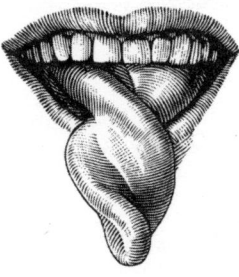

A TONGUE-TWISTER PALINDROME

Top step's pup's pet spot.

A TONGUE-TWISTER LIMERICK

A canner, exceedingly canny,
One morning remarked to his granny,
'A canner can can
Anything that he can,
But a canner can't can a can, can he?'

SEE ALSO: *Eggcorns / Reduplicative Words*

U.

UNRHYMABLE WORDS

¶ A **refractory rhyme** is a word that doesn't rhyme with anything else. Although nothing rhymes with **nothing**, beware the commonly repeated claims for words like **orange**, **month** and **purple**, all of which have rhymes.

¶ To be included here, rhymes must be **perfect rhymes** (or **true rhymes**) with the same vowels and ending consonants. Archaic and scientific terms are permissible, no matter how obscure, but names and places aren't. At least, not in this book.

RHYMES FOR WORDS COMMONLY SAID TO BE UNRHYMABLE

Beige rhymes with *greige* (a halfway house between beige and grey).

Bulb rhymes with *culb* (a retort).

Chaos rhymes with *naos* (inner sanctuary of a temple).

Chocolate rhymes with *auklet* (a small auk).

Circle rhymes with *hurkle* (to draw your limbs close together).

Circus rhymes with *murkus* (lacking a thumb).

Dunce rhymes with *bunce* (money or profit).

Film rhymes with *pilm* (Scottish word meaning 'dust').

Filth rhymes with *spilth* (a quantity of liquid that is spilled).

Month rhymes with *oneth* (with difficulty).

Music rhymes with *anchusic* (a red colouring).

Orange rhymes with *blorange* (colour of blonde and orange) and *sporange* (a spore case).

Plinth rhymes with *synth* (short for synthesiser).

Purple rhymes with *curple* (posterior) and *nurple* (the rump of a horse).

Silver rhymes with *chilver* (a ewe lamb).

Toilet rhymes with *oilet* (a hole in a wall).

GENUINELY UNRHYMABLE WORDS

Amongst	Filmed	Sculpts
Angst	Glimpsed	Sixth
Bilge	Gouge	Spoilt
Borscht	Kiln	Traipsed
Breadth	Kirsch	Unbeknownst
Bronzed	Neutron	Warmth
Comb	Ninth	Whilst
Depth	Obliged	With
Eighth	Pierced	Wolf
Elbow	Plankton	Worlds
False	Poem	Wounds
Fifth	Scarce	

W

The King sent for his wise men all

To find a rhyme for W.

When they had thought a good long time,

But could not think of a single rhyme,

'I'm sorry,' said he, 'to trouble you.'

JAMES REEVES

SEE ALSO: Long Words / Word Records

LEXIPEDIA PEOPLE

HESTER THRALE
WRITER AND SOCIALITE
(1741–1821)

¶Hester Salusbury, born 1741, lived two lives. As Hester Thrale, wife of a wealthy brewer, she was the dazzling hostess and most intimate confidant of 'Dictionary Johnson'. And as Hester Piozzi, she was a diarist, author and lexicographer who scandalised Regency society.

¶As a child, the young Hester demonstrated a precociously sharp mind. Her wings were clipped, however, with her arranged marriage to Thomas Thrale; a union that brought the 'yoke' of a controlling, philandering husband. Then, on 9 January 1765, Doctor Johnson came for dinner.

¶Johnson was to become a frequent guest at the Thrales, enjoying 'Master's' wine and his 'Dear Mistress's' keen intelligence. Less than a year into their friendship, Johnson appeared on the edge of a nervous breakdown. The Thrales, taking pity, gave him a room and a study which he did not relinquish for sixteen years.

¶It was during this time that Hester and Johnson developed their intense friendship. In public, they presided over salons at the Thrale's Streatham home, buzzing with artists and writers. Privately, Hester became his confidant, carer and secret-keeper. She held, quite literally, 'Johnson's padlock' (it was found labelled as such among her possessions). There's little doubt that Johnson was in love with her, and when Thomas Thrale died in 1781, it was assumed by many of his friends that the two would marry.

¶Hester, however, had other ideas. Having lived under the thumb of her husband, and mothered the needy and self-absorbed Johnson (not to mention twelve children) Hester, now a wealthy widow, chose her own path.

When she married her daughter's music master, Gabriel Piozzi, in 1784, it outraged many, including Johnson, who burned her letters and vowed never to speak of her again. Hester didn't care, just as she was unruffled by the scandal many years later around her pursuit of a young actor nearly fifty years her junior.

¶Hester Piozzi's first published work was *Anecdotes of the Late Samuel Johnson* (1786), arriving five years before Boswell's biography. It was a runaway success, with the first four editions quickly selling out. She later published a book about her travels through Italy, a dictionary called *British Synonymy* (1794), and an ambitious if imperfect history of the world, *Retrospection* (1801). Her diaries, *Thraliana*, were published in 1942, and provide a unique perspective on Georgian and Regency England.

¶Hester once wrote, 'In Johnson's intellect mine was swallowed up and lost'. But as Hester Piozzi, it was free to shine, undeterred by the disapproving gaze of Regency society. Remembered today as 'Doctor Johnson's Mrs Thrale', H.L.P., as she signed herself, was a dauntingly impressive woman who proved to the very end that she was nobody's but her own.

VICTORIAN EUPHEMISMS FOR PREGNANCY

¶ The Victorian reputation for prudery meant that even discussing pregnancy required great delicacy. Fortunately the Victorians were accomplished euphemists.

¶ Consider the tact exhibited in the *Globe*'s headline about Queen Victoria's pregnancy: 'The Queen Enceinte'. This fragrant French borrowing suggests nothing to modern audiences, but to Victorians it was a respectful account of the Queen's situation.

¶ Using euphemism herself, Queen Victoria wrote to her eldest daughter about how 'furious' she felt to be **caught**. Sounding similarly irritated were **fallen on**, **gone** and **burdoned**. But given the dangers of childbirth, maybe such sentiments were understandable.

¶ Most euphemisms weren't so negative. The description **in an interesting condition** was common enough for Charles Dickens to write wrily: 'Mrs Dickens being in an uninteresting condition, has besought me to bring her out of London for two months.'

¶ As well as interesting, a lady's state might be **delicate**, or one of **domestic solicitude**. Each communicates both everything and nothing.

¶ Still remembered today is **in the family way**, as in; **advanced in the family way**, or **discovered to be in the family way**. Whatever the precise wording, the meaning was clear, which is more than can be said for **ceasing to be unwell**, which is rather confusing.

¶ To explain: **unwell** was itself a euphemism for having one's period. Thus, a lady who ceased to be unwell had missed her period and might therefore be pregnant. But since a pregnant woman could also be described as unwell, 'ceasing to be unwell' might either be the start of pregnancy, or the end of it.

¶ If unwell was ambiguous, there was no confusion about a woman **heavy with child**, or **great-bellied**, although such robust descriptions were reserved for the working classes. A doctor looking to express the same might say a lady was **gravid** (from the Latin for burdoned), but this was largely reserved for medical books.

¶ After nine months of exhausting euphemism came the **accouchement** or **confinement**, where, God willing, the woman would be **delivered of a little stranger**. All being well, **acts of coition** could then recommence.

SEE ALSO: *Euphemisms for Death*

A GLOSSARY OF VICTORIAN UNMENTIONABLES

BREASTS: *diddeys, manuals of love's devotion, paps, ripe fruit, ruby-tipped globes.*

CLITORIS: *bell, button, dot, little man in a boat.*

PENIS: *arbor vitae, lobcock, prodigious engine, root, steed, stick, stiff sinew, tackle, truncheon, yard.*

ORGASM: *critical period, flood of bliss, sting of pleasure, sweet death.*

SEX: *amorous congress, amorous engagement, amorous rapture, convivial society, nocturnal embrace, storming the mint, the work of generation, tupping, wapping.*

VAGINA: *cloven inlet, downy spring-moss, fairest flower, sable fur.*

❡ *Aristotle's Masterpiece* wasn't by Aristotle and was no masterpiece, but for two centuries after its publication in 1684, it was the leading sex manual for amorous couples in Britain and America. A new edition of the work was published, on average, almost every year for 250 years.

❡ Aristotle's status as the world's first sex-pert arose because of an earlier book, *Aristotle's Problems* (1595) that also contained bold descriptions of sex. With *Aristotle's Problems* and then *Aristotle's Masterpiece*, 'Aristotle' became a most surprising code-word for sexual knowledge.

❡ *Masterpiece* wasn't the first book about sex, and much of it was a re-hash of existing works. It also contained a great deal of non-sense. Why, for instance, do women have longer hair than men? 'Because women are moister than men, and phlegmatic', answers 'Aristotle'. And why is immoderate carnal copulation hurtful? 'Because it destroys the sight, drys the body, and impairs the brain'.

❡ But alongside the old wives' tales, *Aristotle's Masterpiece* offered some sensible information on women's health that was otherwise hard to come by. Rarer still were its 'Directions respecting the Act of Coition or Carnal Copulation', from the 'storming of the mint' to the 'unlading of the freight'.

❡ *Aristotle's Masterpiece* is possibly the most successful book you've never heard of. It remained popular through the nineteenth century, with the last edition published in 1930. Read today, the advice is archaic; but for over two centuries it was prized as one of the few books to talk about sex openly.

A WORD OF ADVICE TO
BOTH SEXES IN THE
TIME OF COPULATION

When the Husband cometh into his Wives Chamber, he must entertain her with all kind of dalliance, wanton behaviour, and allurements to Venery: but if he perceive her to be slow and more cold, he must cherish, embrace, and tickle her, and shall not abruptly, the Nerves being suddenly distended, break into the Field of Nature, but rather shall creep in by little and little, intermixing more wanton Kisses with wanton Words and Speeches, handling her Secret Parts and Dugs, that she may take fire and be inflamed to Venery, for so at length the Womb will strive and wax fervent with a desire of casting forth its own Seed, and receiving the Mans Seed to be mixed together therewith. But if all these things will not suffice to inflame the Woman, for Women for the most part are more slow and slack unto the expulsion or yielding forth of their Seed, it shall be necessary first to forment her Secret Parts with the Decoction of hot Herbs made with Muscadine, or boyled in any other good Wine, and to put a little Musk or Civet into the Neck or Mouth of the Womb, and when she shall perceive the Flux of her Seed to approach, by reason of the tickling pleasure, she must advertise her Husband thereof, that at the very instant time, or moment, he may also yield forth his Seed, that by the concourse or meeting of the Seeds, Conception may be made, and so at length a Child be formed and born.

Thus, Reader, have I finished the difficult Mystery of Generation, as I hope, to the satisfaction of all Modest and Ingenious Persons.

ARISTOTLE'S MASTERPIECE
(CHAPTER 37)

¶ The language of medicine is constantly changing. For over 2,000 years, doctors thought disease was caused by an imbalance of bodily fluids – known as the *four humours* – and that it was spread through bad air, or *miasma*. Both theories were wrong, but it took until the nineteenth century before they were definitively disproved. Today, a doctor who warns of *acrimonious humours* or *commotions of the blood* is best avoided.

¶ But not all language changes arise from debunked theories. Some terms just fall out of fashion, particularly when they have negative connotations or sound like they come from *Lord of the Rings*. One can't imagine a modern GP diagnosing *King's Evil* – said to be cured by the monarch's touch – or *scrivener's palsy*, as much as it would be curious to see.

¶ Many names that seem modern have surprisingly long histories, like *impetigo* and *scrofula*, both dating to the fourteenth century. And while we won't be seeing *bilious derangement* anytime soon, the legacy of the four humours lives on in the words *phlegmatic* (calm), *bilious* (bad tempered) and *sanguine* (optimistic).

GLOSSARY OF ARCHAIC MEDICAL TERMS

APOPLEXY (1386)
Stroke.

BARREL-FEVER (1850)
Alcoholism.

BILIOUS DERANGEMENT (1651)
Liver disease (also, jaundice).

BRONZE JOHN (1862)
Yellow fever.

CONSUMPTION (1620)
(*Also: the white plague*)
Tuberculosis.

DROPSY (1769)
Swellings under the skin, now known as edema or oedema.

FALLING SICKNESS (1485)
Epilepsy.

GREEN SICKNESS (1547)
Hypochromic anaemia.

GRIPPE (1775)
(*Also: sweating sickness*)
Influenza.

KING'S EVIL (1387)
Scrofula.

MILK LEG (1830)
Deep vein thrombosis.

PAINTER'S COLIC (1822)
(*Also: dry bellyache*)
Mercury or lead poisoning.

PUTRID FEVER (1597)
Fever accompanied by a putrid odour; later, typhus.

ST. ANTHONY'S FIRE (1405)
Ergot poisoning.

ST. VITUS'S DANCE (1621)
Chorea.

SCRIVENER'S PALSY (1864)
Carpal tunnel syndrome.

SCRUM POX (1896)
Impetigo.

SHIP FEVER (1758)
Typhus.

THE FLUX (1600)
Dysentery.

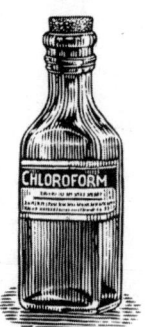

¶ **Syphilis** is an unpleasant sexually transmitted disease that can disfigure the body and send people mad. The word comes from *Syphilis, sive morbus Gallicus* ('Syphilis, or the French Disease'), a medical text written in poetry by Italian physician Girolamo Fracastoro. Published in 1530, thirty-five years after syphilis first appeared in Europe, the book describes how Syphilus the shepherd displeased the sun god Sol, and was punished with the pox.

¶ The story went that Syphilus was angry with Sol. Drought had killed his flock and, blaming the sun god, he made sacrifices to King Alcithous instead. His countrymen followed suit, Alcithous developed a god complex and Sol punished Syphilus with the disease that would bear his name.

> *The all-seeing Sun no longer could sustain*
> *These practices, but with enraged Disdain*
> *Darts forth such pestilent malignant Beams,*
> *As shed infection on Air, Earth and Streams;*
> *From whence this Malady its birth receiv'd,*
> *And first the offending Syphilus was griev'd,*

¶ Syphilus was Patient Zero, but Sol's curse spread across the land, even reaching the king. At this point, the nymph Ammerice stepped in. As well as recommending sacrifices to Sol, she prescribed a variety of remedies to cure the disease. It worked and they all lived happily ever after. Except, the remedies *didn't* work, and now the world had syphilis to contend with.

¶ From the beginning, syphilis was associated with soldiers. It was first recorded in Europe in 1495 during the French siege of Naples, when it was known as the **French Disease**. Except to the French, who called it the **Italian Disease** (and later, the **English Disease**). The English called it the **French Disease**, as well as **Naples Canker** and **Spanish Pox**, depending on who they were fighting. The Russians knew it as the **Polish Disease**, but Poles called it the **German Disease**; Turks had the **Christian Disease**; Persians, the **Turkish Disease**, and on it went.

¶ To doctors, syphilis was the **great mimic** or **great imitator**, because its symptoms were similar to many other diseases. But on the street it had dozens of names: the **pip**, the **pox**, the **canker**, and **Lues Venerea**, the bane of Venus. Even in the twentieth century, when a cure had been found in the 1940s, it inspired new slang, like **cupid's measles**, **garden gout**, **Mississippi rug burn** and **Will's Whiff**.

¶ Syphilis has a curious place in literary culture too. It is mentioned or alluded to by many great writers, perhaps inspired by personal experience. Shakespeare, Dickens, Byron, Wilde, Joyce and Keats are all suspected syphilitics, although with the exception of Byron (who definitely had it) each is subject to debate.

FIG.1 *Joseph Gruenpeck,*
De pestilentiali scorra (1496)

¶ In 1935, Charles H. Voelker of the Dartmouth College Speech Clinic wrote about a 'vocal unpleasantness' that was affecting much of his class. It was characterised by a 'rattling, rumbling, cracking or ticker-like substitution for phonation'. And it was driving him mad.

¶ This was the first clinical description of what would become known as *vocal fry* – also called *creaky voice*, *gravel voice* and *glottal fry*. And almost a century after Voelker, it's still irritating people. As one Reddit user wrote, 'That damn vocal fry... I try not to hate them for it but there's only so much I can take. Such rage.' 'I wanna rip my ears off,' fumed another.

¶ Few areas of the human vocal register have attracted so much attention, or provoked so much ire, as vocal fry. To some, it is the speech equivalent of nails on a blackboard; to others, it is merely the latest way of criticising how (young) women talk.

¶ Caused by the slow, irregular vibrations of the vocal cords, a voice with vocal fry is low – about as low as it can go – and has a creaky, crackly quality. For a time, speech experts thought it was a voice disorder that might even damage the vocal cords, although this is no longer the view.

¶ As Voelker showed, vocal fry is nothing new. From Mae West to Elmer Fudd, it has long been a feature of American English. But when celebrities like Britney Spears and Kim Kardashian started using it in the late-2000s, it created a fashion among young American women for croaky voices. Journalists were soon obsessed with the phenomenon. 'More college women speak in creaks, thanks to pop stars', read a typical headline from MSNBC.

FIG.1 *Word spoken without vocal fry.*

FIG.2 *Word spoken with vocal fry.*

¶ Vocal fry isn't the first speech mannerism associated with young women to provoke irritation. In the 1990s, people were incensed by *uptalk*, where every sentence seemed to end like a question? But vocal fry has inspired new levels of vitriol. Female podcasters have come to expect a torrent of abuse for their crackly voices, and young women have been told that they risk damaging their prospects in the workplace. The feminist writer Naomi Wolf even wrote an impassioned piece for the *Guardian* warning young women that vocal fry would make them sound 'less competent, less trustworthy, less educated and less hireable'.

¶ The problem is that while vocal fry isn't limited to women, the anger it inspires is. This leaves many wondering whether the real issue is vocal fry, or young women. Except, when Charles Voelker first described vocal fry, it was young men who made the 'aberrant' noise.

¶ It's not clear then whether the problem with vocal fry is its creakiness, young women, or young people generally. Perhaps it's all three. Regardless, the vocal fry will continue... until a new annoyance takes its place.

¶ Anyone familiar with the songs 'Flat Foot Floogie (with a Floy Floy)' (1938) or 'Cement Mixer (Put-ti Put-ti)' (1946), will know all about *vout-o-reenee*, the *slanguage* invented by Bulee 'Slim' Gaillard, the American musician, songwriter and hepcat extraordinaire who, performing with Leroy 'Slam' Steward, was one of the biggest names in the 1930s jazz scene.

¶ Gaillard lived quite the life – certainly as he told it. Abandoned on Crete aged twelve (his father, a ship's steward, had sailed off without him) he fended for himself for four years, before boarding a ship that somehow got him to Detroit. Being only sixteen, he was too young to work at the Ford factory, but old enough to transport bootleg liquor for the infamous Purple Gang. Later he may also have been a boxer, a mortician and a bomber pilot. He may even have known Al Capone.

¶ Gaillard's stories weren't always reliable, but his genius was the real deal. He was a polyglot – on top of English, he spoke Armenian, Arabic, German, Greek and Spanish – and a polyinstrumentalist. In one track, humbly called 'Genius', he plays the piano, trombone, guitar, drums and organ. And tap dances.

¶ And then there's *vout-o-reenee* (also spelled *voot-o-ree-nee*), or simply *vout*, Slim's signature jive language, and his lasting contribution to English. Vout was exuberant, nonsensical and infectious. When Bob Hope asked Marlene Dietrich her opinion of Slim, she had only one thing to say: 'Vout!' Even Jack Kerouac said of him: 'To Slim Gaillard the whole world was just one big *orooni*.'

¶ If the meaning of vout isn't clear, *Slim Gaillard's Vout-O-Reenee Dictionary* (1946) might help. Although probably not. The entry for 'vout', for instance, simply reads: 'Used as word substitute or word ending', which doesn't do justice to the word. Vout was money… and good times… and great performances. And anything could be *o-roony*: *Cool-o-roony*, *hip-o-roony*, even *steak-o-roony*. Just take something you like, add *o-roony*, and it's better. *Neat-o-roony*.

—◦•◦—

Voutie-o-roony-mo means super extra happy and good. It means everything is voutie, like roony-o, you know.

SLIM GAILLARD

—◦•◦—

189

SEE ALSO: Bee's Knees / Mary Jane

BLINK-O-ROONY	*sleepy*
BURN-O-VOOTY	*kitchen*
DRUG-O-REE-NEE	*sad*
GLOBE-O-VOOTY	*the world*
MELL-O-REE-NEE	*wonderful*
MUG-O-VOOT	*face*
PUTI-PUTI	*rhythm*
REET	*right*
REP-O-VOUTY	*answer*
ROOT	*same as reet*
SAN-WICH-EE	*between*
SLIM-O-REE-NEE	*sharp*
TICKET-TEE	*watch*
TOOL-O-ROOTY	*fork*
VOOT-O-LA	*joy*
VOOT-O-REE-NEE	*good music*
VOUT-VILLE	*town*
WHAT'S THE VOUT?	*What's the news?*

W.

WEIGHTS AND MEASURES

BANANA EQUIVALENT DOSE (RADIATION)

The dose of radiation a person will absorb from consuming one banana (approx. 78 nanosieverts).

BEARD SECOND (LENGTH)

A humorous unit, inspired by the light year, for the distance a beard grows in a second (calculated to be 10 nanometres).

BRISTOL STOOL SCALE (MEDICINE)

Used by clinicians to classify the firmness and appearance of a patient's stools.

CENTIMORGAN (GENETICS)

Used to measure the proximity of two genes on the same chromosome.

CENTIPAWN (CHESS)

Used by chess computers to measure the strategic value of a player's position. A centipawn equals 1/100 of a pawn. Often used in comparing moves.

COW'S GRASS (AREA)

A measurement used by Irish farmers in the eighteenth century to indicate the area of land required to feed a cow.

CUBIT (LENGTH)

An archaic measurement of length often seen in the Bible. Noah's ark, for instance, was 300 cubits long; the Ark of the Covenant was two and a half cubits. The unit, based on the length of the forearm, is 18–22 inches.

DOL (PAIN)

Short-lived unit for the measurement of pain, from the Latin for pain, dolor.

EDDINGTON NUMBER (ASTROPHYSICS)

The estimate of the number of particles in the universe (10^{40}).

FROG UNIT (PHARMACOLOGY)

The amount of a substance fatal to a frog.

GALACTIC YEAR / COSMIC YEAR (TIME)

The time it takes the solar system to complete one revolution around the centre of the galaxy (approx. 250m years).

HAWKING INDEX (BOOK COMPLETION)

*A humorous unit (given as a percentage) measuring how many people will finish a given book. Named after physicist Stephen Hawking, whose **Brief History of Time** scored 6.6%.*

JERK (ACCELERATION)

Rate of change of acceleration over time, measured in metres per second cubed.

JIFFY (TIME)

Proposed by physicist Gilbert Lewis as the time it takes light to travel 1cm in a vacuum: 33.3564 picoseconds. (Also seen in computing and electronics, but defined differently.)

MEGADEATH (DEATHS FROM NUCLEAR WARFARE)

The number of people killed as a result of nuclear warfare, with one megadeath equalling 1 million souls.

MICROMORT (RISK OF DEATH)

A unit of risk equal to a one-in-a-million chance of death. Walking, for instance, scores 1 micromort per 27 miles, hang gliding is 8 per jump and climbing Mount Everest is 37,932 micromorts per ascent.

MINER'S INCH (WATER FLOW)

The amount of water to pass through a 1-square-inch opening in 24 hours.

MOMENT (TIME)
A medieval unit of time mentioned by the monk St Bede. Thought to be equivalent to 90 seconds.

MOTHER COW INDEX (FARMING)
The number of pregnant cows an acre of land can support.

MOUSE UNIT (TOXICITY)
A measure of the toxicity of a substance, being the amount fatal to a mouse.

NIBBLE (COMPUTING DATA)
*In computing, a **nibble** is half a byte (four bits), or one hexadecimal digit.*

OLF (ODOUR)
The olf, from Latin olfaction, is the emission rate of bioeffluents – i.e. smell – emitted by the average sedentary person with an average skin area of 1.8m², who takes an average of 0.7 baths a day, and wears new underwear daily.

SHAKE (TIME)
A measurement used by nuclear physicists equal to 10 nanoseconds.

SCHMIDT STING PAIN INDEX (PAIN)
A rating scale from 1–4 to measure the pain of insect stings.

SCOVILLE SCALE (CHILLI PEPPER HEAT)
The scale measuring the heat of chilli peppers in Scoville Heat Units (SHUs).

TON OF REFRIGERATION (COOLING)
The cooling effect of melting a ton of ice in 24 hours (=12,000 BTU/h).

COMPARATIVE SCALES

¶ Wales is 20,779 square kilometres; just smaller than Israel but a shade bigger than El Salvador. Because it is familiar, it has become a useful way of making sense of large unfamiliar things, from the scale of rainforest destruction to the size of nuclear blast zones.

¶ An early example of what is known as the **Wales Scale** is R. Montgomery Martin's *China: Political, Commercial and Social* (1847), where Shantung was described as 'about the size of Wales'. Since then, '*[something]* times the size of Wales' has become a common explainer. The BBC's *More or Less* even provided a humorous codification of the scale, including **decawales** (10 times the size of Wales), **hectowales** (100 times) and **kilowales** (1,000 times).

¶ Other countries have their Wales-equivalents. America has Rhode Island, Germany has the Saarland, and the Netherlands uses Utrecht.

¶ Informal comparative scales don't just measure area. Volume can be described in terms of **Olympic-size swimming pools**, **Royal Albert Halls** or **Grand Canyons**; length appears as **football fields**; nuclear catastrophes are a factor of **Three Mile Islands** or **Chernobyls**; nuclear weapons are 'measured' in **Hiroshimas**; and large-scale loss of life is darkly appraised in **9/11s**. And ever since British Prime Minister Liz Truss's time in office was pegged to the lifespan of a lettuce, **Lettuce Time** has become the measure of a short-lived, disastrous appointment.

¶ **Wikipedia** is the fifth most-visited website on the internet. Funded by the Wikipedia Foundation – which itself relies on public donations – it is free to use. This created a major problem for commercial encyclopaedias, but enabled Wikipedia to become, as stated on its own Wikipedia page, 'the largest and most-read reference work in history'. This is a very plausible claim.

¶ The English-language Wikipedia alone contains 4.8 billion words in over 6.9 million articles – around 112 times larger than **Encyclopaedia Britannica**. This would be the equivalent of nearly 3,600 printed volumes. But it would need over 33,000 Britannica-sized volumes to contain the 64,379,724 articles found in all 341 Wikipedias.

¶ There are Wikipedias in **Latin**, **Yiddish**, **Hawaiian** and **Cherokee**, as well as constructed languages like **Esperanto**, **Interlingua** and **Volapük**. However, the **Klingon** Wikipedia was 'locked' in 2005.

¶ Unlike traditional encyclopedias, whose editorial staff commission experts to write entries, Wikipedia uses an open-source model. Volunteer editors – so-called **Wikipedians** – use collaborative webpages, or **wikis**, to add, edit, debate and delete entries. Although there are tens of millions of registered editors, only around 9,000 are regularly active (defined by making thirty edits a month).

¶ **Community-sourcing** has defined Wikipedia since it launched on 15 January 2001. It's the community of volunteer editors that gives Wikipedia its content, peer-moderation and democratic ethos. But all communities, particularly online, have their issues.

¶ Because Wikipedia allows anonymous editing, pages can be vandalised by trolls and spammers, with obscene pictures, advertising or misleading information. (Ironically, Wikipedia's entry on *Most vandalised pages* had to be protected from persistent vandalism, before finally being archived.)

SEE ALSO: *Dictionaries of Interest / Johnson's Dictionary*

WIKIPEDIA PAGE RECORDS

LONGEST ARTICLE
Opinion polling for the 2024 United Kingdom general election

LONGEST ARTICLE THAT ISN'T A LIST OR TIMELINE
Tartan

LONGEST BIOGRAPHY PAGE
Vladimir Putin

LONGEST LIST
List of Falcon 9 and Falcon Heavy launches

MOST-EDITED ARTICLE
List of WWE personnel

MOST-DELETED ARTICLE
The weather in London

LONGEST UNDETECTED HOAX ARTICLE
Donovan Slacks

LONGEST ARTICLE FOR DELETION PAGE
Mass killings under communist regimes

¶ Another problem baked into the community-sourcing model is the reliability of information. Knowingly or not, editors can introduce bias, misleading information, outdated theories, opinions, unverified claims, hoaxes, discredited research, misquotations, misunderstandings, errors of omission and more. Some editing errors are more calculated, particularly when they relate to conflicts of interest or revenge editing (where vindictive edits are deliberately inserted to make someone look bad).

¶ All of this can harm an encyclopaedia's reputation, and in its early years, Wikipedia was lampooned for its unreliability. While this has improved greatly, many schools and universities would disapprove of, even disallow, Wikipedia citations.

¶ A more intractable problem has been Wikipedia's gender bias. While around 50 per cent of readers are female, the number of female editors has hovered stubbornly around 9–15 per cent. This bias then influences editor decisions. For instance, while only 17 per cent of published biographies are about women, these account for 41 per cent of biographies nominated for deletion.

¶ Despite these issues, Wikipedia's achievements cannot be overstated. It is as significant a work as Johnson's 1755 *Dictionary*; arguably more so, given how widely it is used. It may be flawed and subject to abuse and manipulation, but English Wikipedia alone received 130 billion page views in 2024. No other reference work has achieved anything even close to this.

There are around 75,000 lists on *Wikipedia*, including many **lists of lists**. In fact, there are so many lists of lists that there's a **List of lists of lists** page, featuring 872 lists of lists, including the **List of lists of lists** itself. Here's are some of Wikipedia's most intriguing lists.

List of unsolved problems

List of fictional pigs

List of games considered the best

List of replicas

List of people who died on the toilet

List of inventors killed by their own invention

List of fictional US presidents

List of hat-tricks

List of renamed places

List of Wikipedia controversies

List of non-water floods

List of dates predicted for apocalyptic events

List of skeptical conferences

List of poisonings

List of people who have lived in airports

List of sexually active popes

List of most expensive items

List of fictional Jews

List of topics characterised as pseudoscience

List of artificial objects sent into space

List of future astronomical events

List of helicopter prison escapes

BRICKFIELDER
Southern Australia

*A hot, dry, dusty wind that can bring a
sudden increase in temperature. Named after
the clouds of red dust picked up from the
brickworks in Sydney's Brickfields district.*

BURAN
Central Asia

*A powerful wind in Russia and Central Asia
that drives blizzards in winter and torrid
heat in summer, often bringing sandstorms.*

CAPE DOCTOR
South Africa

*A cold, dry wind that blows through to Cape
Town from False Bay. So named because it
clears the city's polluted air. If it also brings
rain, it is called a Black South Easter.*

194

SEE ALSO: Beaufort Scale / Scottish Rain

HABOOB
North Africa

*A strong desert wind that creates large
sandstorms. Although associated with
the Sahara, haboobs can occur in the
deserts of central Australia, Arizona
and other large arid areas.*

HURRICANE BAWBAG
Scotland

*Not a regular wind, just a memorable name for a
cyclone that hit west Scotland in December 2011.*

KHAMSIN
Egypt and the Levant

*A hot, dry wind that carries large amounts
of dust and sand. Khamsin is the Arabic
for 'fifty', a reference to the fifty days of
the year when the wind appears.*

MISTRAL
Southern France

*A strong, cold wind that blows from the Rhône
Valley through to the Mediterranean.*

NOVEMBER WITCH
Great Lakes

*The gales that drive Arctic air across the
Great Lakes, North America, during
November – 'the month of storms' – are
known as Witches. Given the name,
journalists can't resist describing its
'screaming' and 'furious' winds.*

PAMPERO
Argentina & Uruguay

*Strong polar winds that roll over the
pampas in the southeastern area of South
America. The winds can bring relief from
the summer heat, but also heavy storms.*

SHARQI (OR CHERGUI)
Morocco

*A powerful dry wind that blows
from the southeast and can lead
to sudden sandstorms.*

SIMOON
Sahara

*A brief wind, often lasting only twenty minutes,
but which is scorching hot and filled with
dust. Sometimes develops into whirlwinds.*

SIROCCO
Southern Europe

*A hot wind that starts dry in the
Sahara, but becomes more humid
over the Mediterranean.*

THE SNOW EATER
Alberta

*The nickname given by the Blackfoot people
to the Chinook wind, a warm, westerly wind
that drives over the Rocky Mountains.*

THE HAWK
Chicago

*Although Chicago is known as the Windy
City, it's far from the windiest city in America.
Regardless, Chicagoans call the cold wind
that blows off Lake Michigan the Hawk,
or the Hawkins. It's not known why.*

LEXIPEDIA PEOPLE

JAMES HARDY VAUX

CONVICT & AUTHOR

(1782–c.1853)

¶James Hardy Vaux was a rogue of the first order; a thief, fraud and forger, transported three times to Australia, where he ultimately died. He also wrote what is often called Australia's first dictionary: *A New and Comprehensive Vocabulary of the Flash Language* (1819). That said, it's not quite a dictionary, and the flash (slang) was predominantly British, but it was written while he was detained at the Newcastle penal colony in New South Wales.

¶Vaux was born in Surrey but moved to London as a young man, where he became a committed ne'er-do-well. In his memoirs, he lists his criminalities during this time as: 'buzzing, dragging, sneaking, hoisting, pinching, smashing, jumping, spanking and starring; together with the kid-rig, the letter-racket, the order-racket and the snuff-racket.'* What got him transported, however, was pickpocketing a handkerchief, which saw him sent to Australia to serve a seven-year sentence.

¶If transportation was intended to set him right, it failed. Working in the Colonial Secretary's Office, Vaux found he could forge the signature of the colonial administrator and went on a spending spree. He was inevitably caught, 'double-ironed and put to the hardest labour'. It was the first of his many offences committed on Australian soil.

¶His autobiography, *Memoirs of James Hardy Vaux, a Swindler and Thief, Now Transported to New South Wales for the Second Time, and for Life,* tells of his numerous crimes, escapes and punishments. It's a fun read and he was clearly not without charm. At the end there is a 77-page 'dictionary' of criminal slang, dedicated to the commandant of the penal colony, with the wish 'that from the correctness of its definitions, you

may occasionally find it useful in your magisterial capacity'.

¶*The Comprehensive Vocabulary* contains 332 entries, from Alderman Lushington (a lush) to Yournabs ('yourself; an emphatical term used in speaking to another person'). Given his dedication to the criminal life and the villains he rubbed shoulders with, linguists regard Vaux's list as the real deal. There are also traces of early Australian English. Swag, for instance, had long been criminal slang for booty, but Vaux adds the sense of 'a bundle, parcel or package', a meaning particular to Australian English.

¶It was unprecedented to be transported three times to Australia – a testament to Vaux's unfailing ability to make Bad Decisions. His final arrest, for the criminal assault of an eight-year-old, was in 1839. Reporting on the case, one newspaper credited his knack for survival to 'the elegance of his dress, and his specious appearance, and good deal of contrivance.' Although no more was heard of him, his place as Australia's first dictionary compiler lives on.

*A translation of this criminal patois can be found on page 216.

¶ In any poll of the public's most hated words, *moist* will be at, or near, the top. Indeed, results from five psychology experiments concluded that 10–20 per cent of the US population were 'averse' to the word. This number would presumably increase in the case of *moist panties* or *moistened gusset*, with both *panties* and *gusset* widely hated too. Such words seem to provoke a visceral reaction in a phenomenon referred to as *logomisia*, or *word aversion*.

¶ *Moist* has become the poster child of hated words but it's not unique. Words like *luggage*, *discharge* and *slacks* are deeply

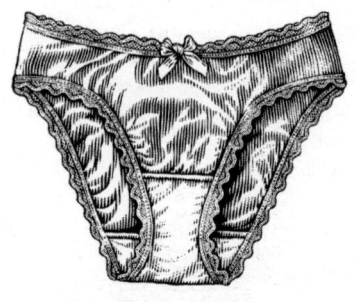

FIG.1 *Gusseted panties*

SEE ALSO: *Word Rage*

triggering for many. While a number of hated words are medical or sexual in nature – *distended, scrotum, residue*, etc – others seem quite innocuous. There's nothing to raise eyebrows about *mulch, casserole* or *tissue*, but plenty of people find the sound of such words icky. (Some even find the word *icky* to be icky.)

¶ The question linguists have been debating is whether a sound can be intrinsically unpleasant, or is it always invested with meaning in what is known as *sound symbolism*, or *phonaesthetics*.

¶ In the case of *moist*, some believe the problem indeed lies in its sound; the long *oy* and sharp *ss* and *tt*. But if so, why is nobody upset by *joist* or *foist*? Perhaps then it's because the facial muscles used to formulate the word are the same as those that express disgust – but again, 'moist' begins with a long *mmm*, more commonly associated with deliciousness, so that doesn't work either. The most likely problem is the word's assocation with bodily fluids, and specifically, female sexual arousal. This was certainly the view of psychologist Paul Thibodeau, who researched the question in 2016. Thibodeau

---

60 TRIGGERING WORDS

Abcess • Albumen • Artisanal • Bilge • Bollard • Bulbous • Chunky • Congeal • Corpuscle • Crampon • Crepuscular • Crotch • Dangle • Discharge • Drippings • Effulgent • Egest • Ejaculation • Engorged • Eructation • Flaccid • Flaps • Fungible • Giblets • Girdle • Glistening • Globule • Goiter • Gristle • Logorrhoea • Lotion • Membrane • Nodule • Ointment • Ooze • Penal • Polyp • Protuberant • Pulchritude • Pustule • Residue • Rictus • Schmear • Seepage • Shrivel • Slacks • Slurp • Slurry • Smear • Soggy • Suckle • Testudinal • Thong • Tumescent • Unctuous • Undergird • Unguent • Wet • Wipe • Yolk

argued that the underlying problem was the disgust response to bodily effluvia. In other words, people are squeamish about words associated with secretions, seepage, suppuration and ooze.

¶ But while the meaning of most nausea-inducing words reflects some common themes, there is something about how these words sound – their *phonology* – that can't be ignored. As well as being synonyms, words like *lotion, ointment, cream* and *unguent* – all noted for causing discomfort – have an oleaginous quality that really brings these words to life. The long vowels, and the facial muscles required to express them, make these words that aren't just said, but felt. And maybe this is the secret of word aversion; the combination of association, sound and facial expression that leaves people wanting to, well, *vomit*.

THE FLANGE

¶ *Flanges* are the projecting rim, or rib, on an object (typically a pipe or valve) used to guide, strengthen or connect with another object. As such, they're essential in engineering and architecture.

¶ Flanges come in different shapes and sizes, including: the *orifice flange, swivel flange, slip-on flange, expanding flange, puddle flange, split flange, loose flange* and *screwed flange*. There is also a variety of flanging tools, like the *hand-operated flange aligner*, the *hole flanging tool* and the *hydraulic flange greaser* (a video of which can be found on YouTube).

¶ None of this is in any way rude. The world needs flanges, and the word is purely technical. But there's something in the phonology of *flange* that makes it sound rather filthy.

¶ Some words sound naughty by association, like *Uranus, mastication* and *ballcock*. But *flange* has a strong claim to being the most filthy-yet-innocent word in the English language.

FIG.2 *4-way flanged cock with square glands, from John Wilson's* Tubes, Pipes & Accessories *(1910)*

¶ Wordle was the world's most-played word game in 2023. Created by software engineer Josh Wardle for his partner, the online word puzzle became a viral phenomenon.

¶ Posted on Wardle's personal website in November 2021, Wordle initially had around 90 daily players, mainly comprising family and friends. As people started sharing the game on Twitter, this number grew to 300,000 by December, and to 10 million over the course of January. By the end of January, just three months after the game first appeared online, *The New York Times* bought Wordle for a sum 'in the low seven figures'.

¶ The game itself was not original. *Jotto*, a code-breaking game from the 1950s, and *Lingo*, a TV quiz format, are very similar. But Wordle was simple, sharable and addictive. And because players can only tackle one Wordle a day, they were left wanting more.

¶ Given the number of Wordle clones, many wondered why *The New York Times* didn't just make their own version. The reason, of course, was Wordle's millions of daily players, who would all now flow to the paper's online game section.

¶ While the high watermark of Wordle play was in 2023, it retains many loyal fans who play the game daily. Whether *The New York Times* paid $1m or $3m to buy the game, it was a canny investment that drew millions of new users to their site.

SEE ALSO: *Spelling Bee Winners*

WORDLE NUMBERS

4.8 BILLION
...number of Wordle games played in 2023, equal to 137 years of play (assuming 15-minute average game time).

29%
...percentage of players who couldn't identify JOKER, the most failed Wordle in 2023.

14,855
...number of words that can be played in Wordle. The quiz setter chooses from a smaller list of 2,315 possible solutions.

1 IN 2,315
...odds of solving Wordle first go. With 1 in 250 games solved in one guess, not everyone seems to be playing by the rules.

8%
...number of Wordle games starting with ADIEU, the most-played opener in 2023.

NOVEMBER 2027
...when Wordle will run out of playable 5-letter words, unless the database is expanded or words repeated.

WORDLE SPINOFFS

DORDLE, TRORDLE, QUORDLE, HEXORDLE, OCTORDLE, DECORDLE
Versions involving multiple game boards: two, three, four, six, eight and ten respectively.

DAYDLE
Guess dates instead of words.

KLINGON WORDLE
It exists, and is as it sounds.

SWEARDLE
(ALSO, LEWDLE)
Players guess swear words.

MOISTLE
A version about 'gross words'.

BARDLE
Featuring words from Shakespeare plays.

ANTIWORDLE
Avoid the answer in the most guesses.

FIBBLE
'Lies to you once per row.'

REVERSLE
Work backwards from the answer.

WORDLE STRATEGIES

TIP #1: THE OPENING SALVO

Choose an opening word with frequently used letters. In order, these are:

E / A / R / I / O / T / N / S / L / C / U / D

The most commonly used starting words are listed below, although some, like *adieu* and *audio*, have a lower success rate than people expect. Perhaps consider suggestions from the game's own Wordlebot (cleverly available to newspaper subscribers only).

TIP #2: THE SECOND BLAST

The second guess is as important as the first. Players who don't use Hard Mode (where revealed hints must be played) should play a second word of high frequency letters.

TIP #3: LETTERS TO AVOID

J, Q, X and Z are the rarest letters in Wordle puzzles. Generally speaking, early guesses should avoid them.

TIP #4: THINK WORD STRUCTURE

Consider how letters pair together at the start, middle and end of words. The most common letter pairs are shown below.

TIP #5: FINDING MISSING LETTERS

When an almost-solved puzzle could be completed with a variety of letters, use a fresh word containing as many of these as possible. For example, a word ending -ROWN could be CROWN, BROWN, DROWN or GROWN. Using BADGE efficiently checks three letters at once.

TIP #6: WORDS TO AVOID

With a few rare exceptions, Wordle doesn't allow plurals or past tenses, so exclude these. Forget rude or offensive words too, since these are omitted from Wordle's dictionary. Finally, since Wordle is based on a list of accessible words, the answer will never be something obscure, so don't count on *fadge*, *borts* or *knout* to be the solution.

TIP #7: MIX UP STRATEGIES

The puzzle setters like to throw in curveballs so avoid rigidly playing the same strategy. Allow yourself to play different starting words and test unusual guesses.

TIP #8: POST-MATCH ANALYSIS

The game's WordleBot provides helpful in-depth analysis after each game.

TIP #9: FORGET TIPS #1-8

Alternatively, ditch strategies entirely and be spontaneous. Use the first word that pops into your head and see where it goes from there. What's the worst that can happen?

WORDLE CRIB GUIDE

WORDLEBOT'S RECOMMENDED OPENERS (IN ORDER)
slate / trace / crate / caret / carte / plate / stare / saint / least / stale / taser / parse / snare

PLAYERS' MOST COMMON OPENERS (IN ORDER)
adieu / audio / stare / raise / crane / arise / slate / train / irate / great / house / heart / ocean

COMMON OPENING LETTER PAIRS
bl / br / ch / cl / cr / fl / fr / sh / st / sl / th / tr / qu

COMMON MID-WORD PAIRS
ea / oa / ou / qu

COMMON END-WORD PAIRS
ck / ed / gh / ly / nd / nt / sh / ve

❡ The American Dialect Society has chosen a **Word of the Year** since 1990 (their first was **bushlips**, after President Bush's promise: 'Read my lips: no new taxes'). Since then, all the main English dictionaries have declared their own Word of the Year to great fanfare.

❡ Some people are niggled by the very idea of 'Word of the Year' as if it implies a stamp of approval. But one doesn't need to use the word, or even like it. It's just a linguistic snapshot of the cultural mood.

❡ Each dictionary has its own system. *Merriam-Webster* measures the volume of online lookups; the editors at Oxford Languages (publishers of *OED*) and *Macquarie* make their shortlist, then have a public vote; and members of the American Dialect Society have their own ballot.

❡ These different approaches achieve very different results, but each is looking for a word of unique cultural import so that we're never, erm, lost for words.

WORD OF THE YEAR, ACCORDING TO...

AMERICAN DIALECT SOCIETY (2023)
ENSHITTIFICATION: *'the creeping decline of a digital platform as user experience become secondary to profit-making.'*

CAMBRIDGE DICTIONARY (2018)
NOMOPHOBIA: *'fear or worry at the idea of being without your mobile phone or unable to use it.'*

DICTIONARY.COM (2020)
PANDEMIC: *'a disease prevalent throughout an entire country, continent, or the whole world.'*

MACQUARIE DICTIONARY (2017)
MILKSHAKE DUCK: *'A person who is initially viewed positively by the media but is then discovered to have something questionable about them which causes a sharp decline in their popularity.'*

MERRIAM-WEBSTER (2022)
GASLIGHTING: *'to attempt to make (someone) believe that he or she is going insane (as by subjecting that person to a series of experiences that have no rational explanation)'*

20 YEARS OF OXFORD LANGUAGES' WORD OF THE YEAR

2004	Chav	2012	Omnishambles	2019	Climate emergency
2005	Sudoku	2013	Selfie	2020	[no single word chosen]
2006	Bovvered	2014	Vape	2021	Vax
2007	Carbon footprint	2015	😂 (tears of joy emoji)	2022	Goblin mode
2008	Credit crunch	2016	Post-truth	2023	Rizz
2009	Simples	2017	Youthquake	2024	Brain rot
2010	Big society	2018	Toxic		
2011	Squeezed middle				

200

SEE ALSO: *Inkhorn Controversy*

¶ People get very cross about language. Bad grammar, misused words, buzzwords, cliches, throat clearers; all can be triggers. There's even a term for it – **word rage** – although this neologism might itself be annoying, which would be ironic.

¶ Complaining about the state of the English language is nothing new. George Puttenham did it in 1589, Jonathan Swift railed at the 'Corruptions in our Language' in 1712, and George Orwell added his tuppence in 1946. While the charges may differ, the essence remains the same: that English is going to the dogs. Too many corruptions and imports, and too few people using language correctly. *Plus ça change*, as Jonathan Swift definitely would not say.

¶ What *is* new, however, is the speed with which English is growing. New additions have always vexed the old guard, but with the *OED* adding around 2,000 new words and senses each year, and many more creations creeping in via slang, there's even more to get irate about.

¶ Corporate jargon is particularly loathed, as is much that young people say, but these are just the tip of the word rage iceberg. It's enough to drive you mad. Like, literally.

CORPORATE JARGON

Actionable	Learnings
Bleeding edge	Reach out
Blue sky	Stakeholder
Circle back	Synergise
Empowering	Talk offline
Going forward	Touch base

TAUTOLOGIES

Added bonus	Met with
ATM machine	Pin number
Forward planning	Prior experience
Free gift	Revert back
Future plans	Safe haven
I personally	

ERRORS

Alot	I was stood
Apple's (etc.)	Literally*
Expresso	Could of
Ironic*	Would of
Irregardless	Should of
I was sat	Specialty
*used incorrectly	

CLICHES

At the end of the day...	Not being funny...
Do you know what I mean?	To be honest... (also: to be fair)
I'm just saying...	With all due respect...
No offence but...	

YOUTH SPEAK

Adulting	Epic
Amazeballs	Funsies
Awesome	Holibobs
Awesomeness	So random
Awesome sauce	This is everything
Bants	Totes vibing
End of	Whatever (or whatevs)

OTHER IRRITANTS

Actually	Iconic
At this moment in time	Like
Basically	Methinks
Completely unique	My bad
Curated	Pre-order
Din dins	Referencing
	So...

SEE ALSO: *Vocal Fry / Word Aversion*

SEE ALSO: *Long Words*

WORDS

LONGEST MONOSYLLABIC WORDS
Scraunched (crunched), *strengthed* (strengthened defensively), 10 letters.

WORD WITH THE MOST MEANINGS
Set, with 430 senses listed in *OED* (2nd Edition).

LONGEST PALINDROMIC WORD
Tattarrattat (12 letters).

LONGEST WORD WITH ONLY ONE VOWEL
Strengths (9 letters).

LONGEST WORD WITH LETTERS IN ALPHABETICAL ORDER
Aegilops, 1. an ulcer in the eye; 2. a Mediterranean oak; 3. a type of grass (8 letters).

LONGEST WORD IN *OED* WITH NO MAIN VOWELS
Rhythms (7 letters).

LONGEST WORD WITH ALTERNATING CONSONANTS AND VOWELS
Taramasalata (12 letters).

LONGEST ENGLISH WORD CONTAINING ONLY VOWELS
Euouae (6 letters). Controversially, this is a mnemonic, but it's in the *Collins English Dictionary* and is playable in Scrabble.

LANGUAGES

LONGEST ALPHABET
Khymer (Cambodia), 74 letters.

SHORTEST ALPHABET
Rotokas (Papua New Guinea), 12 letters.

COUNTRY WITH MOST LANGUAGES SPOKEN
Papua New Guinea (840 languages spoken).

LANGUAGE WITH SMALLEST VOCABULARY
Toki Pona, a constructed language with between 120–137 words.

HARDEST LANGUAGES TO LEARN[1]
Arabic; Chinese (Cantonese); Chinese (Mandarin); Japanese; Korean.

COUNTRY WITH MOST NON-NATIVE ENGLISH SPEAKERS[2]
India (128,539,090 people).

OLDEST SURVIVING WRITING SYSTEMS
Egyptian and Sumerian, from 3300–3250 BC.

LANGUAGES WITH ONLY ONE SURVIVING SPEAKER
Apiaká, Bikya, Bishuo, Chaná, Dampel, Diahói, Kaixána, Lae, Laua, Patwin, Pazeh, Pémono, Taushiro, Tingua, Tolowa, Uru, Volow, Wintu-Nomalaki, Yahgan, Yarawiu.

BOOKS

FASTEST SELLING NON-FICTION BOOK
Spare (Prince Harry, the Duke of Sussex).

US STATE THAT HAS BANNED MOST BOOKS[3]
Florida (5,107 books banned).

MOST CHALLENGED / BANNED BOOK IN AMERICA (2023)[3]
Gender Queer (Maia Kobabe).

MOST PUBLISHED WORKS BY ONE AUTHOR
1,084 (L. Ron Hubbard).

WORLD'S BESTSELLING NOVELIST
Dame Agatha Christie (2–4 billion).

MOST TRANSLATED AUTHOR FOR ONE BOOK
Antoine de Saint-Exupéry, *Le Petit Prince* (translated into 382 languages).

LONGEST NOVEL
À *la recherche du temps perdu* (*In Search Of Lost Time*) by Marcel Proust, published in seven volumes (roughly 4,215 pages).

LARGEST DICTIONARY
The 33-volume German dictionary *Deutsches Wörterbuch*.

ACHIEVEMENTS

MOST WORDS WRITTEN ON A POSTAGE STAMP
2,024.

FASTEST TO TYPE THE ALPHABET
3.3 seconds.

MOST FIVE LETTER WORDS SPELT CORRECTLY IN ONE MINUTE
65.

MOST WORDS BLINKED BY A PUBLISHED AUTHOR
190,185, blinked by author Chen Hung, paralysed by Lou Gehrig's disease.

HIGHEST SCRABBLE WORD SCORE IN A TOURNAMENT[4]
Caziques (a chief or prince), 392 points

FASTEST PITMAN SHORTHAND WRITING SPEED
300 words per minute.

MOST WORDS SPELLED BACKWARDS IN ONE MINUTE
56.

MOST 'FUCKS' SAID IN A FILM
935 (*Swearnet: The Movie*, 2014); 8.35 per minute.

203

Unless otherwise noted, all records are sourced from Guinness World Records.

1 Rosetta Stone
2 2011 Census of India
3 American Libraries Association
4 North American Scrabble Players Association

Y.

YODA LINGUISTICS

When Yoda made his cinematic debut in *Star Wars: Episode 5 – The Empire Strikes Back* (1980), the first thing audiences noticed was that the little guy spoke funny. 'I'm looking for someone,' Luke Skywalker said to the 900-year-old Jedi master, not realising who he was; ***Looking? Found someone, you have***, was Yoda's idiosyncratic response.

The key to Yoda-speak is ***word order***. English requires the ordering of words according to a ***Subject-Verb-Object (SVO)*** structure:

<u>The Force</u> *is strong in* <u>him</u>.

But Yoda uses ***Object-Subject-Verb (OSV)***, a word order so rare that it has only been found in languages spoken in Brazil's Amazonia region. OSV reads:

In <u>him</u> *strong* <u>the Force</u> *is.*

To complicate matters, Yoda doesn't even stick with OSV. In his first seven films, he speaks 169 sentences, using *five* different word orders. In addition to OSV, which he uses most, and SVO, reserved for dramatic lines that need to be understood, Yoda dabbles with three other options:

VERB-SUBJECT-OBJECT (VSO)
<u>Is</u> *the Force strong in* <u>him</u>.

VERB-OBJECT-SUBJECT (VOS)
<u>Is</u> *in* <u>him</u> <u>the Force</u> *strong.*

OBJECT-VERB-SUBJECT (OVS)
In <u>him</u> *is* <u>the Force</u> *strong.*

To the untrained ear it starts to sound like word soup, but there is precedent. The inverted word order is a well-known rhetorical device called ***anastrophe***.

Shakespeare used it – 'The castle of Macduff I will surprise' (*Macbeth*) – as did Winston Churchill: 'Sure I am of this, that you have only to endure to conquer.' Yoda couldn't have said it better.

But Yoda's word ordering must have posed challenges to his colleagues. In the heat of battle, who could confidently parse, ***To fight this Lord Sidius, strong enough, you are not***, or, ***Then now the time is, Commander***? Combined with his habit of separating auxiliary verbs from main verbs (***Begun, the Clone Wars has***) it all begins to feel gratuitously confusing.

George Lucas intended Yoda's speaking style to convey ancient wisdom, but many would say otherwise. 'Break me a fucking give', wrote *The New Yorker*'s Anthony Lane; although linguist Mark Liberman corrected Lane, suggesting, 'A fucking break, give me' would be more accurate. Speaking of which, Liberman did an exhaustive review of Yoda's syntax and concluded that actually there was *no* system, just 'random word scrambling'.

Be clever, it might not; but a fortune has it Lucas made.

SEE ALSO: *Origins of Nonsense / Reduplicative Words*

Z.

ZERO PLURALS

¶ A *zero plural* (also, *invariant plural*) is a plural noun that is the same as its singular. It's one of those linguistic oddities that keeps English interesting.

¶ Zero plurals commonly relate to animals hunted by humans; from *boar* in the forest to *trout* in a stream. But it's not an ironclad rule. No-one hunts *goldfish*, but they do *rabbits*.

¶ Nor is it always animals. One aircraft can be from a fleet of *aircraft*, and regardless of whether something weighs one *stone* or ten, the form doesn't change.

¶ Such quirks can make English a vexing language to learn. If *goose* are *geese*, why not *moose*, *meese*? Obviously it's a different species, but since *species* is also a zero plural, maybe it's time to stop asking so many questions and just accept it.

ONE AIRCRAFT, MANY AIRCRAFT

ONE BISON, MANY BISON

ONE CARIBOU, MANY CARIBOU

ONE CROSSROADS, MANY CROSSROADS

ONE ELK, MANY ELK

ONE GOLDFISH, MANY GOLDFISH

ONE GROUSE, MANY GROUSE

ONE MOOSE, MANY MOOSE

ONE OFFSPRING, MANY OFFSPRING

ONE QUAIL, MANY QUAIL

ONE REINDEER, MANY REINDEER

ONE SALMON, MANY SALMON

ONE SHEEP, MANY SHEEP

ONE SERIES, MANY SERIES

ONE SHRIMP, MANY SHRIMP

ONE SPACECRAFT, MANY SPACECRAFT

ONE SQUID, MANY SQUID

ONE TROUT, MANY TROUT

ONE TUNA, MANY TUNA

SEE ALSO: *Collective Nouns / Double Negatives / Fossilised Words*

FIG.1 *Fish*

FIG.2 *Fish*

FIG.3 *Fishes*

NOUNS WITH NO SINGULAR FORM

Amenities • Annals • Antics • Ashes (remains) • Belongings • Biceps • Binoculars • Bowels • Braces (for teeth or trousers) • Clothes • Confines • Contents • Credentials • Customs (as in border security) • Dregs • Effects (as in personal belongings) • Forceps • Fumes • Goggles • Headphones • Headquarters • Hijinks • Jitters • Knickers • Leggings • Manners • Margins (as in financial) • Odds • Pyjamas • Particulars • Pliers • Premises • Proceeds (as in profits) • Provisions • Quarters (as in accommodations) • Remains • Riches • Savings • Scissors • Scruples • Shambles • Shears • Shenanigans • Spectacles • Suds • Thanks • Tidings • Tropics • Tweezers • Underpants

❡ The **zyzzyva** is a tropical weevil found in South America. It's yellow (ochreous, to be exact), eats leaves and lives in and around palm trees. It is also the last non-numeric word in the *Oxford English Dictionary*. (The last *last* entry is **999**, the telephone number for the British emergency services.)

FIG.1 *Zyzzyva*

❡ Of its etymology, the *OED* says 'origin unknown', but it certainly looks like it was engineered to bag the last spot in the dictionary when it was admitted in 2017. Fans of the ancient Egyptian malt beer **zythum** were no doubt furious.

❡ Zyzzyva would be the last word in *Merriam-Webster* too, if they included it; but the editors weren't buying this particular South American weevil. Instead, the last non-numeric word in America's leading dictionary is **zyzzogeton**, 'a genus of large South American leafhoppers (fam-

ily *Cicadellidae*) having the pronotum tuberculate and the front tibiae grooved'.

FIG.2 *Zyzzogeton*

❡ A cynic might suggest that naturalists are taking advantage of their species-naming privileges. How else can one explain **zyzzyxdonta**, the air-breathing land snail, and the marine tubulariid hydrozoan named **zyzzyzus**?

❡ Strangely, **zzz** – the representation of the sound of someone sleeping – doesn't appear in the *OED* or *Merriam-Webster* (although it does in the *Cambridge Dictionary* and *Dictionary.com*). Were it to make the cut, one can be sure it wouldn't be long before some snail-bothering malacologist 'discovered' a **zzzzyzyk**.

SEE ALSO: *Dictionaries of Interest / Unrhymable Words*

LAST WORDS

A TABLE ALPHABETICALL (1603)
ZODIAK: A circle in the heaven wherein be placed the 12 signes, and in which the Sunne is moved.

NEW WORLD OF ENGLISH WORDS (1663)
ZYGOTAT: One appointed to look to weights, a Clark [*sic*] of the Market.

A DICTIONARY OF THE ENGLISH LANGUAGE (1755)
ZOO'TOMY: Dissection of the bodies of beasts.

ENCYCLOPEDIA BRITANNICA (1771)
ZYGOPHYLLUM: In botany, a genus of the Decandria Monogynia class.

A COMPENDIOUS DICTIONARY OF THE ENGLISH LANGUAGE (1806)
ZYGOMATIC: Pertaining to a cavity in a bone of the temples like a yoke.

AMERICAN DICTIONARY OF THE ENGLISH LANGUAGE (1828)
ZYGOMATIC SUTURE: The suture which joins the zygomatic processes of the temporal and cheek bones.

OXFORD ENGLISH DICTIONARY (1928)
ZYXT: Obs. (Kentish) 2nd singular indicative present of SEE (V.).

GREEN'S DICTIONARY OF SLANG (2024)
ZZZZ: (New Zealand) a prison-made tattoo machine.

MERRIAM-WEBSTER MEDICAL DICTIONARY (2024)
ZYRTEC: used for a preparation of the dihydrochloride of cetirizine.

APPENDIX

The list of collective nouns found in *The Boke of Seynt Albans* (1486) was written in Middle English. Unable to find a modern English translation, the following appendix was prepared. Although the original text is presented as a single list, what follows below has been split into Animal, Human and Other.

ANIMAL

A barren of mules

A bevy of conies
(conies = rabbits)

A bevy of quail

A bevy of roos
(roos = roebucks)

A brace of greyhounds

A brood of hens

A building of rooks

A business of ferrets

A cast of hawks from the Tower
(cast is a hawking term for how the bird is released)

(A leash of the same hawks)

A chirm of goldfinches
(chirm = chattering)

A clattering of choughs
(chough = a bird in the crow family)

A company of greys

A congregation of plovers

A couple of running hounds

A couple of spaniels

A covert of coots

A covy of partriges
(covy = brood)

A desert of lapwings

A dissimulation of birds

A dolefulness of turtle doves

A drove of cattle

A drove of tame swine

A fall of woodcock

A flight of doves

A flight of goshawks

A flight of mallards

A flight of swallows

A flock of sheep

A gaggle of geese

A harras of horses
(harras = an enclosure)

A herd of all manner of deer

A herd of crane / curlews / hart / swans / wren

A host of sparrows

A kennel of raches
(raches = hunting dogs)

A labour of moles

A leap of leopards

A leash of greyhounds

A litter of kittens

A litter of welps

A murmuration of starlings

A muster of peacocks

A mute of hounds
(mute = a pack)

A nest of pheasants

A nest of rabbits

A pace of asses

A paddling of ducks

A peep of chickens
(peep = a chirp)

A playfulness of colts

A pride of lions

A richness of martens

A route of wolves
(route = a company)

A school of fish

A shrewdness of apes

A siege of bitterns
(bittern = a large marsh bird)

A siege of heron

A singular of boar

A skulk of foxes

A sloth of bears

A sounder of wild pigs
(sounder = herd)

A spring of teal

A stode of mares
(stode = a breeding enclosure)

A sute of lyam-hounds
(sute = pack, lyam-hounds = hunting dogs)

A swarm of bees

A tidings of pies
(pies = magpies)

A trip of goats
(trip = a small flock)

A trip of hares

A walk of snipes

A watch of nightingales

An exaltation of larks

An unkindness of ravens

A bevy of ladies

A blackening of souters
    (souters = cobblers)

A blast of hunters

A blast of soldiers

A blush of boys

A charge of curates

A cluster of churls

A condemnation of jurors

A congregation of people

A converting of preachers

A cowardness of curs

A credens of sewers
    *(sewers = servers
    at a meal)*

A dignity of canons
    (canons = clergymen)

A diligence of messengers

A discretion of priests

A dishonour of Scots

A doctrine of doctors

A draught of butlers

A dressing of tailors

A drift of fishers

A drunkship of cobblers

A faith of merchants

A fellowship of yeomen
    *(yeoman = a man holding
    a small landed property)*

A festre of brewers
    (festre = fester)

A fighting of beggars

A flattering of taverners

A fraunch of millers
    (fraunch = privilege)

A gaggle of women

A goryng of butchers
    *(meaning of goring
    not clear, but could
    be filthiness)*

A herd of harlots

A host of men

A kerf of panters
    (panters = pantry-men)

A lash of carters
    (carters = cart drivers)

A laughter of hostelers

A lying of pardoners

A malapert of pedlers
    (malapert = sauciness)

A melody of harpers

A misbelief of painters

A multiplying of husbands

A never-thriving of jugglers

A playfulness of maidens

A pledge of barons

A pluck of shoe-turners
    *(pluck = to pull a thread;
    shoe-turner = the person
    who shapes shoe soles)*

A pontifical of prelates

A poverty of pipers

A promise of tapsters

A proud showing of tailors

A provision of stewards

A prudence of vicars

A rabble of knaves

A rascal of boys

A rout of knights

A safeguard of porters

A school of clerks

A scolding of kempsters
    *(kempsters = wool
    combers)*

A sentence of judges

A sitting of ushers

A skulk of friars

A skulk of thieves

A smere of curriers
    *(smere = smear; currier
    = one who colours
    leather after tanning)*

A soiling of carvers
    (carvers = food carvers)

A squat of daubers
    (daubers = painters)

A stalk of foresters

A state of princes

A subtlety of sergeants

A superfluity of nuns

A tabernacle of bakers

A temperance of cooks

A thrave of threshers
    (thrave = 12 sheaves)

A threatening of courtiers

A trenket of corvisers
    *(trenket/trinket =
    the shoemaker's knife;
    corvisers = shoemakers)*

A waywardness of haywards
    *(haywards = officials
    responsible for the
    fences and enclosures
    in a town or parish)*

A wondering of tinkers

A worship of writers

An abominable sight of
    monks

An eloquence of lawyers

An example of masters

An execution of officers

An impatience of wives

An incredulity of cuckolds

An obedience of servants

An observance of hermits

An untruth of summoners
    *(summoner = minor
    officials who summon
    people to court)*

OTHER

A cast of bread

A cluster of grapes

A cluster of nuts

A pair of bottles

A rage of teeth
    (rage = aching, pain)

ENGLISH ALPHABETS

Tracking the composition of the English alphabet isn't as straightforward as one might imagine. Even as late as the nineteenth century, there were different versions of the alphabet, depending on the compiler's attitude to *J*s, *V*s and ampersands. Although the alphabets below are dated, none – except Augustine's, and that isn't English – can be considered ***standard***, because there was no 'standard' to speak of. Despite this caveat, they show something of the journey the alphabet has been on.

ST AUGUSTINE'S LATIN ALPHABET (C. 597)

A B C D E F G H

I K L M N O P Q

R S T V X Y Z

RUNIC FUTHARC ALPHABET (FIFTH TO TWELFTH CENTURY)

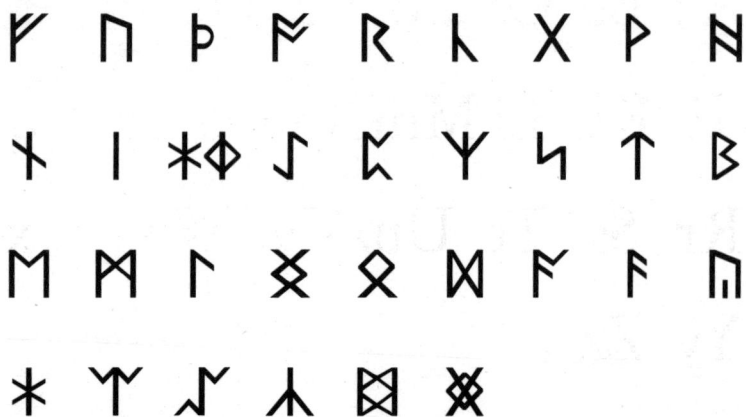

BEOWULF'S ALPHABET (C. 1000)

Aa Ææ Bb Cc Dd Ee Ff Gg

Hh Ii Kk Ll Mm Nn Oo Pp

Rr Ss Tt Þp Ðð Uu Ww Yy

CHANCERY STANDARD (FOURTEENTH CENTURY)

Aa Bb Cc Dd Ee Ff Gg Hh

Ii Kk Ll Mm Nn Oo Pp Qq

Rr Ss Tt Uu/Vv Ww Xx

Yy Zz

ANSWERS

CLASSICAL MOTTO OR AD SLOGAN?
(PAGE 15)

Say thank you. (Andrex)
Live forward. (Just For Men)
Beauty is confidence. (Nivea)
Be Ready. (Macleans)
Strong is beautiful. (Pantene Pro-V)
Now or never. (Nunc aut nunquam.)
Live while you can. (Dum potes vive.)
Today, not tomorrow. (Hodie, non cras.)
See and believe. (Vide et crede.)
Faster, higher, stronger. (Citius, altius, fortius.)

BRANDS AND AMPERSANDS
(PAGE 19)

P&G
1. Proctor & Gamble

Johnson&Johnson
2. Johnson & Johnson

McKinsey&Company
3. McKinsey & Company

TIFFANY & CO.
4. Tiffany & Co

BEN&JERRY'S
5. Ben & Jerry's

D&G
DOLCE&GABBANA
6. Dolce & Gabbana

COMIC BOOK SOUND EFFECTS – WEAPONS
(PAGE 44)

Atomic machine gun .... BRACKA BRACKA BRACKA!
Bullet hitting wood .... CHOK!
Bullet ricocheting off steel .... P-TANG!
Bullet flying through the air .... BWEEEE!
Sound of Nazi Schmeisser
sub machine gun .... BRAAAP BRAAAP!
Sound of M-16 machine gun .... BRRA-A-A-AP!
Sound of M230 chain gun? .... BRRRRRP!
Sound of bullet shot in the back. .... K-CHUNK!
Sound of bullet shot in the head .... POK!

SOUND EFFECTS QUIZ
(PAGE 45)

BRAP!... *belching*

FERRIP ....*a card deck being riffled*

GAGGAK-THOOF.......................*spitting out beetle*

GAK!.................................*coughing up hairball*

PLURP! .... *a bird pooing*

SCHLUCK!........................... *putting in contact lens*

SKLANG! ....*breaking glass*

SLRRRK....................................*drinking soup*

TCHIKIT................................ *a lock being picked*

TPTPTP............................... *feet running quickly*

VIP..*a bullet passing by*

WHRRRRR-TCHAK.............. *spinning revolver cylinder*

CHARLES DICKENS OR PATHOLOGY?
(PAGE 124)

NAMES FROM CHARLES DICKENS' NOTEBOOK:

Ambrosina
Aramanda
Ethlynida
Gentilla
Menella
Rebina
Samilias
Sapsea
Seba

FROM THE CAMBRIDGE HISTORICAL DICTIONARY OF DISEASE:

Cinchona
Marasmus
Melena
Ménière
Noma
Rosacea
Tetany
Variola
Yersinia

PAGER CODES
(PAGE 145)

The translation is Bring Back Pagers.

215

ANSWERS

CLASSIC BOOK TITLES IN PIG LATIN
(PAGE 154)

Oby-may Ick-day = Moby Dick
Ime-cray and-way Unishment-pay = Crime and Punishment
Ave-bray Ew-nay Orld-way = Brave New World
In-yay Old-cay Ood-blay = In Cold Blood

JAMES HARDY VAUX'S LIST OF CRIMINALITIES
(PAGE 195)

BUZZING . . . . *picking pockets*

DRAGGING . . . . *stealing trunks and bales from carts or carriages*

SNEAKING . . : . . . . *housebreaking, or shopbreaking, to steal 'whatever is most come-at-able'*

HOISTING . . . . *shop-lifting*

PINCHING . . . .*lifting small trinkets in a shop while seeming to browse*

SMASHING . . . . *using counterfeit money*

JUMPING . . . . *entering through the lower windows of a home to steal silverware etc.*

SPANKING . . . .*smashing a shop-window at night to steal goods within reach*

STARRING . . . . *noiselessly cutting a hole in a window to steal something*

THE KID-RIG . . . . *defrauding delivery boys and porters to steal their load*

THE LETTER-RACKET . . . . *scamming money from a kind, charitable person*

THE ORDER-RACKET . . . . *scamming goods from tradesmen by forging orders*

THE SNUFF-RACKET . . . . *'Throwing snuff in the eyes of a shop-keeper,*
and then running off with such money or
valuable property as may be within reach'

THE LIBRARY

One joy of writing the *Lexipedia* has been the discovery of many wonderful books about language. It's particularly special that a number of the authors also contributed questions to League of the Lexicon. It is therefore a pleasure to share this library for language lovers. Please browse at your leisure.

808.02

WRITING

DREYER'S ENGLISH (UK EDITION)
An Utterly Correct Guide to Clarity and Style
Benjamin Dreyer (2019)

BABEL
Around the World in Twenty Languages
Gaston Dorren (2019)

808.88

COLLECTIONS OF
MISCELLANEOUS WRITINGS

BLURB YOUR ENTHUSIASM
A Cracking Compendium of Book
Blurbs, Writing Tips, Literary
Folklore and Publishing Secrets
Louise Wilder (2022)

HEMINGWAY DIDN'T SAY THAT
The Truth Behind Familiar Quotations
Garson O'Toole (2017)

821.070804

NONSENSE

**THE ORIGIN OF
ENGLISH NONSENSE**
Noel Malcolm (1999)

**THE CHATTO BOOK OF
NONSENSE POETRY**
Hugh Haughton (1991)

INDEX

CREDITS

ACKNOWLEDGEMENTS

¶ Writing in the *Paris Review*, Anna North memorably described Acknowledgements as 'the only true thing amid a pack of lies.' She meant the ones in novels, but it's a neat quip that reflects the strangeness of acknowledgements generally. And while I've worked hard to avoid lies in this book, the following thanks are truly true.

¶ I'm embarassed to admit that until recently I didn't know what an agent did, not really. Well, I do now. Jennifer Joel and Harriet Poland at CAA have been an author's dream. Both saw how the *Lexipedia* book and Lexicon game were two sides of the same coin and have been tireless champions of both. These are the people you want in your corner and it's thanks to them that the *Lexipedia* found a home with the wonderful people at Bloomsbury and Avid Reader Press.

¶ My editors, Grace Paul at Bloomsbury and Caroline Sutton at Avid Reader Press, have encouraged, advised, indulged, steered and, when necessary, cracked the whip to ensure the *Lexipedia* became the book I hoped it would be. Both understood my passion for design and shared my determination to create something special. Rose Brown at Bloomsbury has project edited me with tireless patience, and Laura Gladwin and Kitty Stogdon made sure the text was free of miskates. But that's just the tip of the iceberg. Bloomsbury's Rob Cox, Marianne Laidlaw, Helen Upton, Danielle Rudasingwa, Ben Chisnall, and Avid Reader Press's Jofie Ferrari-Adler, Megan Noes, Meredith Vilarello, Rhina Garcia, Emily Lewis, Jessica Chin, Ruth Lee-Mui, Allison Green, Alison Forner have done more to make the *Lexipedia* a reality than I can possibly express here. Thank you.

¶ Given my passion for design, I owe special thanks to Dan Prescott at Couper Street Type Co, and Caroline Church, illustrator extraordinaire. Both have been enduringly patient with me and created something which I hope makes them as happy as it does me. Mia Butcher also deserves my gratitude for her role in the beautiful cover design.

¶ Over the last year I've relied on numerous friends, relations, even strangers, to eyeball my work. Damien Morris deserves the deepest of hat-tips for being a Giver of Great Notes – repeatedly, reliably and graciously. Fern Miller too. If either were fed up with my many questions, they never let on. And heartfelt thanks to Dorian Lynskey, Robin Lawrence, Barbara Davidson, Sophie Rouse, Nisha Jani, Carole Conrad, Caroline Blake and assorted Blackburns – Olly, Deborah, Sonny and Jude – all of whom were generous with their time and wise with their feedback. I'm also indebted to members of the *League of the Lexicon* 'Brain Trust' – people I've never met but who gamely assisted when the 'bat signal' went up: Valentino Tedaldi, Andreea Dogar, Andre Hilton, Nurlan Imangaliyev, Agathe Majou, Mark Grand, Llywelyn Evans and Jessika Wolmeringer .

¶ I've also benefitted from the input of people who truly Know Their Beans. Professor Anthony Bale gave me valuable advice on alphabets and the Great Vowel Shift. Keith Houston, author of the marvellous *Shady Characters*, indulged a lengthy exchange about the history of the hashtag. Richard Ovenden, Bodley's Librarian at the University of Oxford, patiently steered me in the right direction more than once. Heather Suttie ensured I wasn't talking mince about Scottish insults. And Katie Walker didn't just advise about putting advertising slogans into Latin, she did the translations. If you ever want a motto, speech or strapline in Latin, contact her agency Latin Rules, because that's what they do. I am especially grateful to Professor Jonathon Culpeper and Professor Jonathan Hope at Lancaster University, and Sam Hollands at Northern Arizona State University, for giving me a preview of their groundbreaking research on Shakespearean coinages. It was a privilege to be given access to it.

¶ I've relied on many online resources that don't need naming, but an exception must be made for the Internet Archive. When the site was briefly brought down by hackers in 2024, I came to realise just how much I relied upon it.

¶ This book only exists because of League of the Lexicon, the game which started it all. This warrants its own honour roll, which I have no intention of supplying here. Instead, I'll confine myself to an omni-thankyou to the thousands of Kickstarter backers, dozens of linguists and lexicographers, army of tweeters, bloggers, podcasters and reviewers, and everyone else who cheered, supported, shared, assisted and advised on the game. You know who you are, and you have my thanks. A select few, however, deserve more than anonymous gratitude: Stephen Fry, Susie Dent, David Crystal and Lynne Truss gave it their support when it mattered most; slang lexicographer Jonathon Green and polyglot linguist Gaston Dorren both authored special editions that took the game to a new level, and the etymology genius Jess Zefarris contributed hugely in the development of our US Edition, published by Adams Media in 2025. Finally, the bookchain Waterstones. They championed League of the Lexicon from the day I accosted an unsuspecting games buyer in the Picadilly flagship store with a prototype. I will be forever grateful for the support of all the above – and many more – because they made the game that made this book.

¶ Which brings me, finally, to the five people I owe most to. My parents, Jan and David; calm, unflappable and almost coy with their advice. They have always supported my adventures, no matter how offbeat. It might not look like I'm listening, but I am. My kids, Sonny and Jude – the two brothers of Two Brothers Games – were the origin of this unlikely journey and the first playtesters of the game. I wanted to kindle their curiosity, and in so doing, fed my own. So all this is their doing. I owe them everything, except royalties. And finally, Rachel. None of this could have happened without your unflagging support, belief, encouragement, indulgence and many kindnesses. You're the bee's knees, the nit's tits and the duck's quack. Thank you.

ABOUT THE AUTHOR

¶ Joshua Blackburn is a writer, designer and Maker of Things. He is also the inventor of League of the Lexicon, the most successful word game in Kickstarter history.

¶ For over fourteen years, Joshua ran the creative agency Provokateur, until he grew tired of making things for other people and started making them for himself.

¶ He has had two books published: *Acme Climate Action* (Harper Collins, 2008), which won a D&AD 'Pencil', and *Launderama* (Hoxton Mini Press, 2019), a photographic portrait of London's launderettes.

¶ Joshua created League of the Lexicon during the first Covid lockdown. As the game's inventor and most prolific question writer, he has become an accidental linguist, appearing on *The Allusionist*, *Because Language*, *The Failing Writers Podcast* and *Butter No Parsnips*. He also writes a newsletter about words and language, The Lexipedian. You can subscribe through his website, joshuablackburn.co.uk.

¶ Joshua lives in London with his family, a neurotic cat and a large taxidermy collection.

LEAGUE

of the

LEXICON

THE QUIZ GAME ABOUT
WORDS & LANGUAGE

LEAGUE *of the* **LEXICON**

WWW.LEAGUEOFTHELEXICON.COM

BLOOMSBURY PUBLISHING

Bloomsbury Publishing Plc
50 Bedford Square, London, WC1B 3DP, UK
Bloomsbury Publishing Ireland Limited,
29 Earlsfort Terrace, Dublin 2, D02 AY28, Ireland

BLOOMSBURY, BLOOMSBURY PUBLISHING and the Diana
logo are trademarks of Bloomsbury Publishing Plc

First published in Great Britain 2025

A catalogue record for this book is available from the British Library

ISBN: HB: 978-1-5266-8934-4; eBook: 978-1-5266-8935-1; ePDF: 978-1-5266-8936-8

2 4 6 8 10 9 7 5 3 1

Design by Couper Street Type Co.
Printed and bound in Great Britain by
CPI Group (UK) Ltd, Croydon CR0 4YY

To find out more about our authors and books
visit www.bloomsbury.com and sign up for our newsletters